REDNECKS & BLUENECKS

REDNECKS & BLUENECKS

THE POLITICS OF COUNTRY MUSIC

CHRIS WILLMAN

THE NEW PRESS

NEW YORK
LONDON

Requests for permission to reproduce selections from this book should be mailed to:
Permissions Department, The New Press, 38 Greene Street, New York, NY 10013

Published in the United States by The New Press, New York, 2005
Distributed by W. W. Norton & Company, Inc., New York

LIBRARY OF CONGRESS CATALOGING-IN-PUBLICATION DATA

Willman, Chris.
  Rednecks & bluenecks : the politics of country music / Chris Willman.
    p. cm.
  Includes bibliographical references and index.
  ISBN 1-59558-017-4
  1. Country music—Political aspects. I. Title: Rednecks and bluenecks. II. Title.

ML3524.W55 2005
781.642'073—dc22   2005047961

The New Press was established in 1990 as a not-for-profit alternative to the large, commercial publishing houses currently dominating the book publishing industry. The New
Press operates in the public interest rather than for private gain, and is committed to
publishing, in innovative ways, works of educational, cultural, and community value that
are often deemed insufficiently profitable.

www.thenewpress.com

Composition by Westchester Book Composition
This book was set in Janson

Printed in the United States of America

2   4   6   8   10   9   7   5   3   1

For Cynthia, the incorrigible Kansas Mennonite.
And for Hadley: May you someday fulfill Roy Acuff's dream and
become the first Opry member to be elected governor.

"Oh, the farmer and the cowman should be friends . . ."
—OSCAR HAMMERSTEIN

Contents

Preface

The Red Carpet

Opening Night in Greenville

May 1, 2003. Tonight the South was supposed to rise again, to show Natalie Maines the meaning of the word *shame*. But the uprising is more modest than expected in Greenville, South Carolina, where the Dixie Chicks will soon emerge from behind their phalanx of security in the bowels of the Bi-Lo Center and come on stage to face the ticket-buying portion of their public. Millions of Americans are peeved at the trio's lead singer, Natalie Maines, for having quipped to a London audience two months earlier that she was "ashamed" to share her home state with President Bush. But a few thousand of the locals who now view the Chicks as enemy combatants got siphoned off by a simultaneous pro-military protest concert being held across town, leaving about only thirty demonstrators to heed the call to picket this evening's tour opening. Roughly the same number of counter-demonstrators have come out to jockey for the attention of the national media, which, naturally, outnumber everybody. Anyway, as microcosms of political agitation go, at least it's a loud and instructive one.

Up on Church Street, where picketers representing both sides are facing the arriving traffic, it's a regular First Amendment smackdown. "My son was in the air force," one sixtyish Chicks supporter, Barbara Sharpe, is barking at a nearby nemesis of about the same age, "and if he was sitting over there in Iraq right now, I would still feel people have the freedom to express themselves without being blasted."

"I love their music," answers Jan Allen, a nurse who came over from nearby Anderson, South Carolina, to protest the group, sounding genuinely rueful. "But when I hear them on the radio now, I have to turn it off."

"I was sorry Natalie apologized," Sharpe announces, upping the ante.

"She *didn't* apologize!" sputters Allen, taking the bait.

"Personally," says the antiwar air force mom, still prodding and pushing her adversary's buttons, "I'm glad Bush doesn't live in South Carolina. Does that make *me* an evil person?"

"Look, I'm not saying Natalie is an evil person. But if I was a soldier, I would feel terrible knowing there were people back home protesting the war we were in."

"Does it make a difference that we weren't at war yet, when Natalie said what she said?"

"We were so close, it didn't matter," says Allen.

"So you never have the right to protest the president when he goes to war? Even beforehand?"

"I wouldn't do it in another country."

This edition of *Crossfire* is starting to choke on its own exhaust fumes, and these two upper-demo adversaries respectfully let it go and return to their respective flanks. Meanwhile, the competing protest signs around them represent all degrees of enraged sloganeering. Some take off from Natalie's offending quote: ASHAMED THE DIXIE CHICKS ARE FROM USA on one side, I'M ASHAMED TOO! FREEDOM OF SPEECH! AIN'T IT GREAT! on the other. There are the song spoofs, naturally, like NATALIE HAS "WIDE OPEN SPACES" BETWEEN HER EARS and TONIGHT THE HEARTACHE'S ON YOU! Names are fair game for satire, as in DITSY CHICKS—SING, DON'T TALK POLITICS or THE 3 FRENCH HENS. (The latter sign-wielder must be a Jerry Falwell fan; the reverend has been making the rounds on TV, claiming credit for coining that one.) Sometimes the punmanship is tortured, as with the sign that reads, HOW MANY LAWYERS DOES IT TAKE TO SCRIPT AN APOLOGY, NATALIE NOBRAINES?

Down a short incline from the boulevard, a little off the beaten track, stands a lonely patch of grass that normally serves a purely decorative function. Local authorities roped off this small lawn earlier in the day and designated it as the official demonstration area for pissed-off patriots. A few conspiracy-minded wags dubbed it "the grassy knoll," in honor of someone else who once faced a chilly welcome in a

Southern state. But the anti-Chicks protesters abandoned this pastoral spot, not to be outdone after their go-Natalie adversaries showed up and immediately headed for more visible positions along the streets. Only two Chick bashers stayed behind on this sad knoll of designated dissent: Charles Crowe, a retired veteran and longtime local Republican activist who is situated in a wheelchair with his breathing apparatus, and his sole companion, Gabriel Gilmour, a teenager. As it turns out, this is a pretty good surveillance spot, now that the queue of arriving ticketholders has backed up nearly as far as the original protest pen.

"I have not seen one person in that line that I know," Crowe declares, proud that his stakeout has yet to turn up a turncoat. Right now he's holding a sign that says LOOKS LIKE DEMOCRATE CONVENTION. "I'd faint if somebody called out to me. This is Republican territory. You couldn't get elected here on a Democratic ticket if you were paying a thousand dollars a vote!" he announces, practically daring Huey Long to rise from the grave with a wad of bills. Still, he's mystified and disappointed by what appears to be a strong turnout, maybe even a full house. "I don't know where all these people are coming from," he says, shaking his head. "Probably Georgia."

Before I have a chance to ask what his beef is with the Peach State, Crowe begins to bemoan his fellow vets' unwillingness to protest. "I can't believe I'm here by myself. I know my friends resent it as strong as I do." Being a Southern gentleman, he believes the brusque tide of today's youth might yet be turned. Gaggles of teenaged girls walk past, snickering at this disabled vet and his misspelled sign—nothing he hasn't experienced before. "These kind of people need guidance," he explains. "I'm from the old school. If you walk down the sidewalk and some kid does something wrong, you correct 'em. You don't worry they'll pull out a gun on you." He talks about how he volunteered years back during the big hurricane in South Carolina, when he was more able-bodied, risking his personal safety to tell young looters that what they were doing was wrong. He views the correction of Dixie Chicks fans with the same sense of civic duty.

"If Natalie knew enough to get involved in national affairs, she should have known we were having trouble getting England behind us. *She* didn't have to worry about stepping on a land mine or a scud missile landing on her heiney." And then comes the inevitable comparison, because this, like so many things in early-twenty-first-century

American life, is really all about a war that ended three decades ago. "I remember Jane Fonda sitting on an antiaircraft gun acting like she was shooting down American planes. She says she's become a Christian and asked for forgiveness, but I'll never forgive her. As far as I'm concerned, this is no different." Really? As bad as Hanoi Jane? "Well," he concedes, "this hurts a little less."

Freedom of speech? Not an issue. "You don't have freedom of speech to go inside the Bi-Lo Center and shout 'fire,'" Crowe maintains. He thinks Natalie Maines's comment about being "ashamed" to be from the same state as the president of the United States is a little ironic coming from someone who recently dropped Texas trou for the cover of *Entertainment Weekly:* "She must not have too much shame." But unlike some of his fellow protesters, he doesn't have a problem with the group's naked cover shot. "That's entertainment. If it helps sell CDs, be my guest! Just don't get involved in politics."

The teenaged neocon at his side doesn't share his elder's tolerance for wantonness. "They showed their ignorance, and now they're showing their tail," young Gilmour mutters, speaking up at last. He was particularly incensed by the Chicks' proud attitude on Diane Sawyer's prime-time show. "They said 'don't forgive me'—that they don't need to be forgiven because they're role models. Maybe it's because I'm a redneck, but around here we don't use that term for people who do pornography"—(that would be the *EW* cover)—"or who break their promise to God by getting divorced"—(two of the three Chicks are on their second marriages)—"or who get multiple tattoos"—(each of the Chicks has a small chicken-foot marking around her ankle for every number-one single they've produced)—"and who cuss and bash the president and don't support the troops. *That's* not a role model here." If only this young buck had ever been fan enough to have some records to destroy. Fortunately, his sister came through and sacrificed her CDs for the cause, so that her brother could put together the collage he now holds up of Chicks records and memorabilia being dumped into a garbage can, above the motto DON'T LITTER—PUT TRASH WHERE IT BELONGS.

His aged companion has switched to a different placard, which reads: WERE THE CHICKS BORN IN THE CHICKEN HOUSE? "What I really meant was 'chicken ranch,'" Crowe explains, referring to the infamous Nevada brothel. "But out of respect for their parents, I didn't use the real words." This might not be the apex of Southern gentility, but in times of contention, you take what passes for courtliness where you find it.

Back on Church Street, it's studies in contrast, everywhere. A couple of Natalie-Go-Home camps shout support at each other from across the traffic jam: "We love Bush, yes we do, we love Bush, how 'bout you?" Turning the volume way down, meanwhile, is a trio of lefties dressed in green medics' garb with lapels reading BILL OF RIGHTS TRAUMA TEAM. At nonverbal intervals—when they momentarily run out of journalists to entertain—they stuff gags in their mouths and brandish blank signs for the passersby. Sometimes it really is a fine line between thoughtful dissent and Halloween pageant.

The man largely responsible for bringing out the pro-Chicks forces is David Bracy, head of the local branch of the Progressive Network. Their chapter is fairly abridged, which is probably no huge surprise in a city legendary for being the home of Bob Jones University, a religious school that overturned its ban on interracial dating only a few years ago. Bracy wasn't even particularly a Chicks fan before now, but he "wanted to make sure that there's some faces that the rest of the country sees in Greenville that are . . ." How can he put this? "Well, I was talking to a police officer the other day who said, 'Greenville isn't all toothless wonders.' He said that, I didn't."

It wouldn't be the left, of course, if everyone involved were remotely of one accord. And so an African American woman standing with the progressives complains to me that the organization is so focused on war issues that she can't get anyone to spend serious time dealing with more locally pressing problems having to do with race.

Anyway, there's not an abundance of manpower to go around on any liberal cause. Bracy says that since the previous fall, when it became apparent that an American invasion of Iraq was imminent, the Network had been holding weekly peace demonstrations downtown, but "since the bombs started dropping, the majority stopped coming." Sometimes it's just him out there. "I have some deep spiritual beliefs that have an impact on what I do. Sometimes I'm holding a piece of scripture and people come by and say 'Fuck you' and look you right in the eye. A lot of people here feel the same way we do, but they're uncertain how to voice that opinion and they're fearful of repercussions. A lot of them work for conservative companies." Tomorrow the circus will blow out of town and it'll be back to the usual ostracization in those forlorn public-square vigils, but tonight, thanks to a visiting country band, of all things, Bracy's acute hometown alienation is briefly in remission.

Just a few paces but about a million miles away, a kid with a crewcut is holding a prosaic (but to-the-point) I REALLY HATE THE DIXIE CHICKS sign. "I wonder if their attitudes would change if they were gassed by chemicals the way the Iraqis were! What if they got shot in the head and put in a factory?" wonders teenager Neil Chaney, whose hypotheticals just keep on comin'. "Don't they have a song, 'Coming Home Soldier . . .'?" He means "Travelin' Soldier," the trio's tender, Vietnam-themed ballad, beloved by left and right until two months ago. "What would they do to a soldier coming home now—spit in his face?"

If this young buck is the picture of righteous disgust, then disgust squared would be a woman named Donna—no last name given—whom I run into along the entrance ramp. Her principal beef is with the Chicks posing with various epithets stenciled onto their skin for that awful magazine cover. Finally, a sort of sixth sense seems to settle in, and she inquires, "So who did you say you were with?" I'm compelled to disclose that I am reporting for the offending co-conspirator in celebrity nudity, *Entertainment Weekly*, and that I wrote the cover story occasioning the display of flesh, which occasions a hostile, Pazuzu-like grin. "That's *pitiful* that y'all would do that for young people! It came in the mail with naked girls on the cover. That's nudity, any way you want to look at it. See those ten-year-olds in line? *That's* what America is taking their children to." I offer to help process the cancellation of her subscription upon returning to editorial headquarters, but she's more determined than ever not to cough up a surname.

Some arriving ticketholders continue to mill about as the sun sets, cheerful, apolitical lookie-loos watching the news media watch the picketers. As opening acts go, this political free-for-all might even beat Joan "One of Us" Osborne, who's already performing inside. What if God *was* one of us? Just a Bob Jones–loving, Rush-listening slob like one of us? Just an ineffectual peacenik-agitator off the bus?

Jane Anderson of Spartanburg has dragged her husband and several middle-aged, upscale, professional-looking pals along to the show. "I don't agree with what Natalie did. She hung herself. But I've done some dumb things in my life, too." And then she explains why Greenville is actually a *great* place to start a tour that's become a flashpoint for freedom-of-speech issues: "South Carolina has a long history of supporting independence rights, from secession on up . . ." This is absolutely the only time all week I will hear someone laud Natalie Maines for carrying on in the proud tradition of the Confederacy.

A fellow named Bob Myers and his nine-year-old daughter, Lisa, are loitering around the newscasters' live feeds. They just made the two-hour drive from Dallas, North Carolina. He thinks the offending comment was "overblown and not taken in context. Anyway, I didn't come here for that. I came for the Dixie Chicks. We have 'em playing in the house all the time. What else are you gonna do, stay home and watch *Mama's Family* reruns?" Well, yes, maybe, if he wanted to escape a lot of grief back in North Carolina. Because, as he goes on to lament, "My friends at work called me a Communist! 'How could you go see the Dixie Chicks?' I said, 'I like their music!' But—"

"Daddy, what's a Communist?" Lisa asks.

"It's kind of a long story," he tells his daughter, rolling his eyes.

Lisa stomps her foot in protest—maybe the single most passionately felt protest I've seen all day. "I *like* long stories!" she insists, a girl after America's own heart.

In the heat of the controversy over Natalie Maines's anti-Bush comments, the Dixie Chicks cooled off by stripping for an *Entertainment Weekly* cover that satirized their detractors' and supporters' "branding" efforts. Many former fans only got hotter under the collar.

Introduction

Row Rage

The Rules of Engagement in Music City, USA

Sooner or later any tale of modern-day Nashville is bound to be summed up as your basic saga of two cities. But for the purposes of examining the town's political divide, we might also call this "A Tale of Two SUVs."

The first sports utility vehicle in question belongs to veteran singer/songwriter Rodney Crowell. Until recently, this lifelong Democrat lived close to Nashville, where some of the neighborhoods have a distinctly bohemian vibe. But not long before the 2004 election, his family uprooted itself to nearby Williamson County, where the suburban sensibility more closely matches the rest of Tennessee and the South in general. His tricks for handling culture shock are simple. "I curse under my breath a lot," he admits, leaning against a console in his upstairs home studio in Brentwood. "You know, if I see one more W sticker . . ." No use completing that empty threat, since he's probably no more than two blocks away from one in any direction on the subdivision grid.

"I don't like bumper stickers, either pro or con," Crowell maintains. But he lost out when it came to branding the family SUV. Repercussions for this sedition came quickly. "My wife had a Kerry/Edwards sticker, and a guy in a Jeep actually pulled up beside her and spat at her through the open window. And I thought, well, *we're in it now!* It's a dogfight, now."

Perhaps, continuing in a Dickensian vein, we could also call this story "Great Expectorates." Anyway, Crowell's off-road revenge against the conservatism he's encircled by has been to record the most overtly political music of his estimable country-rock career. In his home studio out here in the land of deep, upwardly mobile redness, he's been putting the finishing touches on a new CD that will lob a few broadsides at what he considers to be the intolerance and smugness of the right, with pointed song titles like "The Obscenity Prayer." As befits his recent relocation into politically lonelier territory, the album's title is *The Outsider*.

But let's not imagine that the right has cornered the market on road rage. The other targeted SUV in this equation belongs to Chely Wright, who had a very different bumper sticker—a USMC decal—that provoked a run-in with a militant antimilitarist in the liberal part of town Crowell recently left behind. No spit exchanged here; just some accusatory epithets and your basic *digitus impudicus*.

Wright's Marines emblem wasn't intended as a provocation. Several generations of her family have belonged to the military, including a brother now in the corps, who sent her the sticker well before the invasion of Iraq. But it was interpreted as a war whoop by a woman driving her minivan along West End Avenue, in an upper-middle-class neighborhood near downtown Nashville where Kerry yard signs were dominant. The singer says the angry peacenik flipped her the bird, then motioned for Wright to roll her window down, at which point she was on the receiving end of a short but profane diatribe that included loaded words like "killer."

"It's not as if I had a pro-war sticker or I LOVE BUSH or KILL PEOPLE! on the back of my car. Just the eagle, globe, and anchor—that's it," points out Wright, sipping a hot brew in a busy coffeehouse called Caffeine, adjacent to Music Row. "I got flipped off, and I couldn't grab that lady by the throat and bring her over here and buy her a cup of coffee, so I wrote a song about it." That long narrative ballad, "Bumper of My SUV," became an instant hit among a lot of military families who may feel a lack of stateside support for their sandtrapped loved ones in the Middle East.

Welcome to America, where, as Aaron Tippin once sang, the stars and stripes and the eagle fly . . . among other birds.

Bumpers abutting or no, red America and blue America can feel like different countries, or at least separate territories that might like to agree to a mutual secession. As the nation drifted toward opposing corners in the months between 9/11 and the 2004 election, everyone seemed to feel they belonged to the true embattled minority, even when the tide of popular opinion seemed to be with them: the right claiming assault from dismissive media elites, smugly aggressive Hollywood hedonists, intolerant secularists, and—oh yeah—a too easily forgotten miscreant named Osama bin Laden; the left crying foul at the bruising hands of uncivil anti-libertarians, unfair and imbalanced Murdochians and talk-radio maniacs, intolerant religionists, and—did they fail to mention?—a law-flouting domestic terrorist named John Ashcroft. Some of this culture-war stuff was bound to find its way into country music, which, though hardly unilateral as a genre, typically gravitates more toward expressing the fears, beliefs, and hopes of conservatives, who occupy a majority of the artist roster as well as fan base at this point in the music's evolution.

"It *has* been interesting," says Wright. "There've always been politically based songs in country music, I suppose, but never more than since 9/11."

So that would be a positive development, or . . . ?

"That's a dangerous development," she declares, sharply. "Country tends to reflect a major cross section of what's going on in the general population. The thing that keeps country rearing its head above water, just enough to catch our breath and stay alive, or creates those moments where we're the number-one kind of music, is the fact that it's a Polaroid of what's going on in our nation. But I think it would be dangerous if we set ourselves up to be the nation's political voice. That's why I had so much fear when my song started getting out there. My big concern was that people would think"—her voice goes into full-sarcasm-drip mode—"'Oh, another country singer writin' a song about the war.'"

Defensive driving, indeed. Memo to anyone on either coast who ever belittled the heartland as flyover territory: You're missing some pretty interesting sociopolitical interaction by not making a road trip out of it.

America's Accent

Sean Hannity has a dream. As the host of a Fox News chatfest and syndicated radio talk show, not to mention bestselling author, he's a hero to millions, maybe tens of millions, of conservatives. But what he really wants to do is direct America's attention to the glories of country music, maybe by going to bat as the genre's own Casey Kasem. "My goal is to go back and just be a country music countdown host one day," he confides. "I actually mentioned that to somebody in the radio business the other day and they said, 'We can make that happen.' Honestly, that would be fun for me every week. I'm that much of a fan."

That distant sound you hear is the Fox-loathing left collectively chiming in with support: *Great! Get, already!* But abdication of one throne for another isn't likely soon, and anyway, he's already doing his bit for the music. "The Sean Hannity radio show is on nearly five hundred stations now, and a lot of people are surprised that I put these guys on as often as I do. But we've had Martina McBride on, Sara Evans on, LeAnn Rimes, and Chely; Darryl Worley's been on a bunch, as has been my buddy Charlie Daniels . . . and people like it. There's a new audience to appeal to, because in New York City, for instance, where my show is based out of, there's not one single solitary country station." (It's the one major city in the nation where that's true.) "So I get people in New York saying, 'Wow, I never heard this before.'" Right-leaning urbanites dig it, Hannity says, because "the values that we talk a lot about on my show are very similar to the values they sing about in their country songs. There's a common theme of God, faith, family, and love of country."

Hannity has himself a good laugh every time election year rolls around and someone writes a patronizing piece about how the only entertainers the Republicans could drag to their convention are some lowly cowpokes. "Isn't that the problem with that sort of Hollywood elite attitude, that they just don't know how big Brooks & Dunn are? It's that quintessential knee-jerk condescending attitude that I expect from some of the elites." It may be a given that country acts have to work twice as hard and sell three times as many records to get the same exposure in the mainstream national media as marginal pop acts. "But they don't have to prove themselves with the fans," Hannity says. "It's just if they want to get in the elite magazines and that sort of thing, and I don't know if that's even important to them. I can tell you that, as a conservative radio and TV host, I prefer to stay under the radar and not do interviews, myself. Except for this one—it's a topic I like."

That dreaded "E" word just pops up again and again, doesn't it? Country: it's where the elite don't meet, and where those who don't go in for the culture of the Beltway or the Bowery—self-identified conservatives or not—get together to bond over three chords, the truth, and their outsider status. Most of the material will be, as Trace Adkins put it in his transparent attempt to record country's own national anthem, "Songs About Me." But there are also moments, as in the days after 9/11, when the music catches a zeitgeist that goes beyond the breeze of individual validation and rises to at least briefly become Songs About Us.

The most venerable cliché about country is that it's music for both Saturday night and Sunday morning—there to provide a rowdy soundtrack for your wild oat-sowing needs, and suitable hymnody when it's time to pray for crop failure. But it's for Monday morning, too, when another miserable work week is getting under way, and for Friday afternoon, when some less fortunate souls get their unemployment check in the mail, not to mention the occasional Tuesdays when good citizens effect change by voting, and on even more special occasions, like D-day and Memorial Day. More than any other contemporary music, it's a window into every aspect of lower- and middle-class life, the civic by no means excluded.

Reporters and op-ed orators tend to trot right past this wide-open casement. But after the 2004 election, pundits had to confront the possibility, welcome or otherwise, that the red states making up the nation's vast middle represented the mainstream of America. If you follow that line of thinking, you could theorize that country, long marginalized by gatekeepers on the coasts, is actually America's most mainstream music.

Some stats support that idea. In 2004, country album sales were up more than any other major genre, having improved by just over 12 percent from the previous calendar year, versus 1.6 percent for the industry as a whole. And the impact of country on *the* country is far greater than CD sales would indicate. Most fans of the genre aren't big record buyers, partly because it's largely an older audience—folks with families who hear about new stuff slowly or intermittently and aren't camping out at the Virgin Megastore at midnight on Mondays to be first to snatch up Martina's latest. Another reason is the extremely restricted playlists on country radio, which is infamous for being slower to embrace new product than any other format. Taking into consideration that airplay logjam, along with the widespread defection of CD buyers to legal and illicit downloading, country's sales growth in 2004 was a remarkable exception to the music industry's ongoing fiscal woes.

There may be better indicators of popularity than record sales. One would be the ratings for the genre's annual awards shows. The 2005 Grammy Awards drew a total audience of 18.8 million viewers. Compare that figure against the Country Music Association (CMA) Awards, broadcast on the same network, CBS, just three months prior, which drew 18.4 million viewers, a statistically insignificant difference. In other words, if the Grammys had expanded the token country segment—into which they had shoehorned stars like Gretchen Wilson, Tim McGraw, and Keith Urban—to fill the program's entire three hours, the show might have been about as highly rated as it was with J. Lo and Usher thrown in, too.

The best ongoing indicator of country's popularity, though, is radio penetration. As of January 2005, there were 2,028 country stations in the United States. Country music has long been the top format in America and won't abdicate that throne any time soon. Its closest competitor isn't even musical—it's talk radio, with a mere 1,318 stations. (Oldies radio runs a distant third, claiming just 793 outlets, but is still well ahead of such higher-profile laggards as Top 40, rock, urban, and adult contemporary.)

To one way of thinking, there's a certain philosophical overlap between the two top formats, because country radio *is* talk radio—hullo, Mr. Hannity—in the sense that the genre represents middle Americans sharing messages from across staffs of music, as if over backyard picket fences. Plenty of erstwhile rock fans drift over to the format in their old age because, as these converts will tell you, with the exception of Broadway, it's the last place where "the song" matters—by which they usually mean the primacy of the lyric. Virtually every country song is high concept in the same sense that big Hollywood movies are high concept, containing an idea vivid enough to be easily expressed in a single sentence (and a sentence that doesn't always boil down to: *Your pants—off, now*).

The overlap with talk radio extends to the overwhelmingly conservative listenerships of both audiences, and here's where a few of those slumming rockers slip back off the bandwagon. Certainly there are a good chunk of Democrats, even self-professed liberal/progressive wing nuts, in the industry and the audience. But the stereotype that country music has become the house genre of the GOP isn't easily or persuasively disproven.

How conservative *is* the base? Or: How synonymous are the Grand Old Party and Grand Ole Opry? Sara Evans, reigning sweetheart of the country music rodeo, provides what might be telling anecdotal evidence when she recalls a gaffe she made being interviewed before the 2004 election.

"I went on CNBC and they wanted to ask me my response to that ridiculous tour that all those artists did that didn't amount to a hill of beans—the Vote for Kerry tour," she says, meaning the Vote for Change tour that country expats the Dixie Chicks took part in. "And I just said, it's not gonna make any difference at all. George Bush is gonna win . . . Then they asked me something about my fans, and I just kind of blithely said, 'Well, most of my fans are Republicans anyway.' And then, I thought, that was such a dumb thing to say!"

Or was it? Evans is a beloved personality in the genre, with one of its warmest voices and most welcoming musical sensibilities. Though she's known among the faithful for her conservative causes and occasional stumping for Bush, there hasn't been a word of political content in any of her albums that would attract or repel a particularly culturally skewed fan base. So how great was the groundswell of her Democratic fans writing in to say, hey, don't you forget about me? Nonexistent, she says—though she'll allow that, perhaps, not that many people were watching the channel at that moment. (No offense, we're sure, CNBC.) But surely at some point non-Republican members of her fan club must have written in to say they still worship her but wish she hadn't gone all partisan on 'em? "No, not at all. Or at least none that anybody told me about." She's smiling apologetically, as if she almost wishes she did have one or two angry exes on her street team to offer up as anecdotal sacrifices.

Bear in mind that seeming lack of resistance to GOP partisanship among the genre's base (and you *know* rockers like Bruce Springsteen and John Mellencamp are getting unhappy cards and letters each time they suggest swinging the opposite way), combine it with the crushing conservative backlash against the Dixie Chicks, and a feller who's a Friend of Bill could start to feel lonesome at the big barn dance. It would be easy for sensitive Dems to feel left behind in the rapture-like exodus that has seen the Southern and heartland states—the ones that most reliably produce and support country music—shift allegiance from one party to the other in only two generations' time, perhaps for good.

When it comes to country conservatism, "the stereotype is very well documented, and the perception is pretty much the reality," concedes Sony Nashville head John Grady. "When your newly reelected two-term president is the former governor of Texas, that falls within the stereotype of the demographic a little bit. And I guess radio would be considered Republican, if the guys that own the biggest conglomerates of radio stations are also from Texas and are outspoken supporters of President Bush and way up there on his list of givers. It's hard to argue against the stereotype. I'm speaking in generalities, and everyone has his own personal beliefs, but when you have major hit records like [Toby Keith's] 'The Angry American' and [Darryl Worley's] 'Have You Forgotten' all over the airwaves of country radio, at the same time as the Dixie Chicks scenario, where the medium went the other way, the generalities would tell you that that's where it's swung." Not that he'd swing it that way himself, being a Democrat, but "right now, it is what it is."

Not quite everyone believes that country's fans are the mirror image of liberal Hollywood. That's a canard to Country Music Television's editorial director, Chet Flippo, who argues, "The notion that all country fans are totally conservative is rubbish, and it's a result of cable news groupthink. These days everything must be easily labeled, pigeonholed, and categorized, or it's dismissed as nonexistent. If something isn't red state or blue state, it can't be computed." Sharing his chagrin, a majority of artists and the bean counters who rely on them would prefer that the music remain altogether apolitical and not alienate even a single listener whose purchase might provide the next day's per diem.

If party lines are mentioned in song, it's usually for the purpose of declaring bipartisanship: Wright's "Bumper" includes the line "I'm not a Democrat or Republican," and nearly the same party-shunning wording is found in such seemingly ecumenical anthems as the Warren Brothers' "Hey Mr. President" and Big & Rich's "Love Train." The latter duo broke out in 2004 by going musically left of center, even incorporating rap into the act, but they're the same as most of their country brethren in insisting that they're no respecters of politically divisive lines—even if they did accept an invite to perform at the GOP's Black Tie and Boots inaugural ball, where, they insist, there were plenty of Capitol Hill Democrats as well as Bush partisans just there for the party, as opposed to, you know, for the party. John Rich reiterates the splotchy mantra of togetherness: "We're not a red state or blue state act. We're purple state."

Gretchen Wilson, a compatriot of Big & Rich and arguably already the new queen of country, may be the quintessential "Redneck Woman," but she might also rather be dead than definitively branded red, politically. Her don't-tread-on-me attitude extends to labeling. "One of the greatest things about the country music industry and why it's always been more appealing to me than any other genre of music is its openness, and how all the artists really are friendly with each other and there's no competition," Wilson says. (Some of her sistren will gag at this characterization; others will insist Nashville really is that nice.) "I feel like politics go along the same lines. Country music is supposed to unite people. And we all do our own things and we have different opinions, but we all get along and have so many things in common that I don't see red and blue. I just see purple." But here Wilson has an admission to make. "I guess I'm a little bit confused. Do people really think that most country music listeners are either Democrat or Republicans?"

Well, sure, there's a perception out there that . . .

"That what, we're all Democrats?"

Nope, not where we were headed with that one.

"That we're Republicans? Oh. You see how out of the loop I am?" Surprising, but it may have something to do with where Wilson grew up. She was raised in rural Illinois and spent most of her adult years in St. Louis, where politics may not feel quite as one-sided as they've come to in most parts of the Deep South. It's worth remembering that country music is massive in plenty of blue-collar states in the north and Midwest where, quite unlike the nearly union-free South, labor has a strong political presence and the Democratic party hasn't completely squandered the double-digit advantage it's enjoyed in union areas, even though the traditional-values trolley is clearly making plenty of stops at guild strongholds, too.

But let's face it: for all of Wilson's and Big & Rich's nonpartisan mauve talk, country's party gap looks wider than the Gulf of Mexico. Leaving content aside, you can look at who hit the campaign trail for George W. Bush and quickly come up with a list of country heavyweights, including Brooks & Dunn, Lee Ann Womack, and Travis

Tritt. Among the ranks of Kerry campaigners in 2004—leaving out the Chicks, who may be (cue the Eagles) already gone from country, having issued some statements about repositioning themselves in the rock & roll camp—there were exactly zero major Nashville stars. Perhaps that imbalance makes up for the complete absence of major rockers openly harboring warm fuzzies for the Bush dynasty, if you're looking for the political yin to country's twang.

Mike Long, a former *National Review* contributor and speechwriter for Republicans like Senator Fred Thompson, lived in Nashville for a decade and saw firsthand the industry's vitality in attracting and maintaining the GOP's core constituency, and vice versa. "I don't like mainstream country music," Long admits. "But if you do like it, that says that you're not overly concerned about being cool. And people who are Republicans are not too concerned about being cool." The recent return of the long-waning rebel attitude in country fits in perfectly with how the GOP has reimagined itself as the true countercultural party ever since the P.J. O'Rourke revolution, which was arguably as significant as Newt Gingrich's. For much of the Skynyrd set, anyway, it's the triumph of anti-chic cool.

Holly Gleason, a Music Row manager, publicist, and self-professed liberal, says that mainstream musical elitism combines with Democratic political elitism to create a climate that only feeds Southern conservatives' underdog pride. "Truth is, the wider entertainment culture doesn't give a damn about any of these people," says Gleason. "Country music is the one thing that reminds the liberal media about everything about being white and Midwestern or middle American that they don't like. There's a bias against country music, so it feeds into the us-against-them attitude some artists and fans have: 'And by the way, more people like *us*, liberal Hollywood!' It's a very proud red badge." Of courage, or of reverse double-back conformity; take your pick.

Jes' Folk

Country's truest aficionados might feel torn—wanting the music not to fall into a partisan trap, but feeling that perhaps it *should* be political, to the extent that it's always at its best when it's been brutally honest about how real people think, love, and live, and that shutting off the stuff of the culture wars from the rest of what's acceptable to write and sing about constitutes an unreasonable restriction of creative trade. Country music isn't merely talk-radio redux; it's also the new folk music. Which, considering folk's traditional alliance with the left, might strike some as the equivalent of saying white slacks after Labor Day is the new black. But the commonalities become clearer if you throw alternative country into the mix as a balancing factor for mainstream country. Certainly the Grammys are confused on the matter; nearly every album that's been nominated recently in their "contemporary folk" category, from Johnny Cash's *The Man Comes Around* to Lucinda Williams's *Car Wheels on a Gravel Road* to Steve Earle's *The Revolution Starts . . . Now*, can at least loosely be considered alt-country at the core. And the common origins of country and folk make a contemporary reconvergence almost inevitable.

In the early twentieth century, "hillbilly" music and urban folk music appropriated the traditional songs that came from the Appalachias, which in turn were adopted from tunes handed down by Irish and other immigrants. Performed in highfalutin' settings, folk music appeared as something exotic and enchanting; the hillbilly version of the same stuff stayed in the hills, at least until the Carter Family made it viable material for recordings in the late 1920s. Later, around 1940, the name finally got officially changed to "country" by its more stereotype-wary practitioners. Country partisans have always been suspicious of pop crossover, and Woody Guthrie was the original crossover star, making his name in the hillbilly ghetto he soon abandoned for the less woodsy climes of Carnegie Hall when it became evident that his burgeoning political sensibilities wouldn't require such careful parsing up north.

"Guthrie was 'hillbilly' in every sense of the word until he moved to New York in 1940," says Bill C. Malone, country music's foremost historian. "Country people recognized him as that until he went to New York and identified with the radical community there. He cut himself off from the hillbilly constituency, and they pretty much forgot about him, except for a few of his songs. But there was no reason to separate him from the Carter Family or Jimmie Rodgers or any of those people. That's how he thought of himself, until he found out that in New York people were using a different word— 'folk' instead of 'hillbilly' or 'country.' Hillbilly music as a whole was nothing but folk music when it started out. That's where they got their songs, the great body of orally transmitted material, ballads and love songs and fiddle tunes and the rest. That's what they filled up their records and their radio broadcasts with."

From then on, there were important similarities and distinct differences. Most crucially, country and folk both extolled the value of the working class as the bedrock of America and decried the forces that would keep a simple man down. The chief point of divergence is whether the solution to social problems could be found in coming together in groups for reform or by pulling up one's own bootstraps, as it were. Part of this disagreement may stem from environment: If you live in an apartment building, you tend to think in terms of cooperative problem-solving; if you live on the farm and can't see another soul in any direction, your attitude may be more DIY—although the New Deal did sort of derail extreme individualist thinking for a few decades. The idea that every man has to be responsible for himself because there's no one else around may be outmoded in an era when more country fans live in suburbs and newfangled exurbs than on farms, but the sentiment endures even as the landscape changes.

When it comes to the lower and lower-middle classes, "the political anger is offset by some deeply ingrained social traits that have always been part of Southern working-class thinking," says Malone. "It's that individualism, the belief that if there's a solution to be found, it's gonna be found through individual exertion. And if it can't be found, then you just fatally accept it, or flee from it—flee into fantasy or into religion or into the bottle or into geographic movement. If you're not satisfied here, go someplace else, or retreat into anger, violence—all kinds of individual responses outside of collective action. And that's the most tragic consequence of union decline." Well, tragic in one respect, maybe. But what might have been bad for liberal social reform programs has been swell for a genre whose songs have historically been rife with the rich struggles and deep shadows of one guitar-slinging journeyman pitted against the world.

If many of country's leading lights insist that they don't believe in mixing music and politics, topicality can't help but rear its head—that is, when the music isn't mired in one of its periodic pop crossover phases. It's just too inherently blunt to avoid being influenced by current attitudes and events for a very long time. As Kris Kristofferson, whose music has always veered between folk and country traditions, puts it: "I saw some book the other day called *Shut Up and Sing* [by conservative talk show host Laura Ingraham], and my only feeling was: I am singing, dammit—shut up and listen!'"

Fast React

In the days following the terrorist attacks of 2001, the singer/song-writers of the pop world struggled to find relevance in the platform they'd been given and form an appropriate response. And struggled, and struggled.

Finally, the results of all this rock & roll brow-furrowing started to come in. Paul McCartney, one of the half-dozen greatest songwriters of the previous century, delivered a spirited new anthem called "Freedom." It really did unite the divided peoples of a wounded nation, in unanimous declaration that this was the suckiest composition of his storied career (and yes, the masses were quick to multilaterally add, that did include "Ebony and Ivory"). What did the vegan and vaguely pacifistic-seeming superstar mean, exactly, when he sang, "I will fight for the right to live in freedom / Anyone who wants to take it away will have to answer, 'cause this is my right!'"? Was Paul speaking in support of the "just" war philosophy, or was he merely waxing figurative, as bubblegum bards sometimes will? We may never know, because between his halftime appearance at Super Bowl XXVI in New Orleans, when American retaliation for the terrorist attacks was merely theoretical, and his mid-game show at Super Bowl XXIX in Jacksonville, when war had become a messy reality, he'd wisely retired the tune from his set.

Neil Young might have seemed better equipped for such a topical task. Three decades earlier, the mercurial rocker had written a song about "four dead in Ohio" and released it within two weeks of the actual event. But forty-five dead in Pennsylvania seemed to vex him. "Let's Roll," a tribute to the heroic passengers who fought with terrorists on doomed Flight 93, was well intentioned enough, yet the song was curiously unmoving, despite its charged subject matter. Post-9/11 rock wasn't completely a dud: Bruce Springsteen finally stepped up to the plate ten and a half months after the attacks with a rich collection called *The Rising*, but as strong and bittersweet as the album was, its euphemistic approach to the tragedies prompted a mixed, somewhat muted reaction among even hardcore fans.

Into the breach where Macca and Neil had so badly foundered stepped a troubadour who proved to be far more galvanizing, a guy just coming off another anthemic single of a different sort in which he'd addressed issues of tolerance, acceptance, and esteem among society's underclass, "It's Alright to Be a Redneck." It was only natural to look to unassuming honky-tonk hat act Alan Jackson to step up to the contemplative plate and become a funereal America's new poet laureate, no?

Naw, but for country fans already accustomed to seeing Jackson's sensitive side, in between uptempo cuts that take the piss out of contemporary country convention, it was only a minor shock when Jackson rose to the occasion with the reflective "Where Were You (When the World Stopped Turning)." It was a bigger jolt for some city folk, surprised to find themselves acknowledging that this down-home Georgian had modestly assumed the mantle of cataloging the nation's litany of ambivalent, conflicted post-9/11 feelings, and whispering to themselves: *Out of the mouths of rubes . . .*

The rock world was again slow to respond when American forces massed around a defiant Saddam in early 2003 for the second Gulf War. On the eve of major combat, *Entertainment Weekly* critic David Browne wrote a column scolding rockers for being timid or tardy: "Remember when rock stars did crazy, zany things like voice their opposition to armed conflicts around the world? Me neither . . . Are musicians afraid to go against the status quo and risk alienating the public?" Rockers may have been as yellow as Browne suggested, or perhaps they were just baffled in a way they hadn't been in the latter days of the Vietnam era; after all, if the Democratic caucus in Congress mostly believed WMDs posed an imminent threat, maybe Rob Thomas and Fred Durst were legitimately fooled, too.

When rock stars did start turning against the war en masse and in song, their noninterventionist advocacy proved mostly embarrassing, not galvanizing. Take the Beastie Boys, who'd been off the scene for years and reappeared with one of the era's first fresh anti-war tracks, "In a World Gone Mad." Rather than establishing them as musical leaders for a new generation of dissent, the hastily assembled song only made the Beasties seem like naifs who'd lost the plot during their long sabbatical, and tepid reaction to the tune may have even helped keep the album that followed from becoming the predicted blockbuster. Lower-level punks got off some broadsides, but nothing much stuck. Green Day finally had a commercial and critical hit in late 2004 with *American Idiot,* a concept album that contained some basic but highly quotable anti-Bush asides. With Jackson Browne and other old-guard singer/songwriters long since marginalized in the culture, the anti-war left had found a freshly successful spokesrocker in the form of Green Day's Billie Joe Armstrong, although bellowing "Fuck Bush!" at crowds composed of third-generation Mohawks probably counts as a classic case of cussing to the choir.

In mainstream country music, meanwhile, the immediate response to the war effort was not nearly so belated or weak. Nor, for the most part, was it "anti-." "Courtesy of the Red, White and Blue" and "Have You Forgotten?"—both written as populist justifications of America's invasion of Afghanistan—each connected with their audience in an immediate and massive way, even if acceptance wasn't nearly so broad as it had been for Jackson's more passive reflection. If Alan had caused a lot of rock fans to set aside their presumptions about country, the ballads of Toby Keith and Darryl Worley helped the outside world re-assume prejudices about war-mongering rednecks, rightly or wrongly; the word *jingoistic* appeared on cue in virtually every review. The artists' assertions that these songs were written about the early Taliban-rousting, and not as cries to invade Iraq, were widely ignored or disbelieved by critics. Yet for all their militarism, these were essentially folk songs, as broadly defined. Darryl Worley and Toby Keith had come up with the most rousing protest music in a generation, regardless of whether what they were protesting—terrorists, the countries that supposedly coddle them, and, in Worley's case, American amnesia and a perceived lack of will to take the challenge all the way—was deemed an appropriate target by guardians of the troubadour tradition.

Didn't the widespread publicity over these gung-ho wartime songs, occurring hot on the heels of radio's wholesale rejection of the Dixie Chicks after a single offhand Bush-bashing comment, cement country's status as the house genre of the GOP, leaving any self-respecting liberal to slink off to rock & roll, where she belongs?

Whoa, Nellie McKay. This was still everybody's music, according to the eloquent case made by Chet Flippo, in his weekly column on CMT's website. "One of the lessons of the last several presidential elections is that he who has the most country music on his side has the electorate on his side," wrote Flippo shortly before George W. Bush's second inauguration. "Country music is populist music, plain and simple. And it's not just white music or Southern music or rural music or hillbilly music. It's everyday driving to work, drinking a beer after work with friends, dancing on the weekend kind of music. Forget red states versus blue states kind of music: Good country music—as ever—is just about real life and how it applies to daily life." So far, so uncontroversial. "Music should not be a political weapon, which is something that people like to make it be," Flippo's column continued. "One of the national cable news networks has been trying to get the 'real' story about the politics of country artists. I don't think there is a real story there. Like everyone else, country artists are on both sides of the political aisle." Yes, but . . . "There are a lot of intolerant people who seem to live in full attack mode these days," conceded Flippo. "Even so, country is still a genre with a wide embrace. It can appreciate a Steve Earle and a Darryl Worley, can accommodate a Toby Keith and a Gillian Welch, can celebrate a Kenny Chesney and a Bruce Robison. I think it is a lot more tolerant and understanding than any other music genre these days."

He lost a few people there. Was this we-*can*-all-get-along manifesto an uncharacteristic case of wishful thinking on the part of the dean of contemporary country journalists? Flippo made the music sound like a big tent capable of accomodating both the Hatfields and the McCoys, but most observers would see these as two distinct clans who only get together on special occasions, like awkward weddings, and then gravitate toward opposite ends of the reception hall. There *is* a leftish wing in country, but it's generally called alternative country, Americana, roots music, No Depression, y'alltternative, or some other appellation marking it as the less popular, critically more palatable stuff. You might be tempted to view the liberal-leaning "alt" side of country as "separate but equal"—equal meaning far punier, to put things in cynical late-nineteenth-century Supreme Court terms.

Yet setting aside the assumption that your average, conservative, middle-American country radio listener has never heard of Bruce Robison and may hope never to hear the apostate likes of Steve Earle again, there's a good case to be made that these variations *do* exist on a musical and political continuum. Geographically, they share the same base: Even if the alt-country movement still claims Austin as its spiritual home, attempts to root the Americana music industry there in the early 1990s proved less then fruitful, and so the business of roots music is now firmly entrenched along Music Row—even if Texas-favoring Nashville-phobes grumble that this constitutes sleeping with the enemy. Crossover between these two seemingly distinct forms of country has long occurred in all kinds of mundane and spectacular fashions, usually when mainstream stars look to the city's musical fringes for potential hit songs and great pickers.

Fans may still be expected to choose sides between the cool and popular crowds, but Flippo isn't the only lane changer out there. And taken together, the voices of country and alt country provide a valuable conduit to eavesdrop on what's being said in the South and the heartland from every angle—and, ultimately, this is an only slightly skewed subset of the nation as a whole. At least one commentator said that to better understand the electorate, if not to pander to it, John Kerry should have spent less time listening to Eminem (who he claimed, not entirely credibly, as a favorite while on the election trail) and more listening to country. Whether his successors will be wise enough to listen in—to figure out how to better reach across the aisle, or to pick up pointers on which populist formulas could be appropriated to better whup the other side—remains to be seen. But midway through the first decade of the new century, it seems clear enough that country is the only musical forum where all this stuff is even open for discussion.

This book aims to accentuate those voices beyond what's already on record, not to fill some perceived celebrity-yapping void, but because each of these figures, whether they're selling at the multiplatinum or sand pebble level, can be presumed to speak for a wide constituency. The hope is to capture what a few representative middle Americans had to say during the critical three and a half years between 9/11 and Bush's reinauguration, with only minimal editorial interruption and snark. Hope you enjoy a good rant.

Is it possible that opposing flanks might be ready to resume what Bobby Bare, in a song that became an early seventies cult favorite, referred to as a "Redneck Hippie Romance"? Which, in our updated coinage, would be a love affair between crimson-throated conservatives and the alt types we'll call bluenecks? Or is it simply, as Rodney Crowell said, a dogfight? If you're a true believer in the extreme left or right, probably too much seems at stake to savor the back-and-forth of the discussion. If you believe that all abortion is murder, or that all women are about to cede control of their bodies to a theocracy, and if you're pacifistic enough to believe that any military effort is a tragic waste, even if it has some life-favoring side effects, or hawkish enough to argue that dissent should take a sabbatical during the key stages of wartime, then maybe you view dialogue as fatal compromise or a waste of time. But for the majority of us who incline toward the center from those most extreme poles, it might be fun as well as instructive to consider mainstream and alternative country and the political philosophies they reflect as a discordant duet. Maybe it's too much to expect many music fans to find merit in the Dixie Chicks *and* Toby Keith, or to want to hear out Ronnie Dunn *and* Steve Earle, much less such unlikely-to-register-as-domestic-partners bedfellows as Montgomery Gentry and the Drive-by Truckers. Me, I like to imagine this cavalcade of country and alt-country talents on a musical carousel, like the old "America Sings!" attraction at Disneyland—Maines and Worley and Willie and Ricky and Toby and Merle all spinning around till they blend into a joyous blur of patriotic self-expression that would make the Founding Fathers nauseous and proud.

Honk if you agree. If not, you know what that finger is for.

At the Dixie Chicks' 2003 tour opener in Greenville, South Carolina, Natalie Maines made only joking allusions to the ongoing controversy surrounding the band, letting her T-shirt do much of the talking. PHOTO BY RICK DIAMOND

1

Plucked

The Dixie Chicks on the Path to Slaughter

They were supposed to be uniters, not dividers.

So many supposed-to-bes to consider here. The Dixie Chicks' *Home* was the album that was supposed to be an idiosyncratic side project, until the 2002 release proved unexpectedly popular enough to bring together mainstream country populists, alt-country snobs, rock singer/songwriter partisans, bluegrass buffs, hillbillies, hippies, soccer moms, NASCAR stepdads, aesthetes, Austinites, and the disparate populations of Music Row, Manhattan, Topanga Canyon, and Topeka—for about six peaceable months, anyway. Before a world of woe came down on their heads, there was that brief, shining moment when it seemed like the Dixie Chicks might be the three-woman cavalry that would save country music from a recession, from creative doldrums, from excessive inbreeding, maybe even from a seven-decade history of off-again, on-again cultural and musical division. Not to put *too* messianic a point on it, but the album really was that good.

Like many would-be saviors, *Home* had a somewhat humble birth, though expectations could be only so small given that its two predecessors, *Wide Open Spaces* (1997) and *Fly* (1999), earned rare RIAA diamond certifications, awarded for 10 million in sales each. Despite that nearly unprecedented track record, there was little expectation that the group's third major-label album would do even a quarter of that number. They'd just come out of a messy lawsuit over their accounting with Columbia Records, the secret settlement of which won them untold concessions. While they were still in legal limbo, the Chicks—believing themselves to be unsigned free agents (Sony's attorneys would've had a field day begging to differ in court)—entered an Austin studio. Maines's dad, Lloyd, best known to insurgent country loyalists as Joe Ely's longtime guitar player, was at the helm. They used the lull to record a "bluegrass record" that they figured they might release independently as a stopgap project or leak over the Internet.

"You can think about stuff too much," says Maines. "Thank God we didn't have a label at the time, because we would have second-thought the first single, second-thought the length of the songs, second-thought there being no drums. We never once asked those questions of ourselves, ever—because we never thought it was going to get played on the radio. We didn't even think it was going to be sold by retail stores."

"And now it's not!" quips Emily Robison, the trio's banjo player.

"See? Premonitions. Well, we fooled 'em for a while," Maines figures.

Once the legal eagles had their say, Sony kissed and made up with the Chicks and, to the group's surprise, wanted to promote *Home* as the natural successor in a series of blockbusters, with no warnings to consumers that they might want to think of this as a cult favorite. The potentially room-chilling phrase "bluegrass record" was not uttered in public until several million sales were safely in the bag. "Acoustic album"? Seldom, either, were those sales-discouraging words heard.

"Sony didn't want us making a big deal about it being different," says fiddler Martie Maguire. "They were afraid it would scare people away. We kind of wanted to talk about it and be truthful—that we didn't think this would ever see the light of day, that we thought maybe it would be for the hardcore fans to download off the website. Sony settled with us before they ever heard the music, and though I thought Sony would say, 'Okay, this is your little side project and we'll put it out there, but then we need a studio record,' they weren't like that at all. I had much more respect for them after they took this record seriously. They said, 'If radio won't play this, they're crazy.' It helped our relationship with the label a lot."

The conceit paid off. Undistracted by forewarnings about drum-lessness, the public simply heard and responded to as fine a country album as has ever been recorded. Little-noticed ironies were there for anyone with ears to hear. The album's lead track and first single, "Long Time Gone," written by Darrell Scott, has the spirit of a pep talk but is really an elegy for a rapidly disappearing way of life and way of music. The beloved family farm—*"Ain't hoed a row since I don't know when"*—gone. The greatness of classic country—*"They sound tired but they don't sound Haggard / They got money but they don't have Cash"*— gone. Childhood sweethearts? Youthful spiritual convictions? Everything must go!, as the signs read in so many rural downtown storefronts. In singing about intergenerational losses in rural America, and wrapping the rue in the good cheer of fiddles and mandolins, the Chicks managed to revive a chunk of the very traditionalism whose loss the lyrics lament. No song so full of acidic social truths ever sounded so celebratory, and when the tune zipped to No. 1 on the country charts, you couldn't help feeling that everybody won: the traditionalists desperate not to let those bygones be bygones, and the progressives and pragmatists nursing bittersweet feelings about seeing the modern dust storms sweep away all the old customs, mores, and music.

There was more where that came from. Belying the album title, the song "Long Time Gone," in its own wry way, described a state of spiritual homelessness. The same could be said about the heartbreaking title track, "Home," a ballad of romantic remorse. But there was no regret quite as severe as that in the record's concluding track, Patty Griffin's "Top of the World," a song that could send a chill down even a seasoned spine after repeat listens. The lyric's narrator is a grumpy and emotionally distant old man who, we find out two-thirds of the way through the song, is well beyond the point of making familial amends, having been embalmed. But not everything was that heavy: There was grand kitsch in the gallop-tempoed form of "White Trash Wedding"—inspired by Maguire's own low-rent matrimony to an Irishman of modest means—and breakneck bluegrass fun in "Lil' Jack Slade," named after Natalie's firstborn, an instant addition to the canon of instrumentals that old-time string bands would be covering for decades.

And then, becoming the third big radio smash from the album (after "Long Time" and the remake of Fleetwood Mac's "Landslide"), was another profoundly piquant ballad, "Travelin' Soldier." Or, as the song's writer, Bruce Robison, wryly puts it: "the fastest descending number-one country single in the history of the *Billboard* charts."

Wherein lies our tale. "Travelin' Soldier" concerns a high school girl who commences a secret romance with an enlistee right before he ships off to Vietnam. In the tearjerker of a last verse, his name is read as part of a list of local war dead during halftime at the football game, sending the sweet young piccolo player bawling under the stands, the slightly older boy's only apparent mourner. "It's not a pro-war song or an anti-war song," says Maines, echoing the impartial sentiments of its writer. But a lot of country fans took it as supportive of the military, which is why some were surprised and dismayed when Maines, in a much-publicized interview with the Los Angeles *Daily News*, put some distance between that and a more overtly "pro-troops" tune, "Courtesy of the Red, White, and Blue (The Angry American)." Asked her opinion of Toby Keith's popularly beloved go-get-'em post-9/11 anthem, Maines didn't hold back much: "Don't get me started. I hate it. It's ignorant, and it makes country music sound ignorant. It targets an entire culture—and not just the bad people who did bad things. You've got to have some tact. Anybody can write, 'We'll put a boot in your ass.' But a lot of people agree with it. The kinds of songs I prefer on the subject are like Bruce Springsteen's new songs."

Some patriots marked this Toby-bashing down on their mental list of Things That Make You Go Hmmm. Combine that with some mostly unspoken sentiments in country music circles that maybe the Chicks were gettin' above their raisin' by insisting on dealing with Sony's New York brass over the Nashville office, or that their lawsuit had constituted a kind of blackmail or that they were divas for not committing to the heavy promotional rounds that had become de rigueur for genre acts, and you had some of the potential ingredients for a minor Music Row backlash, too.

Home was certified platinum six times over the very week of "the incident," as it continues to be euphemized in the Chicks' camp. At the rapid clip at which the CD was then selling, eight or nine million seemed within easy reach, if not the ten that the more obviously commercial *Fly* had done. But two years after the controversy unfolded, the album still hadn't officially been bumped up to seven million.

London Calling . . . Radio Clash

"Just so you know, we're ashamed the president of the United States is from Texas." It was the between-song rim shot heard 'round the world, blurted out by Maines on Monday, March 10, 2003, at London's 2,000-seat Shepherd's Bush Empire. At least, she was said to have said it in a review that appeared two days later in the *Guardian*, which recounted the insult approvingly, given the paper's leftist bent; critic Betty Clarke added, "At a time when country stars are rushing to release pro-war anthems, this is practically punk rock." Anti-Bush sentiment was so strong throughout Europe at the time that if none of the half dozen other reviewers on hand bothered to mention the impromptu remark, it was probably because it seemed like standard-issue stuff in their world.

A nearly *Rashomon*-like number of recollections have been suggested over the context of the remark, each with its own spin. Some members of the backing band later told friends that it happened after Maines said "We're the Dixie Chicks and we're from Texas!" only to be greeted by booing; both the audience's jeering and the singer's sudden response were recalled as being all in good fun. The Chicks themselves tell a slightly different, not necessarily contradictory version—that it was a spontaneous part of Maines's introduction to "Travelin' Soldier," and that the cheers that inevitably greeted it in a Bush-hostile atmosphere were followed by her sober admonition that the group *did* support the troops gathering in the Middle East, if not their commanding officer.

No big deal, in any case, except that this aside in Wednesday's *Guardian* review got noticed and picked up in an American wire story. By the end of the day, in response to flaring tempers, the band issued an unapologetic, naively courageous clarification of intent: "We've been overseas for several weeks and have been reading and following the news accounts of our government's position. The anti-American sentiment that has unfolded here is astounding. While we support our troops, there is nothing more frightening than the notion of going to war with Iraq and the prospect of all the innocent lives that will be lost."

If the Chicks thought they were dousing a media flame, there was nothing but high-octane petrol in *that* particular fire hydrant. It took a while for their sober but unrepentant meditation on a formerly flippant remark to circulate on Thursday. Friday morning, the treason hit the fan, as a nation of country and talk jocks expressed undying gratitude for being given such excellent grist for a four-hour shift by painting the Chicks as bleached-blond Benedict Arnolds. Never mind that at the moment they had the number-one country single and the top-selling album in any genre, or that less than two weeks earlier, on March 1, they'd set an all-time one-day record for concert grosses by selling $49 million in tickets in less than twenty-four hours. They might have been the biggest act in America, but the smell of toast was in the air. Napalm, too, since radio jocks do love the smell of it in morning drive time.

One radio station that helped get the boycott ball rolling was WTDR-FM in Talladega, Alabama. On Friday, their morning team asked listeners to call and decide whether to "ditch the Chicks" or not. "The phone just went ballistic," recalled Jim Jacobs, head of the broadcast group that owns the station, when I got past the presumed hordes of indignant dialers and reached him that weekend. "I've been doing radio for twenty-eight years, and I've never seen anything get that kind of response." Jacobs said that before the end of the morning shift the station had answered 250 calls—a fraction of the listeners trying to get through—"and 248 of them said 'Stop playing their music' and two said 'Continue playing it.'" Before noon, they'd made a decision to pull all Chicks music and, more important, to alert the media. Once news of this went out over the Associated Press, other stations couldn't follow suit fast enough in making a public show of telling the trio: Your music will never work in this town again.

"We think there is a valuable lesson here to be learned by the entertainment community," Jacobs said. "In all honesty, unless they find a way to put a really neat spin on this, it's my opinion that this woman's killed her career." This statement seemed mind-boggling at the time, considering that less than a week had passed since the Chicks' London gig—their song was still at No. 1 and, for all anyone knew, would stay there—but the reaction was instantaneous. "The general public, especially the conservative general public that tends to be the audience of a country radio station, are sick and tired of entertainers telling us what they think we should believe," Jacobs told me, "when that's not what we use them for to begin with."

I had to ask: "Do the listeners express the same opposition when Darryl Worley or Toby Keith express their opinions?" (Irony intended.)

"Oh, we haven't seen that," Jacobs answered. "In fact, people have been very pro-those types of songs here." (Irony not taken.)

Not every country programmer was champing at the bit to ditch the format's biggest act. At KPLX-FM in Dallas–Fort Worth, program director Paul Williams confessed confusion over what the station's listeners actually thought, because he wasn't sure they had been able to get through the barrage of calls coming in from non-listeners. "There are a couple of websites out there that have programmers' e-mail addresses, and are encouraging people to 'E-mail these people and tell 'em you support our president and hate the Dixie Chicks.' So as far as getting any real listener reaction, it's kinda difficult to tell, except for the request line, which is pretty much fifty-fifty. It's getting harder, because every time one of the talk-radio hosts in this town goes on the air hammering 'em, our phones light up—but those aren't our listeners, those are talk-radio listeners." Williams was unsure then how things would go. "There's a lot of people that came to this format and this station because of the Dixie Chicks. I'm hoping that there is healing and that it gets fixed, because they've been pretty important to us. But if the listeners are going to turn it off when they hear it, then I'd be stupid to play it." He gave a laugh and tried, on their behalf, to look on the bright side: "They may be okay at AC [adult contemporary]."

Cox Broadcasting canceled a syndicated evening show from Jones Radio Networks that aired on six of its stations, simply because Jones initially refused to keep the Chicks' music off the show. By March 18, Jones had complied and offered to supply a Chicks-free version of the show, but this cave-in came too late; Cox said the cancellation still stood, according to the trades.

When I got hold of Chuck Browning, general manager of Cox in Tulsa, he denied that there was any chainwide ban in effect, though he admitted that as a local programmer he wasn't playing them, and was hard-pressed to name anyone who was. He expressed some disappointment over the "hatchet job" other stations were doing on the Chicks, though his sympathy had its limits. "There are places across the country where the whole thing became a 'bit,' and I don't believe in that. But we did some callout research, and the vast majority said *we don't want it*. So we just took it off the air quietly and didn't say anything. As long as the people who listen to this radio station say they don't want it, they won't get it." This would soon become radio chains' line of defense when called on to justify implicit or explicit bans. "I thought that things might start to blow over," Browning added. "If anything, it's gotten worse. We happen to be a country where if someone falls from grace, and recovers admirably, we actually look up to those people more. We love someone who rises from the ashes. But if you don't recover in admirable fashion, you could be damned for life."

On Friday, Maines issued a second statement that aspired toward recovery but achieved only brimstone. This one *did* take the form of a mea culpa. Seeing how much additional damage the Wednesday statement had done, she opted to compose an apology, albeit one that was very pointed in what it did and didn't cover. "As a concerned American citizen, I apologize to President Bush because my remark was disrespectful. I feel that whoever holds that office should be treated with the utmost respect. We are currently in Europe and witnessing a huge anti-American sentiment as a result of the perceived rush to war. While war may remain a viable option, as a mother, I just want to see every possible alternative exhausted before children and American soldiers' lives are lost. I love my country. I am a proud American."

By now, many malcontents, holding out for a more profound penance and looking to read between the lines, took this carefully crafted statement to be Maines's way of saying: *Look, I'm sorry I dissed George Bush, the president. But George Bush, the man—wow, what a tool. I could've probably said it better—dignity, always dignity—but he's still a warmonger, and y'all can go blow yourselves, okay?* In any case, the number of Bush supporters nationwide who accepted the statement as heartfelt contrition may have numbered in the single digits. Which was probably as it should have been; months later, Maines would finally admit to regretting having made any apology at all. And so the game was on.

The heat doubled back on some of the supposed boycotters. Cumulus, the nation's second biggest chain, had issued a directive not to play the Chicks on any of its 260 stations. Rumors quickly spread that Clear Channel, the Goliath of radio chains, had done the same, which the company's Alan Sledge vehemently denied when I put the question to him. He was able to name some Clear Channel stations that hadn't yet banished the group, though he also described a series of advisories by which individual outlets had been told by the parent company to pay attention to their listeners, which some Chicks supporters took as a nudge-nudge wink-wink. "It was very important to let our radio stations know that we as a company did not want to be in a position of censoring. We did not want to appear punitive, as a company, by issuing a company-wide directive," Sledge said. "It's not our job to censor—but it *is* our job to reflect the tastes of our local communities and local audiences." His personal take: "I think it's a classic example of somebody not knowing who their constituency is. Because the middle-American, bread-and-butter folks that were buying their music are also people who most likely voted for President Bush in the last election."

In areas with more diverse demographics than the deep South, such as Southern California, the situation truly was a quagmire. "The Chicks put radio in general in a rather serious lose/lose position," says R.J. Curtis, programmer of KZLA-FM in Los Angeles, the station with the largest total audience in the nation. "If you take the radio method of operation, which is to seize the moment and use it as a promotional opportunity and then jump on the bandwagon, you set yourself up. Because what happens when it does blow over and they do release a new album? You've kind of prevented yourself from being able to play that artist again. On the other hand, if you *do* play them, many country fans that are patriotic will think that you're supporting their statement. Country listeners tend to be more conservative Republicans even here in Southern California, but we received a surprising amount of e-mail and phone messages from people saying, 'You know what? If you *stop* playing them, I'll never listen to you again.' This from people who weren't against the war, but who felt like it would be censorship. I bet I got a little more of that than someone in Alabama or the middle of the country." KZLA was ultimately one of the few country stations to keep playing the Chicks, though they focused on fun, frothy oldies from the group's baggage-free first two albums.

On talk-radio, there was considerably less careful soul-searching. Glen Beck, whose morning show airs on Nashville's WLAC-AM as well as on 115 other stations, expressed the hope that Maines might get a shove into an airplane propeller. Later, he said he was only being "tongue in cheek." In Bossier City, Louisiana, KRMD-FM urged listeners to bring their CDs by the station's parking lot to be smashed by a tractor. Most bands' handlers would be running scared at such a reprise of the classic Beatles record-stompings of the 1960s, but not Chicks manager Simon Renshaw, who declared his relief after someone sent him footage of the Louisiana event. "It's embarrassing. The best you can do is fewer than a hundred people?" he said. "You can get four hundred people to turn out for a car dealership promotion for a country station! It's not exactly Kristallnacht, you know what I mean?"

Milder versions of these events had to suffice in some locales where a 33,000-pound John Deere couldn't be immediately secured, like Kansas City, where WDAF-AM set out trash cans for ex-fans to do a "chicken toss." Back in Nashville, local talk king Phil Valentine hadn't yet decided on an appropriate symbolic destruction when I rang him up the first week into the schedule. "We're looking at the logistics of doing a Dixie Chicks skeet shoot," he said, adding that "some people have wanted to go down to Music Row and picket Sony, and I think that's a bad idea, because we've got a lot of friends there. Fortunately they have people like Travis Tritt who more than make up for Natalie."

Tritt may have been the Chicks' labelmate, but there was no intra-roster loyalty there. "When you say we're ashamed our president comes from the same state we do, it comes off as being cowardly because it was done across the ocean. I dare her to go to the Astrodome and say that," Tritt told a newscaster. He played the no-dissent-during-major-combat card: "To be a good American—regardless of which side you're on—you have to get behind President Bush."

His stance caused an awkward situation at Nashville's Front Page Publicity firm, whose head, Kathy Allmand Best, represented both the mulleted singer and the towheaded targets of his ire. "Obviously, every country artist was being asked about it," recalls Best. "The problem was when I was asked to set up interviews with Travis by shows that were specifically attacking the Chicks"—the conservative-minded Fox News obviously being one—"and that's where I had to draw the line and, unfortunately, finally quit working with him because of that."

The group's other publicist, New York-based PMK-HBH power-house Cindi Berger, didn't have any such ideological conflicts of interest to resolve with her more liberal client list. I was on the phone with Berger shortly after the controversy broke, setting up what would be the Chicks' first interview upon returning to the States, and heard a familiar-sounding voice coming from elsewhere in Berger's limo yelling "Right-wing assholes!" while the publicist tried to explain away the sinister forces lining up against the Chicks. That female background vocalist was Rosie O'Donnell, another Berger client who'd gone from being America's sweetheart to . . . not.

Since the two gatekeepers the Chicks were most reliant on appeared to be Renshaw, an irascible Englishman in L.A., and Berger, whose other major responsibility at that time was shielding America's most renowned lesbian from bad press in the fallout over a Boy George–conceived Broadway musical she produced, you could reasonably wonder whether the Chicks were getting enough input from anyone more plugged into the vast middle of the country to be as panicked as they ought to be. I was doing some surrogate panicking on their behalf, since, in addition to interviewing radio personalities, not even the most charitable of whom would leap to anything as radical as a modest defense of Maines, I was spending hours a day reading the ugliest Internet postings to come down the pike since the Clinton impeachment craze crested.

One posting on AOL, typical of thousands like it, under the subject head THE ENEMY WITHIN!!, was from a user who identified himself as Bill Russell: "What a sickening disgrace and a slap in the face to every military family in the country. My best wishes for the bitch traitor is that their sales go in the toilet, the public throws out their records, public outcry makes CMA take back the awards, and the lousy bitch never gets to sing in public again and her ass gets shipped to Baghdad before the bombs fall, a little fatter target to hit. Chicks, little chickens, right? Yeah, they are yellow. It is time for America to return to the days when the people were proud and the scumbag traitors and enemy sympathizers were put on trial or turned over to military tribunals. We set a bad precedent with Hanoi Jane. YOU ARE A DISGRACE TO AMERICA AND I HOPE YOU ARE BANNED FROM EVERY AMERICAN RADIO STATION. Then see how great you are, you pig(s). THANK GOD FOR THE LIKES OF CHARLIE DANIELS."

A more succinct post: "Eat some of Earls peas Natali LOL" (*sic*)— this one from GNBCOOK, referring to the Chicks' song "Goodbye Earl," a comic number in which a battered wife offs her abusive husband with some poisoned vegetables. Some Internet users, like SKA-MAY2166, felt fooled by what they formerly saw as the group's cuddliness: "Oh, and I loved you so on *Trading Spaces*. When are you entertainers going to understand that we don't give a damn what you think? Ninety percent of you are uneducated and the other ten percent are smart enough to keep their mouths shut. Mark this day, missy. It is the day you killed the Chicks."

Renshaw was less concerned with the crude puns or weight-related insults than seeming attempts at organization in the rightist ranks. "In these forums, they're talking about manipulating radio. They're giving the names and phone numbers and e-mail addresses of country radio stations, saying 'The poll is currently fifty-fifty. Everyone needs to immediately e-mail the following site.' Then, twenty minutes later, you'll see the same person posting, 'Ha ha, it's now eighty-twenty! We're winning! Keep doing it!' It's sinister to me just how in this communications age certain people intentionally aim to affect the media's perception of the mood of the country. It's the great thing about the Internet and the bad thing about the Internet. All of a sudden it becomes very easy for individuals and small groups to start manipulating public opinion. I've talked about this to lobbyists in Sacramento, who say 'That's politics. In any situation, there is 5 percent of the population that is active, and you activate the 5 percent. You don't worry about the 95 percent.' It's what the 5 percent are doing and saying that affects what the 95 percent see and hear, just as in politics."

Country comedians went to town. Larry the Cable Guy—later a huge, less openly crude TV star on The WB—wrote several diatribes against the Chicks for his colloquialism-laden website, sounding provoked more to sexual rage than anything resembling comedy. "They aught a [sic] change the band's name to Two Dixie Chicks and a loud-mouth southern sow," Larry wrote in his self-consciously semiliterate style. "I've had it with this piece-of-crap flubber factory spouting off every time her semi-sized ass hits the stage. People say, 'But Larry, she ain't that fat no-mores, she lost almost 20 pounds!' I say big deal, that's like taking three deck chairs off the Queen Mary! Natalie Maines needs to take her size 78 Wranglers and go back to her old job of smuggling moonshine in her giant canyon-sized ass crack. How dare this first hippo of country music go to a country whose support we're trying to get for a possible war and then attack our President in that country. I hope this starts to mark the end for this singing pork chop. It's a shame them 2 good-looking Dixie Chicks gotta put up with this singing sow's ridiculous rants." On a later occasion, Larry ended a rant against all liberals everywhere by declaring, "I'm madder than a feller playing with himself watching the Dixie Chicks video and just before he has an orgasm they show the little fat one."

Song parodist Cledus T. Judd, who fancies himself the hick "Weird" Al Yankovic, released an entire EP's worth of knocks against the Chicks; listeners could decide whether it was coincidental that this was Judd's first indie release after being dropped by Sony Nashville.

Singing "Natalie," to the tune of Brad Paisley's "Celebrity," he sere-naded his former labelmates: "So go load up your tour bus and pull on out / 'Cause your careers may soon be done / You bunch of multi-platinum jackass millionaires / Hey, hey, rock-'n'-roll, here they come!" All in good fun, he said later, when pressed about these meaner-spirited-than-usual spoofs. "I'm as big a fan of the Chicks as I am of Toby," Judd claimed. "This is just what I do."

More truly impartial observers tried to account for the instanta-neous virulence toward such a beloved act. Martha Hume, editor of the scholarly *Journal of Country Music*, had a theory. "To the fans, their statements came out of left field. Willie and Merle can sing anti-war songs or anything they want and even audience members who are vot-ing for Bush will say, 'They're good men, they can do it.' But when the Chicks did it . . . There's something there, and I don't know if it's sex-ism. My feeling is that it's because their politics are not otherwise re-flected in their work, and with Cash and those guys, their politics *were*, so when you hear what they're saying, it's consistent with the character they've put out there."

Hume is probably on the right track. The polarization of America has resulted in an atmosphere where red types and blue types tend to emigrate where they feel the most camaraderie—if not literally up-rooting and moving across borders, which is the whole story of the ex-urban migration for the conservative set and urban gentrification for bohos and bobos, then certainly selecting churches, private schools, and workplaces where like minds are the norm. With minority views at either extreme cowed into silence in less diverse communities, co-cooning ideologues are free to imagine that anyone smart and friendly in their immediate vicinity would have to be a kindred soul. And if your neighbors all fall in line, why not assume that the Dixie Chicks, talent and good looks aside, are *just like you?* That's the very corner-stone of country music: that the entertainers are no different from their audience, a rule not found in any other genre, not even hip-hop, where a certain amount of ostentatious, super-elitist bling is custom-ary along with the still-down-with-y'all, just-got-shot-at-yesterday street realism. In the Chicks fracas, some country fans may have been wounded by the realization, subconscious or otherwise, that they aren't really so tight with the people who they believed gave a voice to what was in their hearts after all.

A surprise broadside came from an unexpected corner: the website of CMT, the cable channel that continues to be Chick-supportive. Chet Flippo, whose byline was familiar to anyone who read *Rolling Stone* in the seventies, might have been presumed to be a liberal who would automatically take the band's side. Instead, in a sign that many reasonable minds, not just the Internet yahoos and wackos, might take issue with the group, Flippo wrote a wildly controversial editorial asserting that Maines had effectively "divorced" herself from America's country listeners when she courted London's. "What do you expect country fans to say when a country star dumps on the president?" Flippo wrote. "That audience is tolerant of artists' mistakes and foibles: drunkenness, drug use, adultery, no-shows and any amount of indulgent behavior. What that audience will not tolerate is an artist turning on that audience. And Maines's attack on Bush was in effect a direct attack on the country audience. And its values. And its patriotism . . . *Memo to Natalie Maines: You're an artist? And you have a message? Hey, put it in a song. We'll listen to that. But, otherwise—shut up and sing.*" (It should be noted that he used this phrase before Laura Ingraham adopted it as a conservative rallying cry.)

Flippo's column aggravated Bill C. Malone, a country journalist of even longer standing, whose landmark histories of the genre began appearing in the 1960s. Flippo politely ceded his next column to Malone, who wrote: "Old friend, I am sorely offended by your attempts to argue that the country music audience is monolithic, or that some of us are more patriotic than others because of our attitudes toward the current president . . . In your stern lecture to Natalie Maines, you advise her to shut up and put her message in a song. And you conclude with the statement, 'We'll listen to that.' I too would love to hear such a song, but Chet, you know full well that the song would never receive airplay on Top 40 country stations. Corporate sponsors, marketing 'specialists' and other censors would never permit the song to see the light of day."

Malone, a former Texan, is now a university professor in the liberal enclave of Madison, Wisconsin. Coincidentally, the Chicks got some other well-publicized support out of Madison. Half of the town's city council cosponsored a resolution calling for the Dixie Chicks to be played during recesses, and to be given the key to the city, French wine, and other perqs should the trio visit. The resolution also expressed the hope that the band would drop the "Dixie" and change their name to "the Dairyland Chicks."

They certainly wouldn't be given keys to the Lincoln bedroom, even though, bizarrely, the group had played for Bush when he was being inaugurated as governor of Texas. The president himself finally weighed in: "The Dixie Chicks are free to speak their mind . . . They shouldn't have their feelings hurt just because some people don't want to buy their records when they speak out. You know, freedom is a two-way street."

Band relatives felt the heat. Maines's husband, actor Adrian Pasdar, was booed when he played at a game of celebrity baseball in Texas; his Iranian American heritage led to plenty of racial profiling on the Internet. Natalie's aunt, an anchorwoman in Lubbock, had to disappear from the job for a few days. The granddad of sisters Emily and Martie "caught a lot of shit in the nursing home," said Martie, not sure whether to laugh over the intra-elder harassment or not. Maines's dad, Lloyd, learned that every record he'd ever produced (and he'd worked with more than fifty Texas artists over the years) had been banned by a small radio conglomerate based in their hometown, Lubbock, even though he and the offended radio magnate used to be friends.

Liberals stepped up their support. To a chorus of what, depending on the account, may have been wild cheering, boos, or both, Michael Moore finished his famous Oscar speech by shouting at Bush, "Whenever you've got the Pope and the Dixie Chicks against you, your time is up!" Shortly thereafter, *New York Times* columnist Frank Rich wrote a piece devoted to the idea that Moore and the Chicks were weathering their backlashes just fine. Rich cited an *Entertainment Weekly* news story that said the Chicks were holding onto the No. 1 position on the country album sales chart. He failed to notice that this story, which I had written, came at the outset of the controversy, before sales had had a chance to be adversely impacted. Moore took Rich's outdated information and ran with it in an essay on his own site. "The truth is that their sales are NOT down," Moore wrote, with considerable inaccuracy at that late date. "Their song, 'Travelin' Soldier' (a beautiful anti-war ballad), was the most requested song on the Internet last week. They have not been hurt at all—but that is not what the media would have you believe. If there's one thing I've learned, it's that if you tell a free people they can't hear something, read something, or see something, they are going to want to see, read and hear it all the more. So please, boycott the Dixie Chicks, try to start a boycott of Michael Moore, and watch what happens." Moore's ill-timed double-dare was a little like George W. Bush saying "Bring 'em on" right before things got *really* rough in Iraq.

Rich and Moore weren't paying close enough attention to invoke the F-word(s): *free fall*. In the week ending March 2, right after the group appeared on the Grammys, *Home* sold a staggeringly good 202,350 units. The week the story broke, they sold 123,952. By the week of April 13, at the peak of the controversy, sales were down to a mere 33,127 units. Considering that every liberal worth his salt was swearing he or she was headed out to buy the album just to show support, the incredible shrinking numbers suggested a severe vote of no-confidence in more conservative climes.

Music Row, whose denizens had mostly sat back in shock as many of their "friends" at country radio perpetuated the bashing, began to worry that the genre's latest boomlet might go bust, with the trickle-down theory effectively extinguished if the industry's biggest stars were to be banished. I ran into Blake Shelton, who is said to be about as apolitical as they come, and he could only shake his head when the subject of the Chicks came up. "I just wish it had never happened. They're our top act and we depend on them to drive people into the stores. If they're not selling records, what are the rest of us gonna do?"

Another defining moment came in April, when the CMT Flameworthy Awards were held at the Gaylord Center in Nashville. Up till now, the group's backers could say the backlash was being perpetuated by talk-radio-crazed-kooks, Internet nuts, and stunt-happy country radio shock jocks. But an ideologically random audience of rank-and-file country fans booed their Wrangler-packed fannies off when comic Brett Butler made the mistake of saying: "We're in the South, a place of sin and redemption and hopefully forgiveness. So maybe in a couple of weeks, we'll all just try to forgive the Dixie Chicks."

Home viewers had little clue about the cat calls. "They edited out the booing for television," remembers singer Terri Clark. "They had an applause button they hit. I was up there to announce an award right after another announcer had them on the list of nominees, and the booing was just unbelievable. What was heard on TV wasn't half of what it really was. It left me speechless. I was just thinking, holy cow."

Sheryl Crow had come out from L.A. to perform "Picture" with

Kid Rock on the telecast. Her publicist was sorry he joined her. "I hated being there," said Interscope's Dave Tomberlin. "It was disgusting. There were eighteen thousand people there and eighteen thousand people booing. Then you've got these retarded people getting up there to sing these jingoistic anthems and everybody goes nuts." Presumably he meant Toby Keith, going boo-less for the night, who said, "I'd like to dedicate this great award to Mr. Rumsfeld and Tommy Franks and all the people putting it down for us over there . . . God bless the USA, baby."

At a backstage press conference, Vince Gill adopted the same impartial stand just about every other nervous country star was taking, but also made the near-fatal mistake of pleading for calm. "There's political leaders that have said a lot worse things about George Bush than Natalie did, and nobody rips them for it," Gill told the room. "I kind of feel like she's been bashed enough. If she made a mistake, or if she feels that way, it's past the point . . . I can't jump into the fray to say I think this person's wrong and this person's right, because I think being decent and kind and forgiving and all those things are much better things to possess than being right."

Not necessarily the words of an Abu Musab al-Zarqawi sympathizer. But a couple of days later, having been handed his golden tenor and ass on a platter for seeming overly supportive of the Chicks, Gill was compelled to do a follow-up interview with the *Tennessean*, in which he said, "It's pretty imperative that I communicate that I held the completely opposite view of Natalie Maines. The troops and the president don't have a bigger supporter than me."

Other stars learned their lesson from the response to Gill's seemingly harmless statement. Publicists informed inquiring journalists that their star clients were "on vacation," as if the controversy had precipitated an industry-wide spring break. I kept imagining Kenny Chesney in the Caribbean, suddenly being surrounded by schooners holding the rest of country music's royals, all desperate to get out of cell phone range.

"Artists are reluctant to weigh in with an opinion, which is something we haven't seen before," said CMT's VP/general manager, Brian Philips, marveling at the paranoia. "Everybody is being really guarded, and nobody makes a statement without having to issue a press release the next day that further explains their point of view. I think within the artistic community, there are a lot of people who want to reach out and do what they can to help. But there's a lot of trepidation. It's a very strange time, and maybe that's the nature of wartime." And the Chicks' immediate damage-control options? "They've gotta be very careful now, obviously." He paused, catching the incongruity of that thought. "Which, of course, is not in their nature. Which is what makes them great." If only I were allowed to tell him I've just seen them naked.

Goose Bumps

A slight breeze is blowing through Austin. It's April 2003, a month to the day after the London concert. The caution that Brian Philips and others had advised has today been thrown to this modest wind and is now probably floating like a lost balloon somewhere high over Tyler or San Antonio. The Chicks, Renshaw, Berger, and I are milling in the parking lot of a sushi restaurant adjacent to a suburban mall far from the Texas capital city's hip downtown. Tucked into the scenery in our peripheral vision, like well-built Waldos, are some new friends the trio picked up on their return to the States: a low-key private security presence.

"Let's make this story far more interesting than it really is," suggests Renshaw, whose attitude wavers between mirth and righteous disgust, puckishness usually winning out. "We're going to give you the exclusive!" The publicist rolls her eyes, while the manager elaborates: "Let's do it like a *Boys from Brazil* thing, actually deeper than the right wing. The whole deal is, we're gonna be bigger than Jesus. Fuck the Beatles. Michael Moore is a paid guy, and he's already got us big as the Pope. In fact, maybe we could even make this whole thing a papist conspiracy. This was all about us and Michael Moore figuring out a way to promote the Catholic Church!"

"Oh, please," begs Maguire, the group's self-proclaimed worrywart. She's already seen how, in the age of Internet forwards, satire inevitably gets mistaken for reality. "We don't need any more controversy."

"Well," Maines helpfully reminds everyone, "we *did* just pose naked."

I'd seen the test Polaroids of the top-secret shoot while waiting outside the closed set earlier that afternoon. I can therefore attest that—digital erasure of panty lines and skin-tone airbrushing notwithstanding—those really *were* the Chicks' own bodies on the *EW* cover. Soon enough I'll be encountering protesters who'll insist that the magazine was doing its part for the left-wing media conspiracy by grafting the trio's heads onto models' torsos, to make the treasonous sluts more svelte.

There had been a suggestion from someone at the magazine, quickly rejected, that the threesome could wrap themselves in a flag. A setup that did end up being done that day had the group posing with a goat that had the prefix SCAPE painted on it, but those shots were jettisoned in the end as being a bit too on-the-nose. The "nude" shot was Maines's idea. The trio would pose with bumper stickers covering their naughty bits, quoting all (well, some of) the bad things they'd been called. When everyone got to Austin for the photo shoot, FedEx was a day late in delivering the stickers that had been specially prepared, but fortunately, *EW* photo director Fiona McDonagh had played the part of the good Girl Scout and came prepared with an emergency backup plan: body stenciling. Among the words branded on their flesh for the cover: TRAITORS. DIXIE SLUTS. SADDAM'S ANGELS. PROUD AMERICANS.

Not everybody will get the message. There will be feminists on the left as well as moralists on the right who feel the Chicks are merely selling sex with their chosen cover imagery, the stenciled messages just a pretext for, you know, hotness. But the point, Maguire says today, is "to show the absurdity of the extreme names people have been calling us." And to drop a big, fat, thrillingly proactive atom bomb on any remaining notions of traditional "damage control."

From a kamikaze afternoon at the photo studio to a *kanikama* evening. . . . Upon entering the back room of Sushi Saki, the Chicks remove their sensible shoes, not to walk across broken glass as public penance for their sins—as still remains the faint hope of millions—but to sit around the low-slung table and explore some still fairly raw emotions with the raw fish. Tomorrow, they'll meet Diane Sawyer, but tonight is their first domestic interview since "the incident." (Our talk was preceded only by a short interview they did on New Zealand TV to promote their tour stops there, a misbegotten quickie in which Natalie explained away her offending Bush comment as "a joke"—further infuriating her opponents, and dismaying a few supporters, too, coming on the heels of those soberly worded prepared statements.)

Their moods and attitudes *are* in a state of flux, they admit as the saki arrives. "It's sort of like how people say you go through every stage when someone dies or you break up with someone," says Maines. "I have been through every single emotion. One day you feel angry, and then one day you feel disappointed, and then one day you feel confused. And some days I just feel proud."

Of course, the last stage is "acceptance," and it remains to be seen whether the Chicks will have to accept the loss of a certain part of their career. "I feel, in a way, liberated," swears the singer, who's sporting a PEACE, LOVE AND ROCK & ROLL T-shirt, maybe making a statement not just about war but future target-demo shifts. "I had no idea that people thought I wasn't this way. I'm sort of relieved that that's out there, because I don't want people to think I'm something I'm not—on either side; *whatever* you thought I was. No matter what people say, I feel really patriotic. And strong." So that's how it's gonna be, then. "One thing I'm bummed about, though. I never, ever met someone or even had a friendship with someone where I even thought about what their political party was. That didn't determine at all if I was gonna be friends with this person. And 95 percent of my family are conservative Republicans, but they don't *not* invite me to dinner, or—"

"Crush your CDs?" Maguire interrupts, rhetorically.

"—and I don't *not* invite them to dinner. We're family. The other stuff is a part of who you are, but it does not define you as a good or bad person. The thing that bums me out now is, should I look at people and think, 'Are they conservative or Republican?' I was sitting in the dentist chair going, 'Oh, great, if she hates me, she's gonna really do a job on my mouth!' I wish I could stop it, but I hate having to look at people now and wonder, do they like me, or not like me?" Their fears of getting the *Marathon Man* treatment may be unfounded, but there has been some dereliction of professional duties in the furor's wake. Just a few days ago, a month before the start of their six-month tour, Maguire's longtime bus driver told her he would no longer be in her employ. "I can't fathom that he won't drive my bus because of what Natalie said." Wherever that guy's hometown is, he may be a hero, right now.

It's clear now that the apology mollified no one; the right thought it insincere, and the left considered it a cave-in. "One side wanted me not to have apologized and wanted to believe I was forced to do that," Maines says. "And I wasn't. It came from the heart. But I remember thinking, 'Okay, I have to show Martie and Emily that I did everything I could to try to stop this.' At first we were saying, 'It was light-hearted.'

That made people madder. When it was explained to me, that 'you were on foreign soil,' I was like, okay, I can see that, I made a joke about the president on foreign soil. I can see how people took offense to that. So I apologized for disrespecting the *office* of the presidency and the leader of the country. I made the apology I wanted to make and wrote exactly what I wanted to say. The end."

"Hanoi Natalie" still isn't sure how she so adversely affected the troops' morale. "A girl wrote to me: 'Dear Miss Maines, don't you know that when you disagree with the leader of our country and do not show unity with the president of the United States, that is just what Saddam Hussein wants? When Saddam Hussein hears what you've said, he's gonna know he's won.' What—Saddam's browsing our website? Are you serious? We're country music singers. *Don't think he got this in his daily memos.*"

Why them, you might wonder, and not Eddie Vedder, who physically impales Bush masks on microphone stands without inviting the wrath of Rush Limbaugh's legions? Why are the hordes inundating the Chicks' tour sponsor, Lipton Tea, with boycott threats but leaving Martin Sheen and the sponsors of *The West Wing* to another peaceful day?

"That really is an interesting question," says Maguire. "Some people have said it's because we're women, and I don't necessarily believe that. I think it's all about the fact that we're in country music. And the radio people who are doing this are proving that. It's shocking only because we're country. What's the thing you were first called into the office about when we started?" she asks, turning to Natalie.

"Oh, I took a drink of beer on stage."

"Yes. We were playing a club, and she took a swig of beer, and there were some Sony people there, and she was called into the office to have her hand slapped. We'd been playing honky-tonks for how many years, and we were of age . . . It was really hard to conform to that."

"I have always been honest," says Maines, "about saying that I did not listen to country music when I was younger. It was the last thing I would listen to. It was a rebellion, to say 'I do not like this.'" The travails of growing up with a country guitar-hero for a pa. Plus, "especially as a teenager, you're looking for people who ask the questions, for people who have nerve. Country seemed really safe. It wasn't even the music; I didn't give the music a chance because I didn't like the people in it. Then when I became a country musician, it broke down a lot of the misconceptions or barriers I had, because I thought, 'Hey, these people are really accepting of me, even though I don't quite fit into this genre.' I've never fit into country music. But nobody ever seemed to have a problem with that." Her voice drops to a murmur. "So it's just disappointing that now they do."

Time to bite the hand that formerly fed. "We feel let down a little by our industry," Maguire offers.

"Because we sit there and wave the flag all the time—the country music flag," agrees Maines.

"My friends don't listen to country music," Maguire continues. "They're always telling me negative things: 'How can you listen to that? I've tried to listen to a country station . . . ' Criticism after criticism, I'm trying to defend my industry. And then when they do something like this . . . Yes, it's ridiculous, and we have to deal day in and day out with these old-school, backwards . . ." Natalie cracks up. "It's true, they exist. And yes, the audience tends to be older, very conservative. But you have to believe that younger people are making up the country audience, too, and they are saying 'This is bullshit.' "

Robison joins in. "Country radio has been so supportive of us, up until this point. And even though we've had crossover success, especially with this album, I feel like we're some of the most traditional people in country music."

"Maybe that's why we fooled everybody!" says Natalie, laughing. "It had to get really, really ridiculous before anybody in country music said anything. We were starting to think, it's gonna be really hard to show up at awards shows—"

"Where we're not nominated anymore," interjects Emily.

"Yeah, first of all, we probably won't be showing up. But if we do, it'd be hard to be in a room full of people going, 'Y'all didn't say anything!' A few of them have now. But the first people who spoke up were actors and rock musicians, which felt different. Because we always joked on the *Fly* tour about how we'd hear 'Oh, Julia Roberts wants some tickets.' And we went"—gasping—"*'Really?'* And they'd say, 'Yeah, for her niece.' " Everyone cracks up at this familiar-sounding letdown. "So when Barbra Streisand called to wish us well, it was the first time anybody in that world's ever done that. We were surprised. And it just shows you how people make assumptions that if you play one type of music you're a certain way. Because we surprised the country audience as much as we did that audience. People on that side never in a million years thought that we wouldn't want to go to war." A beat. "Did I say 'we'?" she asks, looking at her bandmates. "Do I need to say 'I'?" More nervous laughter.

Misery wouldn't mind a little company right now. "I believe more people feel the way we do than you'd think, not just about politics but about speaking up and being who you are. If more people broke that logjam, people would have no choice other than to accept it. I don't agree with what Toby Keith says, at all. It's not what I like to hear, but I like that he speaks up. And it may be on the safe side of speaking up, because he knows that everyone in the genre is going to agree with him, but still, he's saying something. I respect him more than the people who say nothing."

Doesn't Travis Tritt have a point, in supposing that Maines never would have dared make such a remark in front of anything but an anti-American crowd? "What was funny about that was, we assumed that that whole crowd [in London] was from Texas, because four years earlier when we played the same venue, it was all Texas expatriates," claims Emily.

Natalie adds, "For as many times as we've stuck our feet in our mouths, it could easily have happened in the States. It was so innocent. I think I would have said that in the States, expecting that I would have gotten big cheers—and probably I'd have been enlightened otherwise."

Perhaps there's a gender gap here. Or a maternity gap. "After 9/11, that's the first time I ever had felt true fear, fear that has stuck with me and changed us forever," says Maines. "I remember right after that just being scared all the time, like hearing a plane vibrate and going 'No!' So when I think of those little kids over there, laying in their beds, listening to the planes . . ." Her eyes start to moisten. "How scary that must be. I think when you are a mother, you tap into the big picture of: What are those mothers in Iraq thinking? What are the mothers of the troops thinking? Everyone talks about how this war has ended quickly and not that many people have died, but tell that to the parents of the people who are coming back in body bags. It's just tough for us to think in those terms, because we're mothers now. Not that people who aren't mothers don't care. But the other thing I feel is, I guess, maybe some guilt over how we're just so lucky to be born here. You know? And why are they born there?"

She's weeping now. "It's the luck of the draw. I think of my son, and then a child over there who has such a different life than my child's gonna have. A lot of questions and concern and guilt go along with that. And I have the same tears when they put a face to the name of a soldier . . . It's easier to hear 'six people died,' but when they show you their picture . . ."

"It's a sign of the times," Robison muses, happier to take the long view, as opposed to the view of her front gate, where folks have taken to dumping trash. "I think it will go down in history as an example of what was happening during this time. And I don't know what the outcome will be. Will we bounce back? Will we end up not on country radio? I don't know. But I do think it was definitely a sign of everyone's just being scared right now—scared to speak up, scared to question. And that's unfortunate, because I think our country's based on asking questions. *Especially* in a time of war. *Especially* when people's lives are at stake."

Maines adds, "And people are saying the opposite: A time of war is *not* the time to be asking questions or to not support your leader. First off, to call somebody your 'leader' is almost funny to me. And that's one of those statements where I can't believe people hear themselves saying that. This is *killing* people. Whether you're gonna do it or not, *this* is the time to be asking questions! Why do we have to do this tomorrow? I just feel like we never got an answer for that. I'm not anti-war, period, overall, always."

"I was born pretty much when Vietnam started," says Maguire, "so I don't remember it at all. And because I was in my dingy twenties, I didn't feel the effects of the Gulf War. But I had not felt unsafe in my country until this point—and I felt more unsafe the day we went to war in Iraq than I did after 9/11. If we seemed arrogant, and had pissed off the world before, now we really have alienated ourselves from a lot of countries that we need as allies. And Americans—especially Americans my age—aren't used to that. You grow up feeling so proud that you live in this country, that there's nothing you can't do as a woman. You don't have to worry about the same things that, say, my husband worried about. His family is a Catholic family living in northern Ireland, and they still leave the country once a year because of the marches. My husband was once walking under a bridge when a bomb went off in a police car, and he was thrown to the ground. He tells me stories like that, and I think, wow, I've led a really sheltered life. But now I am living in a vulnerable country. Kids are never gonna grow up like I grew up, knowing that sensation of feeling so sheltered and safe, ever—starting now."

Forget al-Qaeda—the Chicks may not feel safe from their fellow Americans for a while. "Martie had told the story of Emily getting trash dumped in front of her gate, and one of those right-wing talk-show hosts said, 'Well, what do you expect?' My answer was: Not that! Didn't expect death threats! Didn't expect to have twenty-four-hour security outside of my house! I don't feel naive by not expecting that. Violence doesn't cross my mind when I don't like what somebody said." A bitter chuckle. "It was Don Imus who said 'Where's Earl when you really need him?'" Maines stops to reflect on that one—one of America's foremost talk hosts, who's not even on the right, per se, suggesting that there's nothing wrong with the Dixie Chicks that a little assault and battery wouldn't cure. "You know, I can at least say, 'Well, at least I'm not evil.' I know *that* about myself."

Chicken Treks

Joan Osborne has finished her opening set in Greenville. Dan Rubenstein, the Bi-Lo's building manager, is breathing several sighs of relief in one of the private corporate loges. "They brought the bomb-sniffing dogs in Monday and we locked it down after that. Everybody goes through metal detectors and has bag checks. Natalie walked in and they were wanding her, too! That just made them feel better." Considerably more dissent had been expected. "During the week, on talk radio, they were trying to come up with schemes to keep people from coming to the show. One guy said 'Why don't we go down to the Bi-Lo Center and take up all the spaces, so no one can park.' But I don't see too many empty seats. It was really a non-event. Most of the people who might have had an issue were in Spartanburg. Let 'em have their show."

He's referring to an anti-Chicks, pro-Bush protest concert happening simultaneously in a nearby city, organized by talk show host Mike Gallagher. That alternative concert's bill is being topped by the Marshall Tucker Band, seventies Southern rockers whose career has sunk so low that headlining a gig predicated on dissing a more popular act may not have struck them as an act of pathetic career opportunism.

When the Chicks go on, there are no further suggestions from the stage that mortification, not pride, is the proper response to sharing a Lone Star base with the commander in chief, although there are several remarks that have been scripted to address the controversy. "Wait, I hear some booing," Maines tells the crowd. None of the rest of us do, but why let that stand in the way of a good rabble-rousing moment? "We have a plan for that. If you're here to boo, we welcome that, 'cause we welcome freedom of speech. We're gonna give you fifteen seconds . . . On the count of three, you can do your booing. One, two, three!" Screams of glee.

Later, the trio settle in on the lip of the stage for an acoustic mini-set. "I contemplated not wearing a short skirt because I knew I'd have to sit down. Then I thought, 'Hell, these people have seen me naked!'" Ba-da-*dum*.

It's remarkable how many lyrics in the Chicks' old songs seem to slyly anticipate their current predicament, starting with the very title of "If I Fall, You're Going Down with Me," which is performed as a cheerful contract with the 18,000 seditionist sympathizers. The one song in the set list not from an existing Chicks album is a cover of Bob Dylan's "Mississippi," presumably picked for its relevance, grappling as it does with both alienation and loyalty:

> Some people will offer you their hand and some won't
> Last night I knew you, tonight I don't . . .
> Well my ship's been split to splinters, it's sinking fast
> I'm drowning in the poison, got no future, got no past
> But my heart is not weary, it's light and it's free
> I've got nothing but affection for those who've sailed with me

Buried within the song, as it will be every night on tour, is the synth riff from the Who's "Won't Get Fooled Again," which is as close as they come to renewing any barbed presidential commentary on stage. The show ends without a hitch. Lesson from Greenville: If you can make it here—one of the most conservative cities in South Carolina, which was the first state in the South to have flipped to the Republican side—you'll make it anywhere.

When Maines walks back up through the stage trapdoor for the encore, she has some breaking news to pass along. "They told me the president has just announced that the war is over." Huge cheering, along with some awkwardness: Does such a quick resolution to combat in Iraq mean the Chicks were just being nervous nellies all along? "It seems a little strange to keep playing songs," she adds, "but I guess we'll celebrate and just keep going."

Two nights later, the tour decamps in Orlando for gig number two. Time to look around the grounds of the TD Waterhouse Centre to see where tonight's protesters have situated themselves. At last, I spot a guy holding up a sign. Whoops: It says, HUNGRY. GOD BLESS. Eventually two picketers do turn up, both of them Vietnam vets. But the lack of picket signs doesn't mean Orlando has embraced the group with open arms. There are a couple dozen people on the streets leading into the arena trying to unload their tickets; some of them tell me they already tried to give them away to friends but found no takers. These folks aren't quite Nixon's so-called Silent Majority, but they're a quiet plurality, honestly disappointed ex-fans who aren't looking to attract media attention with garish banners but who simply can't go inside, because they feel it would dishonor family members in the military or their own patriotic conscience. The news media have decided the anti-Chicks protests are over—just like the Iraq war!—but they're still there, along scalper row, instead of the dwindling picket lines.

As the tour goes on, the more sensible antagonists tire of the struggle, leaving the front lines outside the performance venues to some guys for whom the term "piece of work" might have been invented. In Tampa, I have the opportunity to chat with Wayne, a demonstrator who has insults for every type of arriving ticketholder. He accuses a pack of women of being lesbian groupies; to couples on dates, he tells the men, "C'mon, guys, you're better than that. Don't be whipped!" His double-sided sign is a doozy: on one side, he's pasted the *EW* cover, surrounded by the following rant: "The Dixie Shits are now accepting donations for . . . 1. Hysterectomies (no need for any more inbred ignorance). 2. A plane ticket to any overseas areas with high levels of SARS. 3. Unlimited food stamps to support their voracious appetites after music career collapses. 4. Lifetime supply of Depends dysentery. 5. Ample amount of duct tape so they can shut the fuck up!" On the other side is a photo clipped from that same issue of *EW*, with a target scrawled on Natalie's white shirt. DISEMBODY THE DIXIE DESECRATOR reads the carefully lettered caption, which gets more profane and scatalogical from there. Accompanying Wayne, a divorced dad, on this protest is his thirteen-year-old daughter, because nothing says "joint custody" like a night of father/daughter dyke-baiting.

In Orlando, things start to get interesting in the vicinity of a radio station's promo van. K92 is a local country station that has banned the Chicks, but—you've got to love the balls of local radio—they've showed up tonight to hand out promotional flyers. Their human shield, so to speak, is a "support for the troops" tarp they've set up for attendees to sign on their way in. But after the show, beer- and adrenaline-fueled Chicks fans come out and verbally berate the unfortunate staffers who are passing out flyers that promote a big cash giveaway on the station's morning show. Some of them bang on the station van and use the flyers to leave notes on its windshield like "Screw you, anti-Chick radio!"

How will radio treat the Chicks when tempers have finally subsided? The women sound like they have a pretty good clue to their own fate, tucked away in one of the verses of that Dylan song they do every night:

> You can always come back, but you can't come back all the way
> Well there's only one thing that I did wrong
> I stayed in Mississippi a day too long

FUTK: Feuds, Uppitiness, Touchiness, and Kittenishness

A year and a half later, with no end to major hostilities in sight after all—and yes, we're still talking about the wars in Iraq *and* country music—another opening night is upon the group. This time's it's a Vote for Change tour the Chicks are doing with pal James Taylor in theaters in swing states. "You know we feel really strongly about something when we're willing to be on stage two months after having babies!" Maines tells the crowd on the first night in Pittsburgh. Later comes the quip she'll pull out every night on the mini-tour: "A lot of people have asked if I regret what I said. And I thought about it. But I didn't want to be a flip-flopper. I knew Bush would hate that."

Maines had taken a more serious tone at the end of 2003, when the group posed with their babies for *Vogue* and offered a postscript to their year of living dangerously. "Our manager will so try to pull the 'Oh, you would have had a natural drop-off in sales after the Grammys,' and it's like, Shut up, No, we wouldn't. Gimme a break. We're not stupid. We're lucky as hell that the tour went on sale before I said what I said, because it would not have sold out in one day and broken all those records. The sales of our next CD will really tell us a lot." Any regrets? Just one, apparently. The apology. "It was all mine . . . but when I look back and read it, I don't stand behind what I said. That will make some people extra-mad, because some were like, Well, at least she apologized."

"What happened was, the whole process politicized them," says Renshaw in 2005, looking back on the group's gradual escalation in activism—first, becoming Rock the Vote spokeswomen, then Maines's solo PSA for the ACLU, then the explicitly pro-Kerry tour of late 2004. "It turned them from being just musicians and human beings into activists. They found themselves at the point where they started to see what was going on in this country and in the world. And they started to develop this kind of 'No, fuck you!' attitude. What had they done wrong? They'd expressed an opinion about the president of the United States of America—an opinion that seems to be shared by about 50 percent of the country and about 90 percent of people outside the country. And for that, they should be vilified and made to suffer? They weren't in any mood to give up and go quietly."

Writing for Salon.com, cultural critic Charles Taylor echoed a genre comparison that had been brought up in the *Guardian* review that started everything. "You would have to be very cynical or very stupid to believe that anyone would choose the kind of publicity that would bring them death threats," Taylor wrote. "Still, it seems to me that the Dixie Chicks are operating now less in the realm of country music than they are in the realm of punk . . . The *Entertainment Weekly* cover, another example of how the band has refused to affect the demure pose that would prove they are backing down, appropriates the tactic used initially by the Riot Grrrl bands, who appeared onstage with words like 'Bitch' and 'Slut' scrawled on their midriffs," he pointed out, adding that such guerrilla tactics are easier on "the fringe" and, "again, it is impossible to divorce the courage of the Dixie Chicks' stance from the place they occupy in mainstream pop." Taylor wasn't timid about taking a big-picture view of the whole fracas. "It's not just the terms of their own success, or even the terms of pop music, in which the Dixie Chicks are causing tremors. It's the very terms in which public discourse is conducted—or not conducted—in America at the moment."

The matter of who controls the flow of discourse was taken up again in Washington, thanks in part to this controversy. In July 2003, Renshaw addressed a congressional hearing on deregulation. That's one horse that couldn't be further out of the barn, but it made for good grandstanding, especially since Cumulus Radio head John Dickey, widely seen even within the radio industry as one of the villains of the story, had the inexplicable cojones to show up and take his beating from a few indignant yet ultimately powerless politicos. Senator John McCain, who still likes to call himself "a proud deregulator," expressed strong concerns about what befell the Chicks, battering Dickey with questions: "Did you not order those stations to take the Dixie Chicks off the air?" Dickey said yes, at last. "Would you do that to me?" McCain asked. "No." "Then why do it to a group of entertainers?"

It was a "business decision," said Dickey, mounting the weakest possible defense. "Our stations turned to us for guidance. There was a groundswell, a hue and cry from listeners."

Senator Barbara Boxer, the liberal California Democrat—possibly, like McCain, under the delusion that this occasion represented a chance to force a happy epilogue to the McCarthy hearings of yore—rose to the occasion with some poetry right out of a Frank Capra movie: "I keep hearing you say 'a hue and cry.' Well, that happens all the time in this country," she lectured Dickey. "There's a hue and cry every time I speak out about women's choice. That's what happens when you have a diversity of views: discourse. A hue and cry is a beautiful sound. It's the sound of freedom."

It's so rare to see opposing forces like John McCain and Barbara Boxer harmonizing, you're tempted to leave a tender moment alone. But of course this lovely Cumulus-bashing duet was a case of bipartisan bull: John Dickey could ban the Chicks *and* John McCain till the cows come home with no fear of censure, ever since the president and Congress let that antiquity known as the Fairness Act go the way of all flesh, along with nearly all governmental media regulation. And who would say it wasn't within his rights to devote his entire chain, should the whim strike, to a 24/7 McCain-bashing format? The "Chicklessness" of the airwaves is the sound of freedom, too, in the land of post-deregulation capitalism, beautiful or disconcerting as that radio silence may be.

In early 2005, the Chicks went into the studio to begin cutting an album with Rick Rubin, the hip-hop mogul who also produced Johnny Cash's last stretch of landmark discs, rumored to be in more of a rock vein. The game plan for this long-awaited followup to *Home*, Renshaw said, was to break the record mostly via TV—getting on any talk show wouldn't be a problem—and if country radio should decide to play it, too, that's gravy. Country programmers, for their part, weren't necessarily looking forward to the day when they'd have to decide which segment of their listeners to confound, by either welcoming the pariahs back into the fold or keeping the doors katy-barred.

"The next time they release an album," wonders Renshaw, "are the right-wing groups gonna conspire together again on the Internet to go, 'Hey, you know what, if they let those bitches back on the air, no one's ever gonna take a boycott seriously again. We've gotta make sure they don't play this shit!'? I don't know. Will country radio play it? I hope so, but there's the betrayal factor to consider. After you do all this work and promote and promote, and these are the very first people to turn their backs on you, to become involved in the whole vilification process and turn it into a stunt, and at the end of the day, is that who you want to be in business with?"

In *Country Weekly* magazine, a prominent radio programmer penned inconclusive remarks that anticipated that moment of decision. "The moral of the story? WE WERE ALL WRONG AND WE ALL LOSE!" wrote Mike Lawrence, program director of KHKX-FM of Midland, Texas, in a commentary filled with more exclamation points than a Shania Twain song. "I would love to have the Chicks back on the air because I know they could have a number-one hit reading ceiling fan instructions! However, this is a very tough situation that goes beyond American or anti-American, Republican or Democrat, right or left, even human or Klingon! The only thing that I'm not confused about is that if I were to play music by artists who no one wants to hear, I, along with a very talented staff, would be out of work!"

Every void demands to be filled, and just when it looked like no one could fill the Chicks' shoes, along came Gretchen Wilson, who even sounds a little like Natalie in certain bits of phrasing. She acknowledges her debt to the band, without whom it's unlikely that "Redneck Woman" could have been the biggest country song of 2004. "Nobody can for one minute say that they aren't unbelievably talented and that they haven't broken down doors," Wilson says. "The Dixie Chicks made it easier for me to say 'Hell, yeah' on the radio—there's no doubt about it. With the song 'Goodbye Earl,' they broke a lot of ground. I'm not gonna sit here and tell you whether I'm Democrat or Republican. But somebody's opinion would never sway how I feel about their music." Wilson *does* think the Chicks crossed a certain church/state line. "Country music should not be about politics. I think everybody's political opinion is a private thing, myself. Everybody is going to lean more toward one side than they are the other, but it has to do with how people feel about birth control and taxes and all these other things that have nothing to do with country music. I grew up in such a small town, but I'll tell you one thing, for being small, they sure were smart. All of those taverns around where I grew up had signs on the barroom wall—every single one of 'em—that said 'No arm-wrestling, no politics, and no religion.' Because those are the three things guaranteed to start a fight every time."

Bruce Robison, the alt-country songsmith who is Emily Robison's brother-in-law and the author of "Travelin' Soldier," still regrets the way the *Home* entertainment revolution was sidelined by the controversy, not just because it cut into his royalties, but because it aborted a real popular-music breakthrough.

"Man, wasn't that the biggest bullshit about it?" Robison grumbles. "Country music had reached one of its low points, and then a freakin' *bluegrass* record is going nuts . . . ? For that to be stopped in its tracks is the biggest shame of all, for a music fan. It breaks my heart so bad. From that point on, this is what we get—less of the Dixie Chicks and more of *these guys*." No naming names, but "any of their critics in country music, I wish they had to get on stage together without their backup bands and play. Most of us can hardly make three chords on a guitar. And those girls could go to bluegrass festivals and stand in a circle and play and bop people's jaws. Let's get anybody else off the country charts, and there's about three of 'em that could even play at all. So to see young girls looking up to them, seeing what they do . . . These are the sorts of role models we need outside of Paris Hilton, you know."

Steve Earle considers them personal role models. Asked who he admires, the country hitmaker-turned-leftist ideologue quickly answers, "Natalie Maines. They took a lot of shit, took a huge hit, and the guy that went after them was a buddy of Bush's and had their career in his hand because he happened to control Clear Channel." (The record isn't as clear on this as Earle supposes, but nevertheless . . .) "They stuck to their guns, and I admire them for that. The apology was coerced, but I even thought they did a pretty good job of wording that. And I *loved* the T-shirt."

Ah, that. As much as the *EW* cover, Maines's stage wear on the night of the Academy of Country Music Awards in May 2003 was a love-it-or-hate-it, camel's-back-breaking moment. The trio didn't attend the Las Vegas event, but they were beamed in live from Austin to perform a song. When they appeared on the big screens in that Vegas arena, murmuring broke out that didn't cease for weeks. Could it be . . . ? Did her shirt really say "FUTK"? Were home viewers just dreaming this latest punk-rock flourish?

Renshaw says the producers of the ACM Awards saw Maines's T-shirt before they went to air and didn't say a thing. The first angry call he received afterward was from the group's Manhattan publicist. "My cell phone erupts. It's Cindi Berger. *'I can't fucking believe . . . What the fuck . . . This shirt . . . '* What are you on about?, I said. What shirt? 'The shirt! The Fuck You Toby . . . ' I said, 'Oh! You mean Freedom, Understanding, Truth, and Knowledge. It's a new clothing line that we're doing.' She was like, 'Are you serious?' I said, 'I don't know. Are you?'"

"People misinterpret. Everyone thought it was about Toby Keith. *Why* anyone would think that was on their minds—no idea. It's like, hey, you go putting Natalie up on a big screen giving Saddam Hussein a noogie in your shows, and you don't think that she's maybe going to take a swipe back at you? We never had pictures of him and Osama bin Laden up there on ours."

Let's hope that hefty Christmas bonuses were paid to the publicists who, with a straight face, had to float the "Freedom, Understanding, Truth, and Knowledge" explanation to hundreds of journalists in the days and weeks that followed. (Detractors came up with their own interpretations of the acronym: Comedian Cledus T. Judd—once again adopting the "when in doubt, call 'em sluts" philosophy—told his audiences that the message on Maines's shirt really meant "Found Underneath Table Kneeling.")

"Look, the girls have got a fantastic sense of humor," says Renshaw. "And occasionally they do things that are cheeky. It may be inappropriate. I'm sorry, I still think it's funny. I don't have a problem with Toby Keith. I know the girls don't have a problem with Toby Keith.

There's no malice or animosity behind it. It was kind of a fun little feud, though. I mean, it's not quite as good as Suge Knight and Puff Daddy—we never did get quite to that level."

More than two years after the fact, it's still not clear to those most closely involved whether to treat the entire brouhaha as an important milestone in the history of the intersection of world affairs and the arts, or as an over-amped exercise in absurdism. Their manager can and does wax on about the significance of it all, how his girls will go down in history as icons of dissent. In the end, Renshaw, being English, does finally gravitate toward a fondness for farce. "It's so funny, when you stop and look at it. You have to think: All of this over something a singer in a band says in some 2,000-seat club in London? It's just a bunch of kids with guitars, for fuck's sake!"

Toby Keith performed for George W. Bush and thousands of backers at the "RNC Victory Rally," held only slightly prematurely at Dallas's Southern Methodist University on November 1, 2004, the night before voters elected the president to a second term. AP PHOTO/TONY GUTIERREZ

During and after his 1976 campaign, Jimmy Carter was the first president to openly align himself with "counterculture" musicians from the rock and country worlds. He and old friend Willie Nelson reunited in Plains, Georgia, in 2004 to tape a CMT special. RICK DI-AMOND/COURTESY OF CMT

Courtesy of the Red, White, and Formerly Blue

Toby, Willie, and the Disappearance of the Southern Democrat

Toby Keith greets his manager at the door of his *Tonight Show* dressing room with some breaking news. "They got Uday and Qusay," he says, nodding in the direction of a TV that's trumpeting the long-awaited deaths of Saddam's sons on this late afternoon in July 2003. Keith wears a poker face most of the time, but even taking that into consideration, he doesn't seem quite as pleased with this development in Iraq as his reputation might have you expect. After all, this is the guy whose "Courtesy of the Red, White, and Blue (The Angry American)," released during the war in Afghanistan, promised terrorist-coddling countries that the United States would not merely "light up your world" but "put a boot in your ass." So surely taking out Hussein's Torture Twins constitutes Tony Lama proctology at its most justified and exacting.

Soon it becomes evident that there's something about the news coverage on CNN that's made his mood less than celebratory. Armchair quarterbacks have already begun to weigh in with reservations about the handling of the mission. "There's people griping already that Uday and Qusay are dead. There was a woman on there going, 'Did they have to *kill* 'em?' Well, if you would've been there, hon, taking that fire . . . If they could've taken 'em alive, they would have loved to, believe me. We want to know where their dad is. But when they're firing at you, you've gotta return fire. You don't know what they've got in there or how many there are. But that's the world we live in: Everybody goes 'Oh, well, they shouldn't have killed them.'" He shakes his head in disbelief. "We don't live in a PC world, so I don't know why people pretend we do. *Reality* is not PC."

Keith never served in the armed forces, but he's pleased to serve as their mascot and stand-in in a culture whose entertainers generally prefer to support the troops from a safe distance. If he has a soldier's attitude, it may come from proximity; he's made frequent trips overseas to cheer the men and women in uniform (or in casts, bandages, and prosthetic limbs). Even a simple stateside after-concert meet-and-greet usually turns into something like a military-family reception, with fans coming through the line to give him photographs of their relatives' divisions and to let him know they appreciate his support. The night before his *Tonight Show* appearance, I stood alongside Keith as he met fans in between shows at a county fair in Paso Robles. Very few of them failed to mention a relative in the service or give Keith a token on their behalf. "Ain't that unbelievable?" he says, proudly. "Now, how could somebody criticize me for meaning that much to those people? If that's what makes 'em happy and keeps their morale up, I'll do whatever it takes to be their guy. It's *amazing* that somebody could criticize that." He mutters the word "unbelievable" again, this time with less good cheer.

If Keith constantly seems to be playing a game of defense, that's appropriate, because before becoming the biggest male star in country music he had a brief stint playing semipro football for the Oklahoma Drillers, as a defensive end. Before that, he was an *actual* Oklahoma oil driller. Don't let all that physical labor and lack of a college education fool you into imagining that Keith is anything less than one of the savviest characters in country music. He graduated from high school with straight A's, but headed for the oil fields because he saw that he could make a better living there than he would at an entry-level white-collar job after four years of higher education. His commercial track record suggests that he's transferred his straight-A skills to a work force where street smarts are almost everything.

His defensive ire has come up again and again in notorious firefights with the likes of Natalie Maines or ABC News anchor Peter Jennings—skirmishes in which he's always claimed, sometimes credibly, to have been the one taking fire first. There's part of him that's Top Dawg and part of him that relishes being the eternal underdog.

Keith may sell four million albums at a pop these days and regularly enjoy number-one country hits, but he'll be the first to bring up how he's pretty much the Susan Lucci of the CMAs, country's most prestigious awards show. That's not even to mention the ever-increasing vilification heaped on him by the nation's left wing. If you polled Al Franken's audience, Toby would probably have a Q rating somewhere between Ron Silver and Don Rumsfeld. It's not entirely clear whether he is delighted or dismayed by all the negative energy directed his way. Both, probably.

I tell him that, earlier, when I'd been preparing to write a magazine article that would provide an overview of the state of country music, a couple of VIPs in Nashville urged me not to focus on Keith, feeling that he reinforced a jingoistic, redneck image the industry was then trying to slough off. When I tell him about this ill will on Music Row, his mood actually seems to lift.

"The kicker is, tonight is my first appearance on *The Tonight Show*, okay? Before that song ["Angry American"], I already had sold ten million records and had number-one country singles numbering in the teens," he points out. "But Leno and Letterman were always a brick wall. These people wouldn't have me. The list would probably knock you out if you looked at the country artists who have come and gone since 1993 and that have all been on *The Tonight Show*, who didn't sell a bucketful of records. How did I get overlooked before 'Courtesy of the Red, White, and Blue'? I come out with one song for the military, during a time when General Jones and everybody thought they needed the support—after selling millions and millions of records that had nothing to do with that—and all of a sudden I'm the flag-waving redneck [the suits] don't want to be associated with in your article."

He catches himself and reconsiders his words. "Which I dig, you know," he says, brightening. "I *dig* being the flag-waving redneck." He's not shy about talking about how it's improved his profile, though he'll insist careerism wasn't a motivation. "Now they finally want me on this show. You know why? Because of ratings. Screw that. I was real reluctant to come on here tonight, but I could tell it meant a lot to the people that work hard around me to deliver this. It doesn't mean jack squat to me. And I'm not dissing *The Tonight Show*, I'm dissing the system." Of course, it's hard to ultimately dis an irony that works in your favor. "Those people in Nashville can say 'flag-waving redneck' is what keeps you off the air, but 'flag-waving redneck' is what got me on this thing."

Keith swears that "Red, White, and Blue" was never even intended to be released commercially, that it was written in honor of his father, who lost an eye to friendly fire while in the service, and who, as the first verse says, flew the flag every day of his adult life. He claims it was only going to be played for the troops, until the brass insisted that the folks at home should hear it, too. When the label did release it as a single, he says, "I knew we were gonna get some opposition to it. But for the millions of letters and e-mails that I've gotten supporting that song, you get about five or six chuckleheads . . ."

Chucklehead A: anchorman Jennings, who in 2002 hosted an ABC Fourth of July special on which Keith was supposedly scheduled to appear. He did not. The network's version is that the singer had never been properly booked in the first place; Keith claims he has the paper trail to prove otherwise, and that it was Jennings's objection to "Courtesy" that scuttled the deal. When the dispute went public, "Everybody in America started sending him boots, for 'boot in your ass,' with their sentiments written on 'em. Jennings's people tried to pass that off as a publicity stunt on my part, but one radio station did it, then another . . . I'm flattered to think that that jackass nut thinks for a second that I'm big enough to coordinate that whole effort."

During the Jennings spat, he questioned—jokingly, he insists—whether the newscaster being a Canadian had anything to do with his refusal to allow a song that America loved so dearly on his show. Now that Jennings, who's been under fire from conservatives a few times before, has recently become a U.S. citizen, and very publicly so, maybe Keith would like to take credit for instigating that patriotic move? "Ha ha, no." But speaking of foreigners . . . "One thing I *am* proud about is that Jennings can speak English. When we let people from other countries in here, I wish they would have to go take English 101 real quick, because this is America, and that's what we operate the best on."

Chucklehead B: the Dixie Chicks' feisty frontwoman, who told a reporter that the song was an "ignorant" black eye for country. "If you're against a cause, then you speak your mind against the cause. But when you single me out personally and attack the craftsmanship of the song . . ." For Keith, that's war. "You know what? She's not a writer; I am. People ask what I think about what she said, and that's like asking

Barry Bonds to respond to a softball player critiquing his swing. If Willie Mays wants to come up and say, 'Barry, you're dropping your elbow a little too much,' he's probably gonna listen to it. But if a softball player is saying 'Barry ain't got no swing, that's why he's striking out a lot,' Barry shouldn't have to respond to that. Just because she's a singer in a band, that gives her credibility to bash my craftsmanship and my writing?"

Predictably, his sympathy for Maines's post-London predicament is limited. "All that freedom of speech guarantees you is that your government won't execute you for running your big mouth. So when people say stuff and then it blows up on 'em, and they go 'Hey, this is America, I can say what I want to say,' listen, nobody said you couldn't say what you said. But they don't say that there aren't consequences or repercussions because people have *their* American right to dis on you."

Keith assumed a truce was in effect after Maines was quoted in *Entertainment Weekly* saying that she respected Keith for being one of the few country stars brave enough to speak his mind. "And then right after that, she went on TV and wore an 'FUTK' shirt. So am I supposed to just sit back and be the good guy? People forget that she started this thing. She said my song makes country music look ignorant and that you've gotta have more tact and be responsible when you do a song. They just had a song called 'Earl Must Die' or something. How hypocritical is that? How can you do a song with the message that if your husband abuses you, you're supposed to kill him and stick him in the trunk, or whatever—I never heard the song, but people told me about it—and then call me ignorant for saying, 'Hey, you flew these planes into these buildings. We're angry about it, and we're gonna come get you?'"

Maines did say that it's easier for Keith to speak his mind because the entire genre lines up with him. "I have it easy because the entire country audience agrees with me?" he sputters. "The entire audience in London was agreeing with *her*. That's why she said what she said. But I didn't know that with 'Angry American,' the entire country was gonna agree with me. In fact, I waited nine months, prayed about it, and put some serious thought and talked to a lot of people before I released my little military song, just because I knew it was gonna take a lot of opposition, and you don't want to fight that fight. However, the fight has been one-tenth of what I thought it would be. I have felt over

90 percent support, and just once every two or three months, some jerk-off will come in with some little letter supporting her or supporting Hollywood actors and that culture."

Keith insists he has no intention of lighting up her world anymore. "My guys thought it was funny to put up on our big video screen an Internet thing somebody made of the Chicks and Saddam Hussein in a fake family picture. I've not got anything against the other two girls, and they have not attacked me personally, as far as I know. So we cropped it and left Natalie and Saddam in the picture. And the crowd went nuts. It was funny for four or five nights, and then it started eating at me. I don't have that mean of a heart, to be able to kick somebody in the crotch like that. That's a little extreme, to put her in a picture with Saddam Hussein. Just because she's young and spouted off a few times, that's a little hardcore. So I put an end to it."

And here comes Keith's pride in craftsmanship again. "If I'm gonna do anything," he figures, "it's gotta be funnier than that."

You won't see a lot of authorized publicity shots of Keith smiling. Clearly he wants to set apart his image from those of the Music Row–bred hat acts who are quick to grin and glad-hand. A projection of sullenness would seem to fit in with the outlaw image he likes to cultivate, and maybe on top of that he's smart enough to realize that choppers as glowing as his are even more effective when flashed sparingly. In his presence, you may find yourself looking for a way to break through the poker mug and bring out that boyish beam. I come up with something that does the trick when I tell him that when the Dixie Chicks played in L.A. two nights earlier, I saw some folks in the lobby of the Staples Center declaring their apparently overlapping loyalties in the feud by wearing homemade "I [Heart] TK" shirts.

"Really?" he says, honestly taken aback. "At their show?" There goes the power grid, as Keith turns the world on with his smile. *"Awesome."*

For Whom Zell Tolls

Have we mentioned that Toby Keith is the face of the Democratic party in the South?

Maybe that's stretching it a little, but Keith's political affiliation is well known among the hoi polloi, and it seems to come up in almost every extended interview he does. It will also come up eventually in almost every conversation about politics you might have with a Democrat in Nashville, although usually it's expressed as a little-known fact being confided, a curious secret that confers hope for a not-entirely-Republican future in country music and in the heartland. The music-biz confidante might lean in just a little and say . . .

"Did you know Toby's a Democrat?"

"Well, not all the stars are Republicans. You may not know this, but . . ."

"I think I heard that Toby's . . ."

It's debatable whether or not this is the hopeful omen that at least a few Tennessee Democrats seem to think it is. After all, retired Georgia senator Zell Miller is still a registered Dem, too, even following his fire-and-brimstone sermon at the 2004 Republican convention (and despite the fact that when a journalist asked Miller if there were any points on which he would choose John Kerry's position over Dubya's, this keynote speaker of the 1994 *Democratic* convention couldn't name a single issue where he still preferred his own party). A lot of the so-called Reagan Democrats simply never got around to re-registering, even though they might have been lost to the party since Lee Atwater's "Southern strategy" took hold in the 1980s, if not since that alliterative phrase first entered the lexicon with Nixon's divide-and-conquer Dixie stratagem of 1968. Anyway, it's votes, not registration rolls, that get counted on election day, right? Toby can come off as being to the right of a lot of moderate Republicans, so it's easy to presume that he's now a Democrat in name and sheep's clothing only, the kind of guy who's too loyal to his family's voting history to admit he's changed sides.

But Keith and the people who know him insist the identification goes beyond brand loyalty. "There's some liberal people in Nashville and the music business that don't understand where I'm coming from," he says. "And once you support the troops or you're outspoken for 'em, people automatically assume you're a right-wing Republican and that you're for the war. As much as the media wants to portray my dad and me as a family of right-wingers, we're very conservative Democrats. My dad was a Democrat every day of his life, but he was for defending his country at all costs. And I support the war on terrorism. All the songs I've had out are about the Afghanistan invasion and have nothing to do with the Iraq war." It's true that he has been quoted several times in the press—even early in the Iraq war, when it was easier to believe that things were proceeding pretty much as planned—to the effect that "the math hasn't worked out for me" on the Iraqi invasion. "But you get lumped into that [right-wing image] as soon as you step out and become *that guy*."

He's put his money where his considerable mouth is when it comes to stumping for politicians on both sides of the aisle. Keith performed in support of Bush at the RNC "Victory Rally" in Dallas on Election Eve 2004. ("It means a lot that he's here," the president told the crowd after Toby's warm-up mini-set. "It sounds like he ought to be running.") Back home he campaigned on behalf of conservative Oklahoma's Democratic governor, Brad Henry, going so far as to hold a press conference with Henry to launch a bill that would expand off-reservation gaming in the state to pay for public education.

If you're to judge a man by the company he keeps, Keith has famously buddied up to country music's most veteran liberal, Willie Nelson, without apparent discomfort. He enlisted Willie to duet on what emerged as something of an instant classic, "Beer for My Horses"—though it could be argued that Nelson did most of the stretching there, since the lyrics' metaphoric suggestion that contemporary criminality and even the crimes of 9/11 might best be dealt with via Old West–style instant justice is distinctly closer to Keith's politics than his new pal's.

Keith's producer and label chief, James Stroud, an unabashed Republican, vouches for his buddy, and says he's not being disingenuous about his core affiliation. "Toby was raised as a Democrat and *is* a Democrat," maintains Stroud, co-chairman of the Universal Music Group in Nashville. "He's not pro-war. He's told me that. He's said 'But I am absolutely pro-servicemen and pro-army, pro-kids that are out there fighting.' And the majority of people in America are that way, Republican or Democrat. Listen, Toby is a very giving person, and a very compassionate person. His beliefs are personal, and I don't want to go to those places. But I will say this: Knowing Toby as my friend, he is a Democrat that is a staunch patriot. He believes in God, he believes that people should give, he believes in helping people—and he believes in separating his politics from the support for his country as far as the troops and his government. I guess he draws that line." In other words, however un-Republican and even bleeding-heart-socialist some of his beliefs might be, we may never find out what those are, because Keith is a single-minded, single-issue voter when it comes to anything involving America's armed forces taking on terrorists.

In that, he's well in line with the history of politics in country music. Through the 1970s, at least, a fan might have assumed that most of the people performing gung-ho anthems, the sort of stuff that now inevitably gets described as "jingoistic," were conservative Democrats, back when that phrase didn't have a contradictory ring. Would any Southerner have bet more than a few dollars in the sixties or seventies on fiery figureheads as patriotic and apparently conservative as the Man in Black and the Okie from Muskogee being registered as Republicans? Not while sober, even though, nowadays, it's not surprising to see Johnny Cash and Merle Haggard show up on Internet lists of supposed GOP luminaries just by virtue of their Vietnam-era support for the military.

Keith, who names Haggard as one of his all-time heroes, likes to cover Hag's "The Fightin' Side of Me" in concert as a prelude to "Courtesy of the Red, White, and Blue." It would be shortsightedness on the part of contemporary northern Democrats to view that as some sort of über-Republican medley. But a Kerry fan might understandably cringe at this moment in a Keith show, because when Haggard in 1970 first sang the lines "When you're runnin' down my country man, you're walkin' on the fightin' side of me," he may have had in mind peaceniks exactly like the fuzzy-sideburned young protagonist of *Going Upriver: The Long War of John Kerry*. Much was made before the 2004 election of how Republicans were using arguably peripheral social concerns as wedge issues to cement their hold on the red states, but there may not have been enough of an awareness among Democrats that, in those same states, patriotism—however it might be interpreted or expressed—was really *the* wedge issue as the war went on.

Or maybe the awareness did exist, and the Dems were merely helpless in figuring a way to argue around it. In the debates, Kerry tried to explain his resistance to the war while trotting out the "I support the troops" line, getting about as far with that nervous syllogism as Natalie Maines before him. The right rejects reasoning along the lines of "Love the troops, even though their mission is immoral" in much the same way that the cultural left dismisses the evangelical canard "Love the sinner, hate the sin" in regard to homosexuality and other purported social ills. Mainstream Democrats like Kerry who were opposed to the war but couldn't argue for a quick pullout were forced into the tenuous position of having to say *Go get 'em, killer!* while decrying the injustice of the troops' cause, an inherently conflicted position that could not help but be seen as hypocritical to much of the far-left and near-right alike.

You could say that by letting the morale of the troops trump their admitted moral concerns about the war effort, Toby Keith and those like him get to come off as the complex characters they are *and* hometown heroes, too. Still, it's reasonable for country fans to imagine that Keith and the stars who go to Iraq to perform at USO shows and visit VA hospitals really *do* care more about soldiers and their families than your average Rock the Vote spokesrocker. Whether or not this is so, when it comes to which celebrities carry the most credibility at election time, regardless of how facile or how complex their actual positions might be, America's vast middle will ultimately tend to favor the ones devoted to cheering up combat-fatigued and seriously wounded Marines over actors and hip-hop stars whose most passionate cause appears to be making it possible for college undergrads to cast ballots over their iBooks from Starbucks.

"They bring dog tags," says James Stroud. "I was with Toby the night before the Super Bowl, and there was a whole company of servicemen that gave him dog tags of men that had died. Handfuls. That's a tough gig," Stroud says, by which he means being made the depository for all that awkward soldierly grief as well as gratitude. "But he's up for it. I'm glad that he's going over there and entertaining the troops. He's one of a few. I wish there were more."

The I ♥ TK Vote

Does the political party that dominated the South through the 1960s (some would argue through the 1980s) have any hope for winning back the demographic we might call the Toby Keith Vote? The War on Terror has been good for the Republicans' hold on the soldier-supportive South. But it would be difficult to overstate how badly things were going for Southern Democrats in the years before 9/11.

It took about a hundred years for the Republican party, which was established in the North in the 1850s with an anti-slavery mandate, to essentially commandeer the South, which was long considered the very heart of the Democratic party. Since the 1960s, of course, they've quickly made up for that century of lost time. Social progressives like to account for that on the basis of the race card trading hands. "We just lost the South for a generation," President Lyndon B. Johnson, a Democrat, is reported to have said after he signed the civil rights amendment in 1964, predicting the widespreed defection of racist Dixiecrats to the other side. As proof of how solidly Democratic the region was at that time, though, the party held twenty-two out of the region's twenty-six available Senate seats—exactly the number that Republicans had following the 2004 election.

The GOP was able to exploit opposition to school busing and affirmative-action initiatives, factors that helped enable a hefty win for Nixon in 1968. This was done with the support of not a few country stars, it might be added, who involved themselves in a national political campaign in significant numbers for the first time ever. Twelve years later, Reagan won over Southern Democrats again. Though the defection didn't become wholesale until the nineties, the 1984 election marked the first time that more Southerners called themselves Republicans than Democrats. Reagan's presidency represented "the turning point in the evolution of a competitive, two-party electorate in the South," according to *The Rise of Southern Republicans*, by Georgia-based authors Earl and Merle Black (who, with those names, really should have gone into bluegrass instead of academia).

After the 2004 election, a study by the *Los Angeles Times* examined just how red the Southern states really were, based on a county-by-county breakdown. (The South was defined as the eleven states of the Confederacy—Alabama, Arkansas, Florida, Georgia, Louisiana, Mississippi, North Carolina, South Carolina, Tennessee, Texas, and Virginia—plus Kentucky and Oklahoma.) In 2000, Bush won 1,047 counties in this wide swath of territory, versus Al Gore's 294. In 2004, it was even more lopsided, with Kerry winning only 216 counties in those thirteen states to Bush's 1,124. Focus on the Southern white vote—which might reasonably be counted as about as close to country music's core constituency as you can get—and things looked even sorrier for the losing side. Of those 216 Southern counties that Kerry did manage to take, 126 were districts where racial minorities are the majority. Kerry carried fewer than 8 percent of Southern counties where whites constituted a majority, according to the *Times*'s math.

(Part of that minuscule percentage, however, most of which represented areas with "college towns," were Tennessee's Davidson County and Texas's Travis County, homes to the two present-day country-music capitals of the world, Nashville and Austin, respectively.)

Progressives might like to blame the transfer of power in the South on racially prejudiced voters, whom they might argue traded one party for another as soon as they realized Republicans would do the most to keep their kids from being bused to schools across town on streets that had been newly renamed Martin Luther King Boulevard. And many social concerns now seen as critical in traditional, religious areas, such as abortion and gay rights, were barely on the popular radar before the Reagan years.

But how to explain the departures from this voting pattern that elected into office Jimmy Carter and Bill Clinton? There's a theory that, in a pinch, Southerners will vote for fellow Southerners, but the adage breaks down when applied to Al Gore, who failed to win even his own home state in 2000. Maybe it's not so much about the party running northerners; maybe it has more to do with the Dems nominating *space aliens*, a category of politico that some might say includes Gore and his successor. "Kerry still comes off as somebody from Mars to somebody in the middle of the country," says Steve Earle, dismissing the very guy he campaigned for. "So it's up to those of us who are from there, who got lucky and happened to be standing in the right place to see the world a little bit differently, to step in. It's up to us"—and not, presumably, whichever New Englander gets nominated next—"to try to educate working people about where their interests really lie."

There is anecdotal evidence that the erosion of support for the Democrats in the heartland isn't permanent yet. Consider the odd, nearly Fortean instances of a few Dems who recently flouted their opponents in gubernatorial races in heavily Republican states. A quick rundown of startling split ballots: In North Carolina, Kerry lost by nine points, which doesn't sound like the makings of a swing state—yet Democrats there held on to the Senate and won back the House from Republicans, and Michael F. Easley won reelection as governor. In a northwesterly direction, but still well within country-music territory, a Democrat in Montana became governor for the first time since 1988, notwithstanding Bush thrashing Kerry by a twenty-one-point margin there.

And in Virginia, Democrat Mark Warner was elected governor in a campaign that used country music as part of his election strategy. One of the guys responsible for making Warner a winner is Dave "Mudcat" Saunders, a rural strategist—or "Bubba coordinator," as he's been known to call himself—for the Democratic party. Saunders, who's also worked on campaigns for John Edwards and many others, may be the only credible political operative in the nation who's advising candidates to hire bluegrass bands and sponsor NASCAR teams.

"Music's influence on things—I don't think you can beat it," says Saunders. He is drawling loudly into a cell phone in a swanky midtown Manhattan restaurant, and with his colorful, mountain-bred dialect, you can't help but imagine a scene right out of *The Electric Horseman*, combined maybe with *Breakfast at Tiffany's* and *The War Room*. When he consulted on Edwards's winning senatorial campaign, the house band was the Lonesome River Band. For Bob Graham, Saunders enlisted Dr. Ralph Stanley's group as the official campaign band. (Presumably, "O Death" wasn't the theme song.)

For Warner's campaign, Saunders and company actually came up with a hit single of sorts: an adaptation of "Dooley," an old moonshining song by the Dillards, a group popularized decades ago on *The Andy Griffith Show*. Saunders wrote new lyrics ("Mark Warner's a good ol' boy from up in Novaville / He understands our people, the folks up in the hills"), retitled it "Warner," and brought in a local group named the Bluegrass Boys to record the track. TV stations delighted in airing excerpts from the track—it didn't hurt that this was around the time the *O Brother, Where Art Thou?* soundtrack was going through the roof—and radio jumped on it, although we aren't talking major Clear Channel affiliates here. "There are fifty-two bluegrass stations in southeast Virginia and up through the valley," says Saunders, "and unbeknownst to us, the company that did the recording sent copies to all of them, and shit, they were playing the hell out of it. It was free media. I personally think you can't beat it, any kind of third-party verifiers you can get."

Of course, not even most of the South, much less the nation as a whole, is Appalachia-adjacent, and one shudders to imagine a John Kerry type cynically trying to ride to victory alongside a Soggy Bottom Boys cover band. Pandering to "the sticks" isn't necessarily much better than sheer avoidance, for certain candidates: that whole "Kerry, get your gun" fiasco that had the senator from Massachusetts going duck hunting shortly before election day in 2004 may go down as almost as egregious an example of pandering as Michael Dukakis climbing onto a tank for a photo op. But Saunders says the key is for candidates to show rural, Midwestern, or Southern voters that they understand them without having to pretend to enthusiastically participate in regional customs. "With Mark Warner we were running a Connecticut Yankee who had moved to northern Virginia and made a zillion in the telecommunications industry. But what we did with the campaign was to say very clearly out front: 'This guy is not a bluegrass music fan, he's not a NASCAR fan, and he's not a hunter—*but* he understands the culture. He thinks that our culture in rural America absolutely is as important as the culture of the Lower East Side.' And so we did not come off as disingenuous."

Signing up the Dillards or Ralph Stanley to move the mountain folk is one thing. Enlisting the real stars of country music to sway a nation is another. But Saunders thinks the Democrats have been remiss for decades in not seriously courting Nashville.

You'll get no argument on that from Joe Galante. RCA's Nashville chief has taken an essentially nonpartisan stance in the twenty-plus years he's been on Music Row, and he's not exactly pushing his acts to be politically active. But he can't believe that one of the two major parties isn't even knocking at their door and giving it the old college try. "It's amazing to me, from a political standpoint, how many of the senators and representatives that are Democrats don't reach out for country acts," says Galante, who was a leader in New York's pop industry before making the move south. "They reach out for the rock acts or the hip-hop acts or the movie stars. It's not necessarily the artists [favoring Republican candidates] all the time. It's that the politicians want to be aligned with Barbra Streisand, as opposed to being involved with Brooks & Dunn."

There are rare exceptions. In early 2004, Wes Clark solicited and won the public support of George Jones, who rarely goes out on a political limb, yet was persuaded to record a campaign ad. Though Jones isn't a Republican, he's been reluctant to do anything that would alienate the Bushes, who are fans. This represented a small coup, though it was Clark's Madonna endorsement that got all the publicity (and probably drove away whatever country voters Jones helped attract).

A more typical example of recent Democrat/Row relations came in the 2000 campaign, when candidate Al Gore made a stop in Nashville to introduce his would-be VP, Connecticut senator Joseph Lieberman. Gore is not completely unaccustomed to the ways of country music: for starters, Nashville was the Tennessee native's campaign base. And he was an acquaintance of Johnny Cash; his elegy at that legend's 2003 funeral was so electric, you can imagine he would have handily won if he'd just gone out on the road paying homage to the Man in Black instead of with his stump speech. Gore is a guy that, on some basic level, *gets* country music. So who did he choose as warm-up act for his Nashville appearance? Jewel.

Granted, marquee-value Democratic country stars willing to wave a campaign banner weren't any easier to come by then than they are now, but at least a few mid-level acts would qualify; some of them, like Sawyer Brown, had played at Tipper Gore's birthday blowout at Nashville's Ryman Auditorium a few years earlier. Perhaps the apparent snub of the town's signature industry wouldn't have stung so badly if Gore's spokeswoman, Mary Perren, hadn't been quite so candid when she explained to the Associated Press: "We're trying to appeal to a young crowd. This is the new Democratic Party. This is the party of the future and we thought Jewel was a good draw for that." Never mind that in 2000 the supposedly futuristic singer in question was already halfway to has-been status. Better to have a slightly shopworn pop star, it was reasoned than someone as octegenarian-skewing as a country luminary. And people wonder why Gore was a prophet without electoral honor in his home state.

Holly Gleason, a publicist and manager whose clients have ranged from GOP standbys Brooks & Dunn to liberals like Mary Chapin Carpenter, says the Democrats have a normalcy deficit, for which Nashville support could seriously compensate. "There are two problems for Democrats when it comes to the average conservative country fan. One is that there will always be a freakish cutaway in the media coverage that challenges their sense of self and family," says Gleason. "And I can speak to this as a publicist. When you're a TV crew and you're looking for something extreme, something not like the same four-hundred hours of film that have been shot covering these things, you find two leather gay guys and five unbathed environmental activists . . . That terrifies middle America. I'm a Midwesterner—so I know, that just freaks people out. And you can *get* those visuals at a Democratic convention . . . The other thing people don't realize about Democrats of the sixties and seventies, as messengers of country music, is that that party was not the liberal freak-out party. It was the working-class party. When we became the catch-all for gay marriage, dreadlocked tree huggers, make up your own schooling as you go along, pass out welfare checks, the welfare queens, etc., we got a bad rap. The Republican machine is better than the Democrat machine. Because we're a party of inclusion, that can be used against us."

Gleason and Saunders can talk till the cows come home about how Music Row and the Democratic party need to get in serious cahoots next time. But where are all these theoretical left-of-center hat acts going to come from, when the only stars who speak up are Republicans like Travis Tritt and Lee Ann Womack? Don't get Saunders started. "I'd say to Travis Tritt and Lee Ann Womack and the rest of 'em that the one thing that they better understand is that their core constituency's getting fucked out here," he says, reasoning that these GOP-affiliated stars are fiddling while Rome, Georgia, burns, as it were. "In job loss, health care, everywhere you look, rural America's getting screwed. And with the big corporate presence in agricultural society, with vertical integration of the food industry . . . I mean, the family farm is gone in Iowa. I'd like to one day ask Travis Tritt what the Republicans have done for rural America. He's gonna say to me, 'They're the party of family values.' And I'm gonna say to him, 'Well, what's the value of cutting the child immunization program? What's the value to rural America of not funding No Child Left Behind?' And he's gonna say, 'Well, we're the party of guns, and the Democrats want to take your gun.' And I'm gonna say, 'I want one example in a state where a Democrat has taken a gun away from a hunter.' And what my partner and I say to 'em is, that's partly why we *are* Democrats, because we *do* hunt—and because of what Republicans have done to the habitat with their bad air and bad stream policies. It doesn't take long to sit down with somebody and explain how they're getting screwed, if you can get off the single issues—you know, the Lee Atwater Southern strategy.

"I mean, take a guy that lives in Henry County, Virginia; he lost his job at the Pillowtex plant; his wife's working two jobs, one at WalMart and one somewhere else; they don't have any health insurance, he's got a sick kid, he has absolutely no future to look at. As soon as his kid grows up, he's leaving the country and moving to the suburbs somewhere, if he goes off to college, because if he comes back, all he'll get is a construction job. And this same guy voted for Bush because some judge in Massachusetts said two gay guys can get married!" Saunders laughs long, hard and—you guessed it—bitterly. "It don't make sense! The Democrats, you know, it's their fault." He's going to change that, with or without Travis Tritt as a convert, one dobro and stock car at a time.

But maybe reconciliation isn't nearly that simple. For some northeasterners and Californians and Seattleites, courting the country audience may seem like a slippery southeasterly slope. You start giving those prodigal Democrat sons a few symbolic sops of the sort Saunders describes, maybe putting gay rights on the back burner along with the gun control bugaboo, and next thing you know, you're offering the more extreme concessions a sometimes Democratic voter like Charlie Daniels wants, resulting in a neo-right-wing package of reconciliatory platitudes that just happens to have a donkey decal slapped on it.

"The Democratic party's just run off to the left of me," says Daniels, who helped campaign for Jimmy Carter in 1976. To find out just how far to the right the one-time "Uneasy Rider" has jogged, you can check out the semiweekly "Soapbox" editorials he posts on his website, dozens of which were collected in a book, *Ain't No Rag*, published by the conservative Regnery Press. "My people always voted for Democrats, from FDR on—until Ike came along, when a lot of people voted for him, because he was a war hero and we had some problems, and everybody felt like he could handle it. But fifty years ago, the South was *solidly* Democratic—I mean, blue all the way through. But they just took the South and its minorities for granted.

"When I talk about Democrats, I'm not making a blanket indictment. There *are* the Zell Millers. And it comes down to a fight between the Howard Deans and the John Kerrys and the John Edwardses, and the other people that say, 'Hey, wait a minute, this is our party too. This is the party of our parents and our grandparents, and you have hijacked it and you're representing something we don't believe in.' I'm not a Democrat or Republican. In fact, I vote Democratic in my state elections a lot of times. I still love Mr. Carter. I wish the Democrats would run a man as honorable as he is. But I can't side with the abortion, with the gay marriage, with the things that the Michael Moores and the Ted Kennedys want . . ."

Getting a guy like Charlie Daniels back into the Democrats' fold may be a challenge even "Mudcat" Saunders wouldn't take on. Here's somebody who, in the seventies, not long before his appearances with Carter, was singing about being stoned in "Long Haired Country Boy"; by the nineties, with "In America," he was advocating the death penalty for drug pushers. Even Zell might find that a little hardcore.

Texas Memories

You know you're an aging, long-in-the-buck-tooth, older-than-Porter-Wagoner redneck if your memory goes back so far you can remember a time when the Democrats and country music seemed perfectly aligned. Dreamlike as it may seem, there *was* an era when "outlaws" walked the earth and found fans among all social strata—not the conservative Kid Rocks and Montgomery Gentrys and Lynyrd Skynyrds that pass for "Outlaws" in CMT specials of the same name today, but counterculturalists like Willie and Waylon, who briefly upended Nashville's social order and yet found entrée into the Lincoln bedroom, thanks to a country-rock-friendly president.

Steve Earle is old enough to recall that now faded era. "There was a moment in Texas, when Rodney Crowell and our graduating class came up, that Texas wasn't the place that it is now," Earle says. "You know, Willie Nelson moved back to Texas in the early seventies, and all of a sudden, rednecks and hippies were going to the same gigs. And I stopped getting my ass kicked all of a sudden! It was like a window that opened up, and then closed."

Why? He's got a theory—Steve Earle's always got a theory. "It's funny. In just a little bit here, I'm playing John T. Ford's country store in Polutus, which is about fifteen or twenty miles from where I went to high school, northwest of San Antonio. Willie played some of his first gigs there after he moved back, at Ford's country store and Armadillo World Headquarters, right around the time *Shotgun Willie* was coming out, when he was on Atlantic. And things almost literally changed overnight. I can remember hitchhiking to see Willie in Luchenbach one time, just sitting out there under the trees and picking my guitar, and some guy in a limo, who worked for some oil company, picked me up. He was going, too, so he took me. It was just this sort of moment . . .

"Keep in mind, times were good in Texas then, at a time when they were not good everywhere else in the country. You know, there was no recession in Texas in the mid-seventies." Oil, that is. "And then all of a sudden I get to Nashville—and I had a trade, I was a carpenter's helper—and when I got there and they weren't building anything, I found out what a fucking recession was. I'd been sort of living in this little bubble in Texas. But then after that, the bubble burst, and times got really hard. And hard times make hard people."

Pancho and Jimmy

Downtown Plains, Georgia, today looks almost exactly as it does in photographs from 1976, when Jimmy Carter launched his presidential campaign in front of the train depot that is now a museum devoted to his presidency. Nearly all of the storefronts in the block-and-a-half-long business district are devoted to selling Carter souvenirs, so it's not at all certain that Plains would have been so preserved in amber without the income derived from a steady stream of tourists to act as protective shield against makeover or decay. But for any Democrats who long for the days before culture wars—or at least when a culture war would have been characterized as fat cats versus populists, instead of baby killers versus holy warriors—it's a nice place to disappear for an afternoon into a quaint, nostalgic dream.

It's easier than usual to slip into that waking REM state today because the former president and Willie Nelson are here, walking the streets. On this October 2004 afternoon they're being trailed by cameras for CMT, which is constructing around their long friendship a cable-TV special, which will climax with a Nelson concert performed in front of the high school tonight.

CMT is owned by Viacom, whose website message boards are sometimes overrun by conservative viewers (or non-viewers) complaining of a New York liberal bias to the channel's programming. I asked CMT chief Brian Philips if there was any concern about spotlighting Carter because of that widespread belief. No, he insisted: "Carter is *the* most popular living ex-president. That's based on an AP/CNN poll. We knew that he was that well-liked going in, or we wouldn't have made the show. He's done a great good around the world over the last few years. I'm not gonna debate the merits of this show, no matter what anybody thinks about it. You can say what you want about what was right or wrong with his presidency, but if you don't like Jimmy Carter in 2005, you've got a screw loose. And the same goes for Willie Nelson."

Earlier today, the pair, accompanied by the cameras, have been out touring Carter's peanut crops, so they've got a little mud on the tires, and their jeans when they get back into town. I'm admiring some decorative peanut-themed fake license plates in the meeting room of Plains' city hall when a handful of Secret Service agents precede the world's most powerful farmer and his braided running buddy of three-plus decades. Ladies and gentlemen, please welcome the men who are, in much of this part of the world, the Last Two Good Democrats.

I start off with an icebreaker: Any truth to the rumor that Zell Miller will be sitting in at tonight's show? (Carter was in the news a few weeks earlier for sending Miller a post–GOP convention letter that ended: "Zell, I have known you for forty-two years and have, in the past, respected you as a trustworthy political leader and a personal friend. But now, there are many of us loyal Democrats who feel uncomfortable in seeing that you have chosen the rich over the poor, unilateral preemptive war over a strong nation united with others for peace, lies and obfuscation over the truth, and the political technique of personal character assassination as a way to win elections or to garner a few moments of applause. These are not the characteristics of great Democrats whose legacy you and I have inherited.")

"He'd be welcome," chuckles Carter, not taking the bait for any further internecine-warfare zingers on such a mellow day. "He's a good country music fan, and so am I."

There's much more to be said about his relationship with the no longer Red-Headed Stranger. "I knew Willie before I was elected president; in the campaign, he was one of my supporters. Then Willie would come and visit me on occasion at the White House—spend the night and get to know all of our children. At that time, he and I were both avid joggers; we would run five or six miles every day together. I've probably been to four or five of Willie's performances over the years. The last one was in Oslo; Willie came over and played when I got the Nobel Peace Prize. The one major concert that he was gonna do at the White House, I was at Camp David with Begin and Saddat, and I couldn't go. That was a big disappointment."

Carter says he just finished a book that he wrote while largely under the influence of Willie Nelson records. In some ways, things for Carter really haven't changed much since the late seventies. "I'm a fly fisherman, and I would tie flies in my study, where Harry Truman used to work, while Willie's songs were playing. When I was in trouble in the White House, when I wanted to be by myself or have some deep thought, I had a very high-quality hi-fi player there, and the number-one thing that I played was Willie's music. So all the good things I did and of course all the mistakes I've made, you could kind of blame half of that on Willie."

Now we know, then: the loss of the 1980 election, the subsequent Reagan years, trickle-down economics, the Bush term that followed . . . a series of (for Democrats) unfortunate events that might all be attributed to a contact high from too many late-night spins of *Phases and Stages* on Pennsylvania Avenue. At least it's comforting to know, given the questionable music known to have wafted down those hallways during administrations before and since, that the ghosts of Lincoln and Jefferson got to hear "Blue Eyes Crying in the Rain" in the wee small hours every now and again.

There will be no policy debates between these two. "Politically we see things the same way," says Carter. "One of the surprising things is how close my early life in Plains was to Willie's life in Abbott, Texas. It's a little town not even as big as Plains. We both picked cotton and pulled plows on a farm; we both learned how to be blacksmiths as young boys and men; we both grew up in highly diverse communities where everybody knew each other."

In an age when presidential candidates are routinely expected to list their favorite pop songs along with their choice of underwear, and when the Bush daughters can startle a national convention by announcing that the homey-in-chief is way into Outkast, it's difficult to remember just how radical it seemed in 1976 when Carter started quoting Bob Dylan and aligning himself with characters like Willie.

"I think that was one of the reasons I won," Carter counters, "because I *did* align myself with characters like these, who were admired by millions of people around the world. It was a very popular thing to do. I knew Bob Dylan quite well; Willie's just finishing a tour with him now. Dylan had visited me at the governor's mansion and spent the night there with us. And of course the Allman Brothers were special friends, as well. Tom T. Hall was a very strong supporter and is still a good friend. He was probably the best friend of my brother, Billy. So we've had a good relationship with country-western folks. Johnny and June came to Plains to visit with us when their little boy was about three. June Carter Cash I always claimed was my kinfolk."

Getting back to the matter of celebrity sleepovers . . . We've all heard about the anecdote in Willie's book about smoking dope on the White House roof. So Mr. President, we have to ask: What did you know and when did you know it?

"Well, I would guess that Willie and my sons knew a lot more about that than I did. That was one of the things that Willie and I never did discuss much. But I don't think there's much doubt that there was—"

Sensing the potential for trouble here, Nelson, who's been pretty quiet up to this point, helpfully interrupts his old friend. "Actually, I don't remember a lot that happened then—short-term memory," he laughs.

Carter laughs, too, clearly grateful to have been cut off. "Yeah, my memory's kind of short on that subject, too."

Enough about pot, back to politics. I'm curious to known how Nelson can be so intensely political in isolated moments, as with his support of Dennis Kucinich, arguably the farthest-left of the major Democratic primary candidates in 2004, yet so apolitical the vast majority of the time. There was the remarkably pointed anti-war song he wrote on Christmas Day 2003 and performed live only once, a little over a week later, at an Austin rally for Kucinich. A departure from Nelson's usual beatific vibe in favor of some real fury, it was called "Whatever Happened to Peace on Earth":

> And the bewildered herd is still believing
> Everything we've been told from our birth
> Hell, they won't lie to me
> Not on my own damn TV
> But how much is a liar's word worth
> And whatever happened to peace on earth . . .
>
> So I guess it's just
> Do unto others before they do it to you
> Let's just kill 'em all and let God sort 'em out
> Is this what God wants us to do?

(It may be strictly coincidence, but an attentive listener can't help but hear an ironic echo in those last two lines of "Beer for My Horses," in which Keith and Nelson sang: "Send 'em all to their maker and he'll settle 'em down / You can bet he'll set 'em down.")

Not too many people ever heard Nelson's first anti-war track, the depressing "Jimmy's Road," written in 1966. Nor will many ever hear "Peace on Earth," which was released only temporarily as a free Internet download; it didn't appear on any CD and he hasn't played it again since the Kucinich rally. He won't tonight, either.

"I think it's important that we have a change in the direction our country is going," Nelson explains. "But I sing to Democrats and Republicans every night. I don't want to do or say anything that's going to make half of my crowd get up and leave the building. Because the election's over November the second, and November the third, I'm still gonna be out there on the highway." They both laugh. "If you really want to stir up the crowd, that's one way to do it, but I think that I'd rather stir 'em up in another way, with another song. So I do what I can do without trying to offend anybody. As I look at it, my job is to bring people together—you know, hold it together and sing 'Amazing Grace' . . ."

"It's one country," offers Carter.

That's arguable, but a fair enough reminder from an ex-president who, at one time, was seen as the centrist in chief. But, somewhat facetiously, I have to bring up guilt by association. Back in 1976, I suggest to Carter, people might have seen you with Willie and wondered: How can a respectable governor emeritus or president-elect hang out with this hippie? Nowadays, people might be more likely to wonder: How can you hang out with somebody who's also friends with a seeming archconservative like Toby Keith?

They both chuckle at that one. "I just talked to Toby a while ago," Nelson informs me, "and he said, 'Be sure and tell the president hello.' He's a big fan. We're all a little closer than most people would even imagine."

Here it comes: that telltale leaning-in, that conspiratorial tone. We know exactly what he's going to say. "Toby's also a Democrat, you know," Nelson shares, in a confiding voice.

A beat. "Kind of."

Who's Your Prexy?

November 2004. Toby Keith plops himself onto a folding chair in a parking lot behind the El Capitan theater on Hollywood Boulevard. A few paces away is a stage with T-O-B-Y in giant letters, where soon the studio audience for the Jimmy Kimmel Show will be ushered outside to enjoy a Keith mini-set. He's in a good mood, as he should be. The first-week numbers for his *Greatest Hits Vol. 2* album came in about an hour earlier, and he sold twice as much as did a simultaneously debuting hits collection from Britney Spears. Naturally, being verifiably twice as popular as Britney doesn't mean he'll be showing up on the cover of *Us Weekly* anytime soon, numbers be damned. But just like "Mudcat" Saunders said, you need all the third-party verifiers you can get, whether you're undersung as a Democrat in a Republican universe or undersung as a country-music star in a world of pop "Toxic"-ity.

Toby has two elections on his mind, both of which occurred during the last couple of weeks. One was the presidential contest. The other was the Country Music Association Awards. One went his way, the other didn't.

"As long as the fans vote, I've always got a chance to win," says Keith, citing shows like the CMT Flameworthy Awards, or the Billboard Awards, which is based strictly on sales. "But with the CMA voters, I bet I have the worst win-versus-nominations ration of anybody, ever. I don't think anybody could be worse than one-for-thirty." He was on the CMA telecast in Nashville a few nights before but went home empty-handed, as usual, despite being country's most reliable male seller.

What is it with Toby and Music Row? You could surmise that maybe there are some voters who don't feel that he's playing to his better angels. Keith is actually highly versatile as a writer and record-maker; most of his singles have a distinctive sound from each other. He can write something as beautiful and humanistic as "Tired"—a weary working-class ballad that was the highlight of Willie's latest album, and arguably one of the best, most sensitive country songs in years—as well as basic, drunkest-common-denominator fare like "I Love This Bar." But since what he calls the "attitude" stuff started setting him apart from the hat pack a few years ago, he's been concentrating on Alpha Male anthems. Here's his double whammy: As someone who's pro-troops *and* pro-partying, he figures he's both too conservative and not conservative enough to be appreciated as a prophet in country music's hometown.

"I would say that some things I do rub them wrong. I'm not the perfect poster child for Nashville," he says, looking very gym-burnished in his usual bicep-revealing, sleeves-forcibly-removed jean jacket. "What they represent is a good, clean, moral kind of lifestyle and all that. And I don't represent all those things, obviously."

The single he's about to perform for Kimmel's al fresco crowd, "Stays in Mexico," is a fast-paced, horn-driven scorcher about marrieds who meet and have a short, torrid affair at a balmy resort. A cheatin' song. You remember those. There've been a handful in country in recent years, but they usually have regret or repentance as the upshot. Keith's song is surprisingly neutral, in that regard. The tune went to No. 1, but in this values-driven era, no one is about to nominate it as song of the year, and the CMA board asked him to do a more innocuous number, "Mockingbird," a duet with his daughter, on the family-friendly telecast. You could also thank or blame him for a lot of the redneck mania happening in country right now; supernova of the moment, Gretchen Wilson, might not have been possible without Keith. When he graduated from mere star to superstar around the turn of the millennium, it was with songs like "Who's Your Daddy" that challenged a prevailing sense of political, musical, cultural, and especially sexual correctness. At the time, country as a format had pretty much been handed over to soccer moms, whose sensibilities were presumed too delicate for country's former poetic realism. For better or worse, Keith made it okay again to be rough. They can thank him for that later, when the history books are written, but at the moment, his are not the kind of accomplishments that win industry accolades.

Some of the bias in Nashville comes down to sheer arithmetic, too, he figures. "If you look at who's won over the last years and look what labels they're on, I think you can figure out what's going on. There'll be thirteen of the fifteen awards every year won by the same organization. It's unfair, but that's the system we live under." Translated: he's affiliated with the Universal Music Group, which isn't as well-represented as BMG's dominant Nashville division (home of winners like the "safer" Alan Jackson and Kenny Chesney). It could also have something to do with the fact that he sounds suspiciously like he's bragging when he publicly repeats the fact that he's "never lived a day in Nashville in my life," as if one of the very reasons for his massive success was remaining outside the Davidson County bubble.

And there's another factor: inside that bubble, despite country music's ultra-conservative image, four of the five major labels in Nashville have outspoken liberals among their top executives (UMG's Luke Lewis, Sony's John Grady, Warner's Paul Worley and Capitol's Mike Dungan). And it's safe to assume that their staffs may be well stocked with underlings who aren't likely to cast CMA votes for somebody they think reinforces a politically reactionary image, even if Keith's cheating-and-drinking songs might be considered the antithesis of a certain kind of moral conservatism.

"I'd say there's some liberal people in Nashville and the music business that don't understand where I'm coming from. I support the war on terrorism. So I probably get some people voting against me just because of that. There's probably some liberal musicians in town who won't vote for me just because they think I'm a right-wing maniac. I think most artists shy away from politics, especially during an election year. That's when you should stand up the most. By not speaking your mind, and staying out of it, all you're doing is protecting your career. And I would rather be endeared to the ones that appreciate me for what I stand for than to try to fake somebody out and keep my mouth shut."

And here's where that other election comes in, the one whose results were more gratifying. When it comes to Bush's victory, he says, "I think that's America speaking up, saying, 'You didn't bring us a good enough candidate to unseat the one we don't like'—the one they *supposedly* don't like. I mean, if you'd have told me Monday night, before the presidential election, that eight or nine million more people are gonna get out and vote, I would've said, well, that's gonna be the MTV crowd and the college kids, and Kerry's gonna win by a landslide. Well, all those extra people did get out and they did vote, and the MTV crowd slept in, and Bush won by almost four million votes."

Is he actually wallowing in the Kerry loss? Yes, upon inspection, this is definite, verifiable *gloating*. But it's understandable. If Bush can be the scourge of the elite and ride that uncoolness into reelection, maybe there's hope yet for a fellow over- and underachiever like Toby Keith to finally win that Entertainer of the Year award.

The "Black Tie and Boots" balls at President George W. Bush's inauguration festivities in 2001 and 2005 were headlined by country performers, many of them fellow Texans, like Lee Ann Womack. SHAWN THEW/AFP/GETTY IMAGES

3

Opryland, D.C.

Visits with the GOP's Favorite Stars

It's January 2005, the gala-crammed week of George W. Bush's second inauguration. So what *is* Ronnie Dunn doing at home in Tennessee? Surely he belongs up in Washington, leading the musical victory celebration with his partner Kix Brooks, as country's leading duo did four years earlier. "We were invited to do some things for the inaugural. But nah," says Dunn, with surprising nonchalance for a true believer. "I think we gave at the office this year."

Brooks & Dunn's contributions to charity last fall included a headlining gig at the Republican convention in Manhattan, where they were easily the biggest-name entertainers on the dais. Content to rest on his laurels after all that barnstorming, Dunn is kicking back in the hundred-year-old barn that he's converted into a business center and Southwest-styled den behind his homestead in Brentwood, Tennessee. But if today he seems almost blasé about serving the president, he was quicker to answer the call a couple months earlier.

"I got a call two nights before the election. They told me they thought that Wisconsin was gonna be the final swing state, even more than Ohio. I was like, *Shit*. I had a bunch of stuff going on, but we dropped everything we were doing and headed for Milwaukee to do a rally with Bush there the next day, because I thought it must be important. Janine was talking with some friends the other night, and she goes, 'To talk to Ronnie, you would think that we were single-handedly gonna win or lose the election because he flew up there and sang!'"

As it happens, Dunn's wife has just ascended to the barn's second floor, bringing some chicken soup up. Ribbing him about the emergency Wisconsin barnstorming gig "was so hard to resist, because he was so serious," Janine laughs. "I was like, 'Well, sure, I want to go, but it may not be *quiiiiiite* as critical as you think.' You know that old gospel song, 'He's Got the Whole World in His Hands'? He thought he had—"

"But everything at that point was so intense," her husband half protests, smiling. "And we were emotionally in the middle of it, with everybody telling us it was the new swing state. Now, looking back on it, we laugh."

This may be the point at which Democrats allow themselves a deep sigh, wistfully recalling those brief few hours when there was real panic in the other camp; when even Republican operatives were e-mailing friends that their side had lost the electoral college; when home viewers could see palpable dread on the president's smiling face as he was videotaped leaving his local polling place; when some political operative had a fever dream that it might be up to Brooks & Dunn to make the Midwestern difference and give the party its best, last shot at beating Kerry in a squeaker. And for the winning side, what a crazy, silly hoot, to remember ever having doubted the mandate!

Are there any worries that some fans among the losing 48 percent might not approve of their favorite country twosome throwing support behind a polarizing president in two successive elections? "I think that's possible, highly possible," Dunn allows. "We probably play to more Democrats than we do Republicans—I don't know! Had I not believed the way I do, I wouldn't have done it. There were members of my management team that were dead against it. And I had as many Kerry guys in my band as I did Bush fans. But I feel firmly that at this time in history, it's important to take a stand, at all costs."

Even at the cost of becoming an easy target for East and West Coast media types who examine both parties' lists of celebrity supporters and make snippy jokes about the inordinate number of country stars lined up on one side, as if that's the best the poor Republicans could do. "You know what?" says Dunn. "I think in some ways that's an underhanded blow dealt by the left-wingers to stigmatize this regime. There were a lot of rock and pop guys that were behind Bush. Steven

Tyler was one of 'em." Really? "Well, they were calling him, and at first he was ready to get involved. He backed away, for whatever reason . . ."

Convention-goers and whistle-stop campaigners were thus denied the chance to ever hear Aerosmith perform "Dude Looks Like a Leader." What they did get, in the form of Bush's recorded intro and exit music—along with an occasional live rendition straight from the horsemen's mouths—was Brooks & Dunn's "Only in America," the unofficial Bush theme song. Funnily enough, that number was cowritten by a buddy of theirs, Don Cook, who went on to found a fledgling organization called Music Row Democrats. Having "Only in America" drafted as the new "Hail to the Chief " wasn't really what Democratic activist Cook had in mind for his song (which isn't even that gung-ho—listen closely, and there's an ambivalence about the American dream to be found in the lyrics). But in Nashville, even if you're on the other side of the aisle, sometimes it's hard not to give at the office.

The Grand Old Genre

It strikes many observers that the GOP has commandeered a musical genre that the opposition used to have at least sharin', if not braggin', rights to. Or maybe it's not Republican musical imperialism so much as complacent Democratic leaders having allowed the entire country music contingent to drift away without so much as a struggle, kind of like the classic case of a record-label exec who forgets to renew an old-timer's contract. There will be no such oversights on Karl Rove's watch, rest assured.

Even in the days when it would have been assumed that most country artists and fans were Democrats, you'd find GOP dabblers, like Roy Acuff, who unsuccessfully ran for Tennessee governor on three occasions in the fifties and early sixties. But the current love affair between country and Republicans got going in earnest with some heavy petting in the Nixon years before blossoming into betrothal in the Reagan and Bush eras. It's hard to imagine California boy Nixon spinning Ferlin Husky platters in his spare time, but he was the first president to regularly invite country performers into the White House, and many loved him for it. When the Grand Ole Opry moved from the historic Ryman Auditorium to new digs out at Opryland in 1973, Nixon was present on opening night, trading jocularities with Acuff and giving the singer's trademark yo-yo a try. The president even took a turn at the piano that evening, playing "My Old Irish Rose" and, in honor of Pat, "Happy Birthday." Nixon was, weirdly enough, the first country music president, never to be confused with George McGovern, the first Warren Beatty–anointed candidate. Flash forward several generations and the dynamic is only more pronounced.

Loretta Lynn has always remained true to her dirt-poor roots no matter how far from them she's traveled in life, so you might expect her to associate with what used to be the party of the working class. But she loved the Nixons. On record, in the humorous hit "One's on the Way," Lynn joked about the unlikelihood of ever making "the White House social scene." In real life, the coal miner's daughter was one of the first country luminaries invited in, a significant milestone for a strain of music that then enjoyed little snob appeal.

Nixon wasn't Loretta's favorite, though. That might be a tossup between 41 and 43. "If George and Barbara Bush have got something going on, they'll call me or send a letter about it," she says. "I love them people. And I call the president Little George, and his dad Big George, because Little George ain't that tall. And my assistant said, 'You're gonna have to quit saying Little George and Big George!' But I don't do that around just anybody. I just sometimes do it in front of the family; I get carried away . . . But to me, our president's one of our greatest presidents," Lynn insists. She means Little George. "They haven't given him a chance! They didn't give George Bush a chance, either—you know, the first one. So I've been a little upset over that. Here Clinton could walk in the White House and pull everything, but all our President Bush had to do was say 'Read my lips,' and that's all you heard. That made me mad. I think for a president to go in and have girlfriends all the time in the White House is a heck of a lot worse than 'Read my lips.' Because he"—we're talking Big George now—"didn't know what he was walking into when he said that, you know."

The elder Bush's support was particularly welcome in country circles because Reagan hadn't been overly appreciative of the genre, even though, if only on the level of shtick, the music should have gone perfectly with the wood-chopping image he liked to perpetuate on his California ranch. Joe Galante, longtime chief of the RCA family of labels in Nashville, was president of the Country Music Association during the Carter and Reagan years. "The White House under Jimmy Carter was a whole lot friendlier to country music than the Reagan White House was," Galante says. "Loretta and Jimmy and Rosalyn Carter were on a first-name basis. The Reagans understood country music but didn't have the same kind of warmth, in terms of relationships, whereas the Carter White House was more willing to bring country music in on a regular basis to entertain, and just more familiar with everybody. Then, obviously, Bush Senior was very strong on country music again— and Christian music, at the same time," he adds, referring to Nashville's other primary musical export. "Bush Senior had that warmth and those relationships with people like Michael W. Smith or Randy Owen from the group Alabama." This time, the mutual validation stuck.

There were doubters who never believed that either Bush had ever seriously gotten below his Northeastern raisin', and who couldn't swallow for a second that such obviously patrician Yankees weren't hoodwinking everyone with their supposed love of country music. Did the elder Bush really put on Lefty Frizzell to unwind after a hard day of poring over intelligence reports from his old friends at the agency? And did W. whose favorite political philosopher is Jesus, also ponder the philosophies of Waylon Jennings, down to and including whether Hank done it this way? Probably not, but if the Bushes' tastes did run more toward the middle of the country road, their affection for the genre seemed genuine to the stars they've invited to the White House.

Bush the father even wrote—or had ghostwritten for him—a personal appreciation that first appeared in *Country America* magazine in 1990. The *Washington Post* reprinted it, under the patronizing headline "George and the Oval Office Do-Si-Do: Heck, a President Ain't Nothin' but Just Folks." "So many country songs have that upbeat, optimistic sound to them, you can't help but tap your toes and hum along," Bush's piece began. "In fact, I enjoy country music so much that the carpenters built a stereo right into the desk in my study at the White House." Reference was made to presidential pooch Millie enjoying the sounds emanating from the hi-fi, too. But from the playlists mentioned, it didn't sound like Carter had left behind his collection of Willie vinyl. The piece went on to say, "I find myself more relaxed with Reba coming over the airwaves. Country music hits all the right chords—like caring for your family, remembering the good times and keeping faith in God. There's nothing better than hearing the Oak Ridge Boys singing 'a little story of an American family' at the end of a long day. Or Randy Travis telling about his love that's 'deeper than the holler.' Or the wonderful harmonies of the Gatlin Brothers and Alabama." Moe Bandy and Lee Greenwood got presidential shout-outs too, and Bush also mentioned how fine an antidote Anne Murray's "A Little Good News" was for those nattering nabobs of negativism on the evening news. It was a rousing endorsement that was utterly convincing in making country sound like a sub-Hallmark line of greeting card aphorisms set to slightly if not particularly twangy music—a fairly accurate portrait, in those days.

The music has gotten a lot better since the first George Bush wrote that paean to Nashville in the dog days of 1990. To a large degree it's become tougher, funnier, more realistic, and even more heartfelt when it does inevitably run toward sentiment and emotionalism . . . in other words, closer kin to all the things that great, classic country used to be before the post–*Urban Cowboy* gold rush spoiled things for a while. Despite this remarkable recent upsurge in the overall quality of country music, the Republicans have stuck with it anyway. So remember: you *can* question what it says about the party when Bo Derek is trotted out at GOP functions year after year, lending something close to but not quite resembling starpower. But poking fun at the party's roster of country supporters? To paraphrase one of Lee Atwater's favorite bluesmen, the late, great Willie Dixon: the metrosexuals don't know, but the little redneck girls understand.

Wahhabi Horse

Here is something you probably didn't know about Ronnie Dunn: he is a boot-scootin' foreign policy wonk.

"I was at a party with Steve Earle on New Year's Eve," he relays. Sounds juicy already. The gathering was at the home of local legend Tony Brown, a conservative producer-cum-label-head who somehow managed to give most of Nashville's most liberal artists their first big breaks, including alt-country provocateur Earle. Perhaps Dunn managed to wangle an invitation to be a guest on Earle's weekly Air America talk show?

Uh, no. "Steve's supposed to be pretty politically active. And I asked him if he was familiar with Wahhabism, which is *the* radical sect of Islam, responsible since the 1700s for threading itself through the Middle East and the Islamic religion, positioning itself politically with especially the Saudi family, and playing a huge role in what's going on right now in politics and history. In 1962, they were allowed to take over the educational system in Saudi Arabia, through the *ulama*, which is their version of our parliament or congress. It's absolutely responsible for what's going on now. The pop phrase is to say, 'Hey, America's in the Middle East because of the oil.' We *are* there because of the oil, but there's an underlying factor that supercedes oil a hundredfold. And that is what's coming at us"—meaning, terror. "I think if you were to broach that subject behind closed doors with the Bush administration, you'd probably find that that's their real motive: *fear*."

So, about that Steve Earle confrontation . . .

"Oh. He didn't know what Wahhabism is. But he's against war, whatever the reason is. 'I'm against us being over there. I'm against us deploying troops in any way,' or whatever. Good," says Dunn, sighing. "The end result of that won't be pretty. Shit, since the late seventies and early eighties they've systematically and methodically gone about hitting us, not necessarily on U.S. soil, but via very extensively planned terrorist acts." I'm hoping to hear about how he and Earle might've rung in the new year by taking it outside and giving each other black eyes, but Dunn has already moved onto the book report part of the program. "One of the books I'm reading right now is *Hatred's Kingdom*, written by the former ambassador to Saudi Arabia, which gives detailed historical accounts of how the Wahhabi sect came about. *What Went Wrong* is another great book, by Bernard Lewis, a Princeton historian. I don't think we have really delved into just how much we are at war and what a well-planned regime we're up against."

Where is Dunn's partner in all of this? He's scooting out the door as I arrived—and not because Kix Brooks isn't every bit as conservative, or that he doesn't enjoy a good political tussle himself, but associates say he prefers to play his cards closer to the vest in public, out of fear of being misrepresented by the media in sound bites. Dunn, however, welcomes all takers when it comes to a political discussion—occasionally even visiting journalists. Some liberal Nashvillians who've gotten into it with him see his eagerness to engage as friendly scrapping, while those who haven't welcomed the chance to debate, like Earle, see it more as aggression. Anyway, today he's on a friendly tear about terrorism.

"My biggest problem with what comes out of this genre is mindless rednecks, that stigma, popping off and touting that image when they're not necessarily informed or even reading anything beyond the pop-culture news outlets. The public is much more apt to take the bait from a song that's talking about a boot up your ass, and that kind of surface-value stuff, than they are from one that deals with the under-lying factors behind what's going on. I don't know why the Bush ad-ministration doesn't actually come out and try to define who the enemy is. They call it bin Laden and the Taliban. It's because they do not want to incite the Islamic world as a whole. They're running away as far as they can from the words 'holy war.' That's the one thing that will ignite that whole Muslim faction. They hate one another, and they're shooting at each other from one tribe to the next, but that's the one thing where they'll all stop, stick their heads out of the cloud and smoke, and go 'Wait a minute—holy war. Let's go at 'em.' I think that's why our guys don't put it out to the mainstream.

"Looking back in hindsight, this war, maybe it could have been planned better. But I'm afraid to say in public that, hey, if you were going to set up a strategic position in the Middle East to monitor what's going on, in terms of this underlying assault right now, Iraq's pretty central, isn't it? Probably the easiest country to walk into and set up camp. The Wahhabis will not allow the Saudi family to align themselves with us, so they have to play both sides against the middle. The Turks aren't gonna help us that much, though they're the most westernized over there. And Iran's dead set against us. So if there's an underlying war being waged, I'm not sure I wouldn't agree with where the U.S. went to set up shop. Let's take it to them, because it's sure as hell coming here."

Unlike Alan Jackson, Dunn can tell you the difference between Iran and Iraq. At length. But he's even more worried about other climes. "I'll tell you what scares me right now: hearing that Russia and China are talking about doing some kind of military alliance. Shit! I have some friends in the intelligence business, and they don't see the Middle Eastern situation becoming as big a threat as the China card—economically, militarily and everything else. That's on the verge of going down, and there's nothing we can do to stop it. The underlying factor in all that stuff, just to completely take us under the water, is historical global migration. The human population has taken its turn migrating, now to the Pacific Rim. You can't stop that. Theirs is already the fastest growing economy on the planet. They could gain access to oil probably in Russia and the Balkans, and that's gonna ramp 'em up in a hurry."

This kind of talk may sound borderline apocalyptic. And Dunn can be so evangelistic about this stuff, you might mistake him for an evangelical. But unlike some of his country brethren who stumped for Bush, the fear of God isn't so much a motivating factor for him. In fact, he can sound as distrustful of the mixture of church and state as a lot of lefties.

"It scares me when any time, in anything, you start letting specific religious beliefs interfere and dictate your politics. It's hard not to let it, almost impossible, but that's a danger. I went to school for a while to become a Baptist minister. I studied theology. But right now, religion scares me to death. Historically, it's probably the cause of more deaths than any other force on the planet."

After 9/11, he cowrote a song called "Holy War" that appears as a hidden bonus track at the end of the duo's *Red Dirt Road* album. There are reasons why it's not prominently billed. The music is pure uptempo gospel, and if you didn't know better, you might suppose the artists in question are giving their approval when they sing:

> Some say a holy war is comin'
> Gonna be the end of mortal man
> There's a TV preacher sayin'
> Armageddon is at hand
> Sayin' the Jews, the gays, the junkies
> The politicians and infidels
> Have conjured up the devil
> Upon the gates of hell

"I got a reaction from a programmer right off the bat, before it was even released," says Dunn. "He said he had played it over and over to his staff, and they thought it was anti-semitic. And it's not at all, but he was reacting to that line in the chorus. The Taliban had been representing western culture as all homosexuals, saying the streets are filled with nothing but drugs and corruption. But I did a 'we say'/'they say,' 'they say'/'we say' thing where it's intertwined, a radical viewpoint from both sides. The lyrics aren't clearly defined enough to really say who I'm talking about each time—on purpose. I talk about the TV preachers too. One of the biggest ways that the Ayatollahs circulate their sermons is on cassettes and via little independent TV transmitters. Here, you turn on the TV and see these TV evangelists going at it, and you want to say, Give me some air. Back away from the pulpit, dude! The song a jab at radicalism from every end of the equation." Nevertheless, "Ask Joe Galante about it and he'll go 'Nah, never mind, it's a stupid song.' I'm amazed he let me put it on the record. You just can't say, 'The gays, the Jews, the junkies'—not in this genre. I got a lecture from my manager Bob Titley, the liberal Democrat, on how dangerous it was for me to put that out. They took off running with a firehose to squelch that song."

Galante doesn't deny having lobbied Dunn to keep the track off the album: "I wasn't crazy about 'Holy War,'" says the BMG Nashville chief. "I thought there were some lines that could have been taken wrong. I told him, 'Ronnie, if you have to explain it to me, I think it's a big problem. Its meaning should be self-evident, in this format. The audience shouldn't need a college education to understand the music.' I wasn't sure what it was doing in the middle of the record. And then he made it the hidden track, and certainly he was entitled to do that. I think he expected it to stir up more controversy than it did."

Given the overlap between the red states and the country-music states, and the voter's concerns that were expressed in the exit polls, is it right to put two and two together and think of country as the genre of moral values?

"I don't see it as that," Dunn laughs. "I always see it as hell-raising good times. It's always been a good outlet for the blue-collar working-man to go out and punch the jukebox on a Friday night and come up with a song that says what he needs to hear. I don't look at my audiences and see a lot of Sunday morning devout churchgoers. If there are, they're in drag!"

Red Dirt Road, widely regarded as the duo's best album, included some more personal reflections, like the title song, in which the dusty lane in question is proclaimed as "where I found Jesus"—shortly followed by "where I had my first beer." Juxtaposing religious conversion and an initial sip of alcohol sounded just a little bit provocative in the context of country music. In moments, Dunn can wax nostalgic not just for that old road but for a more creatively open time in country. And a rowdier one.

"The business side is gonna tell you, stick to painting by numbers—we'll get you there. They don't want you to make any statements. I do miss being able to step out and try to take a swing at something. We can't even be good, consistent, beer-drinking cowboys anymore, you know," he laughs. "All that stuff with those guys like Cash and Willie and Kristofferson and Waylon is just amazing to me. I wonder if an artist like that—that rowdy, kick-ass kind of artist—would be allowed to make it through the ranks of a label these days. Hasn't been one in a long time. Hank Jr. was the last one. Saw him up on stage with a bottle of whiskey in Kansas City.

"I come from such a conservative religious background, it's like, shit, I'd love to overcompensate and go the other way. But I don't know what would be gained in the end. Either dying or going to therapy, for years—again," he chuckles, slapping his leg. "Going down the middle is not as much fun as it could be, but it's not as destructive, either . . . It wouldn't be hard for me to grab a bottle of tequila and just"—he mimes taking a swig—"play that role. But I wouldn't last long. I don't think any of us would. Even Willie has to back off pot every now and then."

Dunn is heading off to D.C. this week, after all, not to glad-hand with the reinstalled administration he supported, but to dine at the Russian embassy with 150 or so of the top Fortune 500 execs, who are meeting to discuss how they can strengthen business relations between the former Soviet states and the United States. Also, he's lent a couple of paintings to a Russian-themed exhibition jointly sponsored by the Smithsonian Institution and the National Gallery. Though he might have been tempted to go the way of the bottle, it turns out that Dunn really has only two vices: art collecting and spook-friendly doomsday tomes.

Sara Evans, Country for Life

Sara Evans *did* play at an event to celebrate Bush's second inauguration, as part of the country roster at the Black Tie and Boots ball. The following night, she is already back on tour, sitting on a bus parked in the snow outside an arena in Reading, Pennsylvania, where she and co-headliner Brad Paisley are shortly to go on. On her bus, it's a family affair, as always. Her brother is in the band. Her sister is nanny for Sara's three-month-old baby. Evans's husband, Craig Schelske, a political activist and sometimes politician, is welcoming a handful of visitors who've flown up on a Lear jet from Nashville, including a couple of the top brass from her record company and a few trade journalists. There is a little loose talk, off the record, about the Washington gig the night before and which well-known names in behind-the-scenes Republican politics were being a little too obvious—at least for her husband's taste—about checking out Evans's figure, which, as even a moral watchdog couldn't help but notice, is already miraculously back to its pre-pregnancy curviness.

How was the ball? "It was great," she says, "although . . ." There was the small matter of having the set cut short, very short, by the president's arrival. They'd gone on late, and she'd sung only two songs when Bush came on stage to thank the crowd, after which it was time to move on to the next act. The entourage endured a lot of flying and moving and shuffling to end up only doing a two-number cameo—not that anybody in this camp will really complain too much about having the set end with the commander in chief bum-rushing the stage.

"Sara went on late because Neal McCoy, who was on before her, was running twenty minutes over," someone on the team points out.

"Well, you know that Neal McCoy is, like, Karl Rove's best friend, right?" says a visiting trade editor. Crickets. No one is going to run with that as a conspiracy theory just now.

By most bragging rights, Evans should have been the one running into overtime on that bill. She was country radio's most-played female artist in 2004, thanks to a series of singles from her *Perfect* album that began with the sober ballad "Back Seat of a Greyhound Bus" and climaxed with an enthrallingly goofy slice of neotraditionalist froth, "Suds in the Bucket" (which, contrary to every expectation about how well such an old-fashioned song would perform in the marketplace, turned out to be her biggest hit to date).

Maybe, I jest, the set got cut off because the Republicans didn't want her sending out the wrong messages to the party faithful. After all, "Suds in the Bucket" celebrates youthful impetuousness, with its tale of a barely legal-age girl in a small town who suddenly ditches her backyard laundry duties to run off to Vegas with her boyfriend to get hitched. Doesn't eloping violate the general spirit, if not the letter, of the principles of parental notification? And then, of course, "Back Seat of a Greyhound Bus" is about a young lady who has a baby out of wedlock. Quickie marriages, illicit pregnancies . . . Are these the sorts of bedrock values the heavy donors should be exposed to?

Evans knows I'm kidding but, joking aside, at least one of those numbers *was* widely misunderstood by her fellow conservatives. "'Back Seat' only went to number twelve on the charts, and I think it's because a lot of people didn't listen to the words, so they thought I was saying she had sex on the backseat of a Greyhound bus. Really," she laughs, "a lot of people were like, 'I can't believe that Sara Evans song!' But to me, rather than it being about an out-of-wedlock pregnancy, it's a song about the miracle of a baby being born—and the terrible choice she could have made to terminate the pregnancy. The song says she found true love for the first time when she looked into the baby's eyes. That's why I was drawn to it. There are so many people in the conservative world who would blackball a single girl who got pregnant. In the church, there are a lot of judgmental people, and for that reason some girls don't want anyone to know about their pregnancy. So, yeah, the song is a little bit rebellious, and yeah, she got pregnant out of marriage, but who knows what this beautiful baby girl could turn out to be? I wanted to make a video that implied all of that stuff, but everybody was afraid of that—too controversial."

From girls who are late, to latte: there's a show to do, so we continue the discussion later at a Starbucks close to Evans's home in Franklin, Tennessee.

"Who all have you talked to so far?" she asks. "I'll be the nicest one—I guarantee it!" she laughs. And darn if she isn't probably right. It dismays Evans that people on the left say such hateful things about Bush, and she insists that conservatives never speak in those sorts of nasty terms, which suggests that she tends to travel in circles that are, well, nice, and that she probably has never tuned into, say, the stream of spite that is the Michael Savage show. Her convictions are nothing if not heartfelt, especially when it comes to helping unwed mothers find safe havens where they can avoid abortion. She's worked with people on the other side of the political fence in town, including producer Paul Worley and cowriter Marcus Hummon. Despite some long nights of debating with these Democratic collaborators, she's still genuinely—*genuinely*—baffled by why bad political parties happen to good people.

"I don't understand a lot of Southern Democrats," she says. "They confuse me. Because socially and morally, they tend to be very conservative—but in other ways, they're Democrats. Paul and I would talk about it a lot, because he was for Al Gore, and I would give him so much grief—but at the same time, many of his viewpoints and mine were the same. There were people from my hometown back in Missouri, and in the church I grew up in, who were Kerry supporters. I'm confused about that, because if you're a born-again Christian and you believe that certain things are sins, how can you support a candidate who wants to push those agendas? I think a lot of people in my hometown are just Democrats because of tradition. Many of them are farmers, and they still view Democrats as being for the working man, for the poor man. But the two don't go together. The working man is a man who has a family. He's about family values—working hard, loving his wife, raising his kids right."

As Evans sees it, the Democrats "do not relate to the average person, as we saw in this election. And there's definitely a similarity between country music and the red states. That's why we have the electoral college, because New York City and Los Angeles cannot decide for the rest of America what your values are gonna be. The Democratic party is shrinking, in my humble opinion, because America is not ready to accept gay marriage. John Kerry was so out of touch with mainstream America. Most people don't live like Brad Pitt and Jennifer Aniston. These people have so much money and fame and live such bizarre lives that they don't relate to the mom or the factory worker in a small town in Kansas. In country music, we sing about love, and normal, everyday things. I heard a song on the way in here called 'That's What I Love About Sundays.' Great song. Mainstream America lives that way.

"One of the main reasons I come out so strongly for conservative values is not only because of my religious beliefs, but because it scares me to think how much divorce there is in America today, how many babies are aborted, how many broken families there are. I believe for America to stay strong there's nothing more important than for the family to stay together. I love the fact that some laws are coming into place now to make it harder to divorce." She means the voluntary "covenant marriage" statutes enacted in the last decade in Louisiana, Arizona, and Arkansas. "I come from a divorced family, so I know what it can do."

"The Democrats definitely have a lot of revamping to do with the party. Because America does not care what Bruce Springsteen has to say about it. And they may not care what I have to say about it. But the fact that the Democrats felt so strongly that John Kerry would win because of his support in Hollywood . . . all these left-wing radicals . . . we're just

not ready for that in this nation. If anything, we are going in the opposite direction."

The Christian music community, ever on the lookout for any spiritually inclined rock act they can loosely call their own, hasn't really
picked up on how much Evans shares their values, since country acts
tend to be not quite hip enough for their evangelistic purposes. But
that's fine, since she has no intention of going gospel or even necessarily courting that crowd.

"One little girl sent me an e-mail saying, 'I just love your music and
what you stand for and what you write on your albums. But my mom
won't let me listen to any secular music, because she says you can't be a
Christian and be famous at the same time.' What?" she laughs. Did
Evans ever consider doing Christian music? "Never. Because I think
my music *is* Christian music because I'm a Christian, and I'm a singer. I
get offended when people say, 'Oh, are you ever gonna make a Christian album?' It's like asking, Are you gonna ever become a Christian
trucker? If you're a trucker and you're a Christian, you're a trucker—
that's your job.

"I became a Christian when I was twenty-one, but that doesn't
mean that I don't still have passion and that my life hasn't been full of
drama. Because my life *has* been full of heartaches and stress. We grew
up poor, me working my ass off on the farm. So I do have a lot of grit.
And I like to be sexy. And I like to drink beer. I'm a real person, and a
sinner, so I want to show people that I'm just as normal and fallible
and vulnerable as anybody else. Our single 'Tonight' is a song about a
woman who's torn about doing something that's wrong; whether she's
having an affair or she just wants to spend the night with him—it's
open to interpretation. She's being pulled by this desire but wants to
be a good person at the same time. I know there'll be a lot of Christians up in arms: 'That's such an immoral message.' No! Because if you
deny you have these feelings, you're lying. Anyway, I'm not just gonna
sing vanilla songs that don't say anything."

Conservatives in country seem to go two ways, oddly: those who
mix politics with their music but don't generally hit the campaign trail,
and those who happily stump for the GOP but don't have a whit of
politics in their music. Evans is among the latter. "I never talk about
politics in my concerts, I never push anything down people's throats.
But I did want to do all that I could do, using my celebrity status, to

help President Bush, when I was called. Other artists and entertainers are a lot more bold and outspoken than I am. It's not in my personality to record 'Have You Forgotten?' That's mixing my art too much with world events and politics. I would rather just sing about love and emotion and heartache."

Within the realm of country, she's as mass-appeal as it gets. Even if Evans's music itself is apolitical, haven't there been those who wished she wasn't so vocal in favor of causes not everyone believes in? "I've never had any negative feedback. I try not to be offensive. But how can that be offensive, when the things I'm mostly concerned about are family values—keeping the family strong, and women embracing motherhood. These radical women's libbers, who just want to say how terrible it is to be home with your kids and make your family your life, it just kills me. To me, the opposite viewpoint is offensive. Even if you don't believe in totally banning abortion, the people that are out there really promote it and want it, to me, that is offensive. I don't think that the things I stand for are that different from most of the people in America."

Her husband ran for Congress in Oregon in the late nineties and lost. As the couple has homes in three states, including her native Missouri, they're still trying to decide where he will run next. "Tennessee is a state where he is very electable. Oregon is a different story. I don't know if Oregon is just too far gone to ever, even in Craig's lifetime, see a big change. It's a frustrating state. The Republican party's not very strong there, and that's one of the reasons Craig has such a passion for it."

He will not be running on an anti–Dixie Chicks ticket, at least. Evans didn't comment much on that controversy at the time, but she now says, "I think what happened to the Dixie Chicks is ridiculous, because they did not deserve everything they got, though it could have been handled better on their part. They kept upping the ante and arguing. I love the Dixie Chicks and I do think people were way too harsh on them, but in my opinion their career is, sadly, over. I can understand people being angry that she said that in England, but for radio stations to never play their music again—that might be a little bit too harsh. Because it *is* America, you know."

Though they have some mutual friends and collaborators, it's clear she hasn't been keeping up much with Natalie. She's a little bit tighter with some other singers in town. "Are you going to talk with Lee Ann Womack? She and her husband are really good people."

Cheatin'—Not Just for Taxes Anymore: Lee Ann Womack's Honky-Tonk Basics

With apologies to Evans, sometimes goodness has nothing to do with it. You don't need to hear more than than a verse and a chorus of Lee Ann Womack's *There's More Where That Came From* to sense that you're probably not listening to a Sara Evans record, because the "more" in the title comes down to more sinnin'. Unlike the conflicted protagonist of Evans's "Tonight," who may or may not have succumbed to temptation, the wayward woman in Womack's title song has certainly already been around that bend and is booking some return trips.

And then there's the first single off the album, "I May Hate Myself in the Morning," a song that a good half of the people in Music Row circles seem to have already penned in as their favorite of the year. Technically, it's not a cheating song, as there's no mention of aggrieved spouses per se when Womack describes old lovers who should have moved on long ago cheerfully backsliding. But it's retro in every way—with its cheerfully guilty follow-up line, ". . . but I'm gonna love you tonight," with the fiddle section that acts as a sort of wordless Greek chorus in the middle eight, with an electronic keyboard sound that's redolent of the early seventies, and the most retro element of all, a return to country's former tolerant attitude toward lovers' everyday transgressions. After so long a period of moral anti-relativism in country, Womack's acclaimed collection is helping make iniquity "in" again.

It may be just as well that Womack is skipping the 2005 Bush inaugural festivities, though she was on the bill in 2001, because how do you get up in front of a crowd of pols, major donors, and PAC bigwigs and say, "I'd like to dedicate this to everyone who worked so hard to keep our guy in office, and it's called 'I May Hate Myself in the Morning'"?

"Wouldn't fit like 'I Hope You Dance' did, huh?" she agrees with a hearty laugh. "Although I bet Dubya would like it."

When it's mentioned that her new release bucks the trend that characterized country in the late nineties, which might have been described as "all uplift, all the time," she volunteers, "I'll admit my role in that, as well. 'I Hope You Dance' was seen as being so positive, I think, because I had the girl in the video and everything; it was sweet, and then you just heard a lot of things like that and just this real, real positive stuff. I had a friend who one night at dinner said, 'Isn't there a contemporary *Christian* station that can play some of this stuff?'" That remark made her laugh—and maybe encouraged her to accentuate the negative. "It just seems like when everybody zigs, I want to zag. So when stuff just got so positive, I was like, '*Gol,* what happened to the cheatin' songs? What happened to the country music I grew up listening to?' That was a big part of why I cut a lot of the things I did for this record. I felt like things were going a little too much in that other direction."

"I Hope You Dance" was the crossover hit that boosted her from a honky-tonk singer with a middling career to, momentarily, a pop star. However, Womack made a follow-up album, *Something Worth Leaving Behind,* even more squarely aimed at an adult-contemporary, middle-of-the-road audience, and it flopped. Which was a blessing, all told, because it gave her the license to go back and do something completely and determinedly retro. "You don't have to twist my arm to get me to make a real country record. If that's what you want," she says, her Lone Star accent growing stronger with each excited syllable as she cheerfully discusses returning to her roots, "then I got it. I can tap into it, and I can deliver it!"

But country *is* still the music of moral values, right?

"Which is ironic, to me," she answers. "Isn't that funny, that people say that? I grew up listening to George Jones and Merle Haggard and stuff like that, so I didn't necessarily think of country as being wholesome. I thought of it as being very real and very representative and not afraid to talk about subjects that affected people. I do know that, stylistically, country has been influenced by gospel music, as far as the harmonies and things like that go. But when you're talking about people like Merle Haggard and Johnny Cash—great, great men who eventually, especially Cash, came around to Christianity and spirituality—I don't necessarily think of 'wholesome.'"

So why re-embrace country's other traditional values—that is, how much fun it is to sing about adultery, alcohol-related fugue states, and so forth—at the same time you're aligning yourself politically with the putative party of moralism?

"I won't go into all of the issues and where I stand on different things. But you'd be surprised, I think, with me, and some of the places I fall on certain issues. That's why I've never really considered myself to be a Republican or a Democrat. I have different views on different things and I either believe in a person . . . or not. And I do believe in where Bush stands as far as terrorism and things like that go. I've heard it said before that people consider themselves more fiscally conservative but, in terms of compassion, more on the liberal side. I don't necessarily line up with everything that the Republican party would stand for. There are just some views that I have that would not be *Republican*. So I would just have to go down each list to tell you where I stand—and I don't really do that anyway. It's that I really believe in Bush. In *him*."

Her stand on celebrity endorsements seems to be self-contradictory. Or is it? "I thought it was very interesting, the number of celebrities that endorsed John Kerry, and the lack of celebrities that endorsed George Bush, but look at how everything turned out. It just goes to show you that celebrities don't—even though they think they do—speak for the general American. And their . . ." She hesitates, realizing that there's something incongruous about her use of the third-person. "I'll throw myself in the mix: *Our* opinions about those types of things don't really matter, when it comes down to what box they're gonna check. And I love that! Because celebrities are not normal, everyday people, no matter *boooow* much we wanna say we are!" She gives a good, Texas-sized chortle. "And I mostly mean really big, big celebrities, people who have lots of money and carry entourages around with them and always fly private. So far, even the small amount of celebrity that I have experienced is so different from what the general public experiences; I don't see how they think they can speak for the everyday American. That's why I'm hesitant to speak out about politics."

Of course, there's a critical difference between how most Americans look at their favorite movie, TV, or rock stars and how country fans perceive their heroes. In the country realm, many of the hardcore faithful don't even look at their heroes as celebrities but—thanks to the closer proximity granted at such events as fan fairs or meet-and-greet lines—as actual neighbors. And who wouldn't want to hear some friendly advice about who to vote for from the girl next door, or even that cheerful divorcée down the lane that you envision listening to Womack's album, as opposed to Tim Robbins or Janeane Garafalo, those creepy social studies teachers?

Craig Morgan, Travelin' Soldier

That new song that Sara Evans liked? The singer in question was Craig Morgan, whose "That's What I Love About Sundays," enjoying a multi-week run at No. 1, has been the biggest indie-label radio hit in the country format since the mid-seventies. It's a red-state grand slam, invoking everything that you could possibly love about the Sabbath—assuming you don't live within a five-mile radius of a skyscraper, that is—from jasmine and baptisms to ground round and after-church coupon clipping. His latest album also has other songs designed to hit middle America where they live, or would like to, including a ballad about a little boy who tithes his lawn-mowing money (it comes as no surprise when the boy in the song does the local widow's grass for free). Morgan's vision of America on its day of rest might strike some city slickers as ridiculously idyllic, but to middle Americans, a description like "idealized" might not even occur.

There's nothing vaguely militaristic or patriotic on this latest album of Morgan's, unless you take as such a line that expresses hostility toward hip-hop and a favorable allusion to gun ownership. But Morgan is one of a very few country stars—certainly the only one currently peaking—with a military record that includes combat during the first Gulf War. Accordingly, national defense is on his mind, even if he isn't singing any new ballads about homeland security.

"What's really cool about the country format, in my opinion, is that it represents and stands up for America more than any of the other formats, and the soldiers are very aware of that," he says, leaning across a conference table at the HQ of Broken Bow, the indie label he's helping put on the country music map. "Compared to rock & roll and hip-hop, it's a more people-oriented format with a belief system that's not quite as . . . *free*. But I've always looked at it from a personal, rather than a business, perspective. I *am* glad that my personal opinions tend to fall in line with what my business tends to demand, you know what I mean?"

He can speak firsthand about what country music means to the war effort and to morale. "As a soldier, I can say that there was nothing more disheartening than having some of these Hollywood superstars or rockers bashing what we were doing over there. It's aggravating to hear people say, 'I don't support the war, but I support the soldiers.' As a solider, you cannot make that statement. That is not acceptable. We *do* support the right for you to speak your mind. I think people like— what's her name with the Dixie Chicks?—Natalie, and people like her, abuse that privilege, based on ignorance. In this war that's going on right now, America, for the most part, does not understand what is going on. You hear so many people say 'It's all about the money, it's about the oil.' The bottom line is, it's about terrorism, and I think it's odd how quick we forget what happened on 9/11 as soon as we start losing men and women in another country. But the fact is, if we were not fighting terrorism over there, we would be fighting it here. What happened here on 9/11 is just the tip of the iceberg of what was planned.

"The president of the United States got beat up over not finding any nuclear weapons or whatever. I can't give you my professional opinion, because I have information that's not readily available to everyone and I'm not able to speak about certain things." He gives a slight if-you-only-knew chuckle. "But he made a decision based on the information that he had received. If it was not one-hundred-percent factual, that's life. And we're over there now, and again, based on the information that I know . . . I have friends that are in Delta Force, the Special Forces, the Ranger Patrol, and the 82nd and 101st, right now. They're very confident about what we're doing. We've truly liberated another country, and we are keeping terrorism at bay. But there's so much that they do know that they cannot share with the country. That's the bottom line."

It's a bit of a catch-22, then: Americans on the left are speaking out of ignorance, yet they can't become better informed because intelligence is being dispensed to the public strictly on a need-to-know basis. Morgan has been out of the service for years but still carries that crucial soldierly cockiness, the assurance that fathers who know best are in charge, and that civilians should stay civilians, and that doves and non-interventionists shouldn't play at being armchair generals, which he sees as a sorry excuse for popular punditry.

He's not desensitized, however. "It's scary to think that my son will do what I've had to do. I've experienced things that most people only read about. And it's horrific, some of the things that I've seen. But I'm flabbergasted by the American citizens who have witnessed some of the atrocities that Iraq has committed, and yet still find it easy to step away. This thing is not gonna end overnight. Even for a soldier, sometimes it's hard. I get frustrated, because I want this thing to end so my friends can come home. We're losing guys. But that's the great thing about this country: We have people that are willing to make those sacrifices."

Oddly enough, Morgan has a personal rule against writing or recording material having to do with soldiers or war. Or maybe not so oddly—it's a matter of honor and humility. "As a soldier, it's difficult to bring light to something that you do for a living. You don't brag on yourself. We all like to have our backs patted, but it ain't something we want to do to ourselves. If I had never experienced any of that stuff, I think I'd be writing a lot of songs about it. I don't think it's a bad thing that other guys do."

After his previous record's "God, Home and Country," Morgan publicly vowed he would have a patriotic song on each album. He's already broken that vow, since the new one doesn't have any. "With everything that's going on in the world, I didn't want that to be the focal point of my album," he explains. "I didn't want everybody to think that I, too, was trying to capitalize. Because people say it about different artists no matter what. I've had soldiers tell me that Toby, Darryl, Chely and these guys were doing it just because." Apparently, even military types can get suspicious about a careerist aspect to the tunes that cheer them on. "Which made me nervous about putting something patriotic on my record, so rather than fight off all the crap, it was easier for me to not include one.

"I had some very dear friends in Afghanistan who got killed. If you remember, when we first went over, there was a helicopter full of Special Forces soldiers that crashed. A friend of mine was on that helicopter. I was doing my show for the troops, and when I finished, I walked off the back of the stage, and there was a gentleman there with a full beard. He walked up to me—and I knew he was with Special Forces—and shook my hand and said 'Craig, I want to talk with you. We both had a mutual friend. He was killed in a helicopter crash. What you don't know, though, they were killed on that mountain right there'—he pointed over across the way—'that's where the helicopter went down. Something else you didn't know. Every day before they went on a mission and every day when they'd come home, they played your song "Paradise." And he had said that he wanted your song played at his funeral. I thought that you should know that.' That tears you up. So he and I stood there and cried for about three or four minutes, and then I went up and did an encore. But that's tough stuff to hear. And that's why I say it's okay for a guy to write a song about what's going on, even though I don't."

The Grass Is Red: Ricky Skaggs's High, Lonesome Republicanism

Ricky Skaggs may be the most vocally conservative guy alive who still manages to maintain a sizable contingent of liberals in his fan base. That achievement has mostly to do with the peculiar makeup of the audience for bluegrass—which is the area where Skaggs has been plying his wares since the mid-1990s. Dismayed by the Garthification of Nashville, he quit the contemporary country scene and went back to his acoustic roots, becoming a small-business owner in the process with his own Americana label, Skaggs Family Records. Ever since the *O Brother, Where Art Thou?* phenomenon took off in 2001, bluegrass has had a huge following among the high-income, post-collegiate urban set, as well as with rural Appalachian folk (who still claim it as their birthright) and conservative country fans (who like the music's traditional and often religious messages). There's probably no other genre that can claim quite so many lefties and righties, both. In much the same way many right-wing rock fans still love Bruce Springsteen, even if he is a stinkin' socialist, Skaggs counts among his fan base progressives who'll swear he's the sole flaming reactionary in their collection.

"I'm really glad that the NPR crowd has come over and embraced bluegrass," says Skaggs. "And yeah, they're a much more liberal crowd. But I think it'd be almost like people turning their back on James Taylor because he did some dates on the pro-Kerry tour. When you hear that guitar and hear his voice, you forget the guy is a Democrat," he laughs. "I certainly do. He's my buddy. Same with Bruce Hornsby, who I'm doing an album with now. They didn't support President Bush, but we're friends and we certainly can look at each other's politics as personal."

Not that there aren't tense or awkward moments in the diverse circles he travels in. "It's a lot easier for me to say I'm a born-again Christian than it is to say that I'm a conservative Republican. Because it made people's hair stand on end, sometimes, if I talk about my politics—but then," he says with chuckle, "I could talk about religion all day long."

Rodney Crowell is evangelistic, too, when it comes to his liberal views—but in the company of someone like his old pal Skaggs, with whom he played side by side in Emmylou Harris's Hot Band in the seventies, he just doesn't go there. "I would never talk politics with Ricky Skaggs," Crowell says. "I know exactly what Ricky's Christian beliefs are. For me to enter into a political discussion with Ricky would be a waste of his time and mine. I don't want to change Ricky. He's who he is. Nor would I open my mouth around Charlie Daniels. I don't know that Charlie's intense conservatism is based so much on religion; I think to him that's what a true patriot is. So I wouldn't want to try to introduce my sort of high-minded liberal spirituality to a gentleman like that, because it would insult his intelligence. So a lot of it, you just let go by. It's a matter of understanding their commitment to what they believe—I don't want to change it."

Skaggs appreciates that. "I love Rodney. He and I are old friends, and I couldn't convince him, either, or Steve Earle. These people have very direct belief systems, and they have their reasons for believing their politics. Mine is based on more than politics; it's based more on a morality thing and what I believe pleases God, and I try to look at what the Bible says about certain things. You know, when you read in the Bible that God hates the shedding of innocent blood—what's more innocent than an unborn baby? That's the real kicker for me there, the abortion thing. But other people are not as convinced of that, and that doesn't make them bad, and it doesn't make me an overly good person because I believe that way. . . . I appreciate the fact that I have the respect of people like that here in town. That's a good thing to know. I saw Emmylou a couple of Sundays ago over at Earl Scruggs's birthday party"—this was a couple of months after the polarizing election they were both so passionate about—"and we sang 'If I Could Only Win Your Love' together, and we hugged, and I didn't say 'Nya na na nya na, you wasted your time!' None of that."

Skaggs is a believer in single-issue voting—not that he isn't in line with the GOP on plenty of its other planks. "The Republicans today are what the Democrats were in the forties and fifties," he says. "I had grandparents and people in my family who were hardline Democrats because, in those days, abortion and all that stuff I abhor wasn't an issue. And you'll see guys like Zell Miller who still is a Democrat, because he hopes that one day there'll be some sort of movement back to the middle of the road. When the Democrats quit voting to kill babies,

I might have an ear to listen to what they have to say. There are a lot of really good Democrats, and I know 'em, and they have a real heart for America. But when it comes down to the morality issues, gay marriage and abortion, that's a line some of us just can't cross. If they even had a candidate who lived what he said . . . I think George Bush lives what he says. I think the man gets up and prays, I think he spends time with the Lord. He don't just lip-service it. Because Christianity ain't a suit of clothes that you wear to church and then put in the closet and then wear 'em again on the weekend. The other candidate made it sound like his religion was like that. He said 'I'm a Catholic and I pray and really believe in God.' Yet he was for abortion, the very thing that Catholics are strongest against! It almost sent a signal to people that he had turned his back on his whole faith, his whole denomination.

"There is still a lot of morality in America. We see a lot of stuff on TV that's not good for kids, video channels that are basically soft porn, but there's a lot of conscience left in America. When people sign up to become a Democrat, they get all the baggage that goes with it. And Republicans—my God, we've got a lot of problems ourselves in a lot of areas."

Around the time of the 2004 election, Skaggs came out with a new album fronted by a single called "Spread a Little Love Around." He wished he'd released it a little bit sooner, to help alleviate some of the poison in the polarized air. As big a Bush backer as he's been, he insists he's not a political creature. "Every politician speak with forked tongue. '*Poli* means many and *tics* are bloodsuckers'—that's what my grandpa used to say about politics." He's a trickier one than he looks, that Skaggs, trying to end on a point of glaring consensus.

Nashville Star

We'd be remiss in not profiling the biggest country star of them all these days: George W. Bush. It might sound facetious or reductionist to talk about the frontman of the free world as if he were a mere contemporary of George Strait and Randy Travis, but there are any number of ways in which he might be considered the ultimate hat act, part of it being the way country singers talk about him in nearly the same terms that their fans talk about them: as someone who is larger than life and yet simultaneously approachable, who doesn't put on the airs that he clearly has rights to, who is a star but not a Hollywood star.

"I guess he's the most politically incorrect politician," says neotraditionalist crooner Mark Chesnutt with a laugh of satisfaction, using a term he would hope the fans would use about him. Chesnutt plays flat-out honky-tonk music and isn't about to get into a Ronnie Dunn–level policy discussion; he prefers to go with his gut on the subject of his love for the president. "He stands up for what's right, and he says what he means. He's not like a *celebrity*." He can barely bring himself to say the dirty word, which he pronounces with the level of disgust once reserved for "communist."

Country's stars rarely get tarred by fans with that particular C-word. They're too accessible for that, and it's not necessarily the illusion of accessibility. "In country music, fans not only believe that they will get to meet their favorite artists, they expect it," says publicist Paula Erickson. "I don't think teenagers actually expect to ever get to talk with Britney Spears. But it's actually pretty rare to find a hardcore country fan who hasn't met at least one, if not several, of their favorite artists, between the meet-and-greets at every show and the strong membership numbers in the fan clubs." It's that humility—even if it's an enforced, mandatory humility—that would seem to grant some of the genre's luminaries the privilege to preach just a little, for the right kind of cause.

By the same token, it may not be possible to overstate the disdain most heartland folks feel about someone who's perceived as above it all deigning to tell them how to think or vote. Something has gone seriously, almost laughably wrong when populist liberals are viewed in exactly the opposite way they imagine themselves coming across to the masses. Michael Moore—or Satan, as he's known in the South—clearly believes he's standing up and standing in for the little guy with no voice; Janeane Garafalo, fretting over Kansas, has said, "Over the last thirty years, the right has managed to agitate and frighten the citizens of the heartland into consistently voting against their own best interests." But rather than seeing Moore or Garafalo (or others) as empathetic modern-day Tom Joads, your typical middle American sees something akin to the face of Harry Dean Stanton in *Repo Man*, intoning the immortal words: "Ordinary fuckin' people . . . I hate 'em." It's the definition of disconnect.

Part of being a country star is identifying your constituency and not wasting time trying to break through to the wrong markets. Bush has done that; in his first term, the administration moved to suspend drilling off the Florida coast, scoring points in a swing state, but went the opposite way when it came to California, which, of course, isn't his demographic. Democrats can and will say he's no friend to the working man and farmer, but tell that to the people positively affected by his $190-billion farm bill, which helped shore up support in key states like Iowa and Missouri, or the administration's stiff tariffs on imported steel, which told the folks in heavily contested West Virginia and Pennsylvania that he was looking out for their interests.

But most Music Row–like of all, he's the proverbial somebody you'd want to have the proverbial beer with. Near-beer, in his teetotalling case, but you get the point.

This drives Nashville's eternally beleaguered Democrats crazy, and they can't believe that anyone is taken in by what they see as an affectation befitting a freshman act. "I've met Bush and the Dixie Chicks both," says CMT head honcho Brian Philips, "and I guess I'd rather hang with the Chicks and the Robison brothers and Kelly Willis and those people. They're more like people that I think most people in our audience would like to hang out and have a beer with, coming at it from a Texas point of view. I don't know how many members of our audience are billionaires or people with huge defense contracts or people who got the keys handed to them and never had to do anything by themselves. That's not typical of who we are. There's a real dichotomy between the raising of the son, George W., and the way most of our audience has been raised. But God bless Karl Rove if he was able to connect those two and make people feel like he *was* one of us."

Here's songwriter Bobby Braddock on the subject: "I think a lot of people in the South are like my brother and his family, in the little redneck town in Florida where I come from. These are good people, patriotic people. They like to go to football games and barbecues, and they think George W. Bush is a good ole boy just like they are. A lot of it has to do with reality TV. People think of politicians as somebody they can imagine being in their home. At one time, people wanted their leaders to be somebody that maybe stood apart from them, somebody they could look up to. Now it's more like 'Well, hey, let's go get somebody just like us and vote for 'em.'"

This cynical view of Bush, as a fox who's dressed up as (and even carefully adopted the dialect of) a hen, is summed up in song by alt-country favorite Robbie Fulks, released in the summer of 2005. "Countrier Than Thou" is mostly a hilarious indictment of the type of reverse-snobs who are often really into, well, alt-country cult faves like Fulks, namely, northeastern wannabes who imagine they have a better, purer sense of what country music is than their undiscriminating cousins down south. But Fulks uses the last verse and chorus to take a jab at the president for also being a northeastern poseur:

> He's got a ranch, he wears a Stetson
> He's a hip-shootin' ex-oil king
> Even talks like Buddy Ebsen
> But he's sittin' in the West Wing.
> Frankenstein, I'm well aware of,
> But won't somebody please explain
> How you get a county sheriff
> Walkin' with a frat boy's brain?
> Countrier than thou, countrier than thou
> If you went to Andover, what's the banjo fer?
> You wasn't raised in a shack so you better not act so
> Countrier than thou.

As amusing as digs like this might be, anyone who spends enough time in the South will come to sense that telling the locals they've been hoodwinked by a brilliant faker and then attacking his stupidity is a doubly losing sales proposition, as well as a logical fallacy. Who's the man brave enough to tell a no-nonsense roughneck like Mark Chesnutt, who's met the president on several occasions and chewed the fat with him about hunting and fishing, that he got suckered by a master dilletante? Don't kid a kidder, comes the response.

"Country singers don't like to put up with a lot of bullshit. That's why we're not in Hollywood," Chesnutt says. "He's a genuine guy. I've been in the entertainment business all my life and been around this side of it for fifteen years now. And believe me, I can tell when somebody's bullshitting. You *learn* that in the music business."

Alan Jackson sang "Where Were You (When the World Stopped Turning)" with an orchestra at the 2002 Grammy Awards while children's drawings of the traumatic events of 9/11 flashed on a screen behind the stage. KEVIN WINTER/GETTY IMAGES

4

Of Boots and Bumper Stickers

War Whoops, Peace Anthems, and Funeral Songs

Looking back on the long buildup to America's invasion of Iraq, Clint Black gets credit for being one of the very first to enter the war-music fray. And not much else. Black's "Iraq and Roll" didn't turn out to be the song that galvanized a nation and its armed forces, but it wasn't for lack of trying:

> Iraq, I rack 'em up and I roll
> I'm back and I'm a high-tech G.I. Joe
> I pray for peace and prepare for war
> And I will never forget there's no price too high for freedom
> You can stay behind or you can get out of the way
> But our troops take out the garbage for the good old U.S.A.

Not everyone in Nashville thought that precipitant tune was un-toppable, and even more germane and humane efforts followed this ice-breaker. So many, in fact, that by late 2004, pro-troop sentiment was rapidly approaching musical burnout.

"There comes a saturation point," said BMG's Joe Galante, wondering in early 2005 if it was time to pull back and give election-hardened, war-weary listeners a break. "The song 'Letter from Home' spoke to the feeling of families and troops, and people responded to it. I remember when it came in the building, before John Michael Montgomery recorded it, we asked ourselves, Do people really want to hear this? That was a long debate, internally: Do we really want to put this in front of people's faces one more time? And we decided to pass. Obviously, we were incorrect, because it went on to be a major hit"—a number-one hit, in fact, in 2004. "But how many people really want to sit and hear that song over and over again? I think we're going to find out."

It was a remarkable run of topicality, while it lasted. What follows is a song-by-song examination of eight country singles that might belong in a time capsule if we wanted to illustrate for future generations the efforts made by mainstream Music Row tunesmiths to capture the national mood in the critical forty months between 9/11 and the second Bush inauguration: Alan Jackson's "Where Were You (When the World Stopped Turning)"; "Travelin' Soldier," written by Bruce Robison and covered by the Dixie Chicks; Darryl Worley's "Have You Forgotten"; two by Toby Keith, "Courtesy of the Red, White, and Blue (The Angry American)" and "American Soldier"; "Come Home Soon," by SheDaisy; "What Say You," a duet between Travis Tritt and John Mellencamp; and Chely Wright's "Bumper of My SUV."

Meanwhile, "Iraq and Roll" probably won't be making anyone's time-capsule cut, even if it is the most Hank Jr.-ish of all the contemporary battle anthems. Sorry, Clint, and better luck next war.

Alan Jackson's Skivvies Hymnody

When Alan Jackson sings "Where Were You (When the World Stopped Turning)," the world doesn't actually grind to a halt, but things do tend to move a lot slower. Especially when it's less than six months since 9/11 and all the feelings the ballad evokes are still fairly fresh, as they are on this February 2002 afternoon, the day before the Grammy Awards. Jackson is standing in front of a small orchestra at L.A.'s Staples Center, rehearsing lyrics that by now are familiar to the ear of any country aficionado, but which will be heard for the first time by many non-country viewers the following night.

> Did you stand there in shock at the sight of that black smoke
> Rising against that blue sky
> Did you shout out in anger, in fear for your neighbor
> Or did you just sit down and cry . . .

Inevitably, a lot of the scurrying among construction workers and sound people on the arena floor slows to a halt as Jackson sings the verses of a ballad that, in just under four minutes, manages to hit just about every emotion the tragedies provoked, from sobbing to shell shock, gun-hoarding to survivors' guilt, nihilism to Nick at Night binging, patriotism to prayer.

> Did you open your eyes in hope it never happened
> Close your eyes and not go to sleep
> Did you notice the sunset for the first time in ages
> Speak to some stranger on the street

After two run-throughs of the tune, Jackson is satisfied. So are the Grammy showrunners. A heaviness has settled over the stage. "That's great, Alan," calls out the telecast's veteran producer, Walter Miller, breaking the tension. "It'll be even better when the clog dancers come in."

A little inside joke there. The acerbically inclined Miller also produces the Country Music Association's annual awards show each November. It was on that telecast, three and a half months earlier, that Jackson premiered "Where Were You," a bit reluctantly. That night, he'd been scheduled to perform a more lighthearted, Southern-fried hit called "Where I Come From." In keeping with that tune's keepin'-it-real, keepin'-it-rural theme, Jackson had enlisted the help not just of banjo legend Earl Scruggs but the Melvin Sloan Dancers, traditional mountain cloggers whose delightfully cheesy choreography is a staple of the Grand Ole Opry. Jackson loves to tweak the sensibilities of those who might prefer to bury the music's yokel past. In 2000, he'd released a single called "www.memory," so for his appearance on that year's CMA Awards, he raised some eyebrows by having a set constructed of laptop computers perched atop hay bales. "They weren't real happy about the hay bales," Jackson laughs. "I've always thought it was funny that Nashville is always apologizing for its roots and trying to get away from the wagon wheels and cowboy hats." The following year, Jackson was prepared to up the kitsch ante and stick it to 'em again with the dreaded hoofers.

But kitsch became a moot point a few days before the November 2001 broadcast, when Jackson's manager and label head called the CMA brass into a conference room to play them a possible alternative,

"Where Were You," which the singer had written and demo-ed just a few days earlier. Awards-show producers are notorious for fighting with artists who want to debut new material instead of nominated songs, but this would obviously be an exception. By the time the playback was over, most of the men in the room were crying, because it *is* a tearjerker. (They may also have been weeping from joy that they wouldn't have to parade a bunch of square dancers in big wooden shoes past a confused and divided nation after all.) Still, "I felt terrible," Jackson says in his deeply laconic Georgia drawl, "having to call back Earl Scruggs and the dancers and tell 'em to cancel."

Not as bad, of course, as he did on the late October night when he sat bolt upright in bed with most of the sad ballad already composed in his head. "After 9/11, I was pretty disturbed, like most people," he says, kicking back in his tour bus outside the Staples Center. "For a few weeks, I thought about writing something—I'm sure a lot of people who write songs felt the same way—but I didn't want to write a patriotic thing and couldn't think of anything that didn't feel like I'd be taking advantage of it commercially." Then, in what he describes as a sort of lucid dream, the melody, opening lines, and chorus came to him. "I'd just gotten this girl who works for me to buy me one of them skinny little digital recorder things, so I went downstairs in my underwear and put this thing down so I wouldn't forget it the next morning.

"It's been overwhelming, the response to it, and a little scary, really. I've had so many people come up to me, and I don't know what to say, other than that I just feel like it was a gift from God. I don't know why He picked me to send those words to, but I'm glad it's become a healing song for some people."

With anybody else, you probably wouldn't buy the "aw, shucks" humility, but look up "reticence" in the dictionary (as Larry King used to say) and you may find a picture of Alan Jackson. Along with the shyness, though, is a good measure of take-it-or-leave-it defiance.

"A handful of pop or adult-contemporary stations were playing it or threatening to play it, but they wanted to know if we could take off the fiddle and steel." The label commissioned just such a mix, but Jackson refused even to listen to it. "Somebody'd have to really be into music to even know those instruments are on there and recognize 'em, between the strings and the whole production. It's not like there's a big country steel lick in the middle of it. If it's offensive, they just shouldn't play it, I guess."

Despite the song's gentle tone, there were some who took offense to a lyric or two—primarily the following lines:

> I'm just a singer of simple songs
> I'm not a real political man
> I watch CNN but I'm not sure I can tell you
> The difference in Iraq and Iran

To some Southerners, in particular, this admission was the equivalent of the hay bales and clog dancers, or worse—a willful demonstration to an already prejudiced outside world that country folk are proud of cutting themselves off from the free flow of information. Maybe honesty is usually the best policy in songwriting, this thinking went, but for the sake of the rest of us down here, couldn't you have been just a little less frank about your international myopia?

Expressing some of this frustration, Texas-bred producer T Bone Burnett—who made his own Grammy appearance the following year, picking up awards for the bluegrass-based *O Brother, Where Art Thou?* soundtrack—says: "With all due respect to Mr. Jackson, who is a very good country singer, if someone doesn't know the difference between Iraq and Iran, I'm not interested in anything else he has to say on the subject. Country music has always been conservative in many important ways, preserving a part of us and our history without which we would be impoverished. These days, people are frightened that we are going to lose something about our country that we will not be able to recapture. But if Mr. Jackson doesn't know the difference between Iraq and Iran, why doesn't he just look it up on the World Wide Web? The information is right under his nose. To not look at it, to ignore it, by definition creates ignorance, and ignorance does not further us as a country. Ignorance did not put a man on the moon."

"I'm sure there are people who criticize it," says Jackson, who let candor take precedence over the discretion that a less self-revealing second draft might have produced. "I just wrote what I felt; I didn't premeditate anything. I'm just a singer of simple songs, and that's the truth. And I *don't* know the difference between Iraq and Iran." In 2001, he probably wasn't the only one. "Some people that aren't real religious probably don't want to hear it, and that's all right, too," he chuckles. Jackson's referring to the line "I know Jesus, and I talk to God," and his paraphrase of II Corinthians' text on the supremacy of love. "I didn't sit down to heal the world or anything."

Plenty of critics from outside the country camp thought his balm was just fine. Writing the day after the Grammys, Salon.com's Eric Boehlert called Jackson's song "a reflective hymn that Americans will be listening to well into the second half of this century."

Jackson was true to his vow not to exploit the song, and he refused to license "Where Were You" for any of the myriad patriotic country compilations that have been released since 2001, content to let Lee Greenwood's ever-popular "God Bless the USA" take up the slack in its stead. Though he included it on his *Drive* album and continues to sing it in concert, he rebuffed further opportunities to perform it on television, including offers that have come in every Fourth of July.

Says Joe Galante, "We had lots of conversations with Nancy Russell, Alan's manager, about the use of that song. Obviously, everybody and their brother wanted to license it for everything—patriotic compilations, put this in the campaign, please sing this here. Alan and Nancy were very firm about it not being a political statement. That song came out in time for the CMAs and was the number-one record in the country for six weeks. Not that the New York and L.A. wings of the music industry knew that. When he did it on the Grammys, most people in the audience had never heard it before. We had to fight with the TV committee to get it on, because they weren't familiar with the song either. I think, if you paint everybody with that brush"—the country-is-jingoistic one—"here comes Alan Jackson with something that was on our minds but that none of us could articulate. It wasn't about a political statement. It was about healing."

Bruce Robison's Reversal of Fortune

Bruce Robison's "Travelin' Soldier" will always be associated with a time in which the healing unraveled: the controversy over the Dixie Chicks. But on its own terms, his composition is one of the most touching ballads in the history of country music. It's a simple, tragic narrative: Girl meets boy; boy is shortly to ship off to 'Nam; boy dies; girl cries alone when death is announced. The song is perhaps even more moving because it's not about an indisputably great love that ends in an act of heroism, but a simple teenaged crush thwarted in its earliest stages by mortality.

> One Friday night at a football game
> The Lord's Prayer said and the anthem sang
> The man said folks bow your heads
> For the list of local Vietnam dead
> Crying all alone under the stands
> Was a piccolo player in the marching band
> And one name read and no one really cared
> But a pretty little girl with a bow in her hair

This was one of the first tunes Robison ever wrote. While he was working as a fry cook during the buildup to the first Gulf War in 1991, a much younger coworker of his, who was in the National Guard, was called up to go to Kuwait. "It was a long buildup, if you'll recall, and the media were preparing us for all these casualties that were gonna happen whenever we invaded," Robison recalls. "They were saying Saddam had the third biggest army in the world and all that. We found out that it was a paper tiger, but they were giving these projections that we were gonna have thousands of troops killed and wounded. I couldn't get my mind around all the stuff that was about to happen. So I wrote a song about one person going off to war and not coming back—and I purposefully made it an unpopular guy.

"It's a song about compassion and about the cost of war in a very intimate sense, trying to personalize the cost of war down to one person. I don't really see it as an anti-war song. From my point of view, all those sorts of questions are too complicated for simple bumper-sticker things. I'm not anti-war or pro-war or anti-this or pro-that. I've never written anything 'charged with topical themes,' and this one isn't, either. The greatest protest song I've ever heard, 'Blowin' in the Wind,' I still feel is a bit simplistic," he says, laughing at his own apparent hubris. "I say that as the most enormous Dylan fan. I'm just saying a three-and-a-half-minute song is a very hard place to talk politics, and you're giving it short shrift. I feel that way about love and death or anything else, too. In my songs, I find one little sliver of the gray area, and I investigate that. People asked me if I was gonna write a song about 9/11, and I didn't see how. I was stuck in Nashville and I took this rental car and drove it all the way home to Austin, and I didn't know if I was gonna make it. I didn't know if there were gonna be more attacks, if there was a gas panic in Arkansas, and it was terrifying. My first child was about three months old at the time. I thought about writing a song about trying to get home. But writing about three thousand people dying? I wouldn't know how to do that—though Alan Jackson did a beautiful job of it."

Robison recorded "Travelin' Soldier" on his own first solo album, where it attracted no special notice. It came to the Chicks' attention for obvious reasons: Bruce's brother Charlie, also a singer/songwriter of some renown, is married to Emily Robison. Bruce, meanwhile, is married to Kelly Willis, Americana's sweetheart. Together they form one of the first families of Texas music. The day Bruce found out "Soldier" was going to be a single for the Chicks was also the day he learned he and Kelly were expecting twins; they decided to semi-retire from performing for a while to raise their children, and live off royalties. In this way, he did have a personal stake in the song's success, and its dive off the charts was doubly aggravating.

"I won't lie. I lost a whole shitload of money because of it. I'm not made of stone. But the album did sell six million copies, so I can't complain. I write songs because I love it, and then something will happen where I just make money off of it, which keeps me able to do what I love. A lot of people said, 'Why couldn't Natalie just keep her mouth shut for you?'—thinking that's what you want to hear. That's the sort of thing that happens a lot with me and Charlie. Somebody will come up to one of us and say, 'Hey, I like you so much more than your brother.' And you say, 'Well, thank you—and fuck you! That's my brother!' I have to stand by her right to say what she wants to say, even if it is gonna cost me money, frankly," he laughs. "But the good has outnumbered the bad, ninety to one—people coming up to me, veterans sometimes, and a lot of people have a political view that colors what they say."

He's worried about speaking out in the wake of the Chicks' controversy, because, even though he's in deep-blue Austin, he depends on having his songs farmed through Music Row to people like George Strait ("Desperately") and Tim McGraw ("Angry All the Time"). "I'm a fairly liberal person, and I'm in country music. And I probably feel like some of those conservative guys in Hollywood: Will I lose my livelihood if I speak my mind? Will I be boycotted? And then you go, wait a minute, nobody gives a damn what I think—I'm a lowly song-writer. So, woo-hoo!"

The irony—or maybe just the bitter pill—for Robison was that when the brouhaha doomed the longevity of "Travelin' Soldier," it was immediately replaced at No. 1 on the country chart by a tune with a far less ambiguous message called "Have You Forgotten?" "I would like to talk to the writer of that song," Robison says. "I take the song personally because I had serious questions about what was going on at that moment—the setup to go to Iraq and the justifications for the war, what precedent we were setting, what are we doing in that part of the world. The song questioned whether I had forgotten about 9/11 if I specifically didn't support the invasion of Iraq. I don't think that song was about Afghanistan. It seemed to claim to know what the people who died that day would have wanted. And I think the song says Hussein was behind 9/11, when it says 'those behind bin Laden.' Then I saw Darryl Worley professing to not want to have a political voice. To me, that song is nothing but political."

In the end, no one has forgotten Robison's song, even if it did have a riches-to-rags chart trajectory. "There was a lady here in Austin who said she loved the song and had it played at her husband's funeral, who died over there. They had a young child, and I can't even tell you what that feels like. There are no words. That song is twelve or thirteen years old, so I can just let it go and be whatever it is to whoever I'm lucky enough to have hear it. I damn sure didn't think that it was gonna be any kind of hit song, or heard at all. I'm thankful for any kind of comfort that it gives anyone—red or blue state."

Toby and Darryl Remember Alamo 2.0

As a producer and the head of DreamWorks Records' Nashville of-fice, James Stroud is one of the town's most prominent Republicans. (And one of its best-liked; he's good buddies with fellow label chiefs Paul Worley and Tim DuBois, both Music Row Democrats.) Stroud played an intimate role in the creation and promotion of Toby Keith's "Courtesy of the Red, White, and Blue" and Darryl Worley's "Have You

Forgotten?"—two songs that were greeted with hosannas in the country world but often derided as mindlessly militaristic outside it.

"When Darryl brought in 'Have You Forgotten?,' he told me the story of a man he worked out with who, on 9/11, couldn't find his daughter in New York. He finally found her, but he was so angry and wanted badly to lash out at people, to go get the terrorists and all that stuff. Then, after the war in Afghanistan started, Darryl had come back from tour and was working out in the same gym, and the TV was on, and the very guy who'd been so scared about his daughter being lost said to him [in response to a news report about Afghanistan], 'I don't know why we're over there. What are we doing as a country?' Darryl looked at him and said, 'Well, have you *forgotten*? Have you forgotten about your daughter?' Darryl got so upset that he left. Then he met with his cowriter and they wrote the song.

"When he told me the story, I said, 'Look, I want to say that through *my* talents. What can I do?' He said, 'Well, of course, produce it for me, but will you play drums on it?'" Stroud did both duties, and you can see him on the skins in the video for the song. "I wanted to participate because I wanted to express to people, through my music— and my emotions, too—Don't forget. It's *not* embarrassing to be angry still and to want these guys dead and out of our world."

> Have you forgotten when those towers fell?
> We had neighbors still inside
> Going through a living hell . . .
> They took all the footage off my T.V.
> Said it's too disturbing for you and me
> It'll just breed anger that's what the experts say
> If it was up to me I'd show it every day
> Some say this country's just out looking for a fight
> After 9/11 man I'd have to say that's right

"As far as Toby, 'Courtesy of the Red, White and Blue' was about his father. After his father died, he had a dream, and the part about his dad in the song is a true story. Toby's father served his country, and he lost an eye in its service. His family flew a flag out in the front yard, like the lyric said, and Toby was raised to be a patriot. Now, Toby is a Democrat. He was raised as a Democrat. But he's told me a thousand times, 'I'm not necessarily pro-war. But I am absolutely pro-servicemen and pro-army, pro-kids that are out there fighting.' So that's where he goes. And that's where I go."

> Now this nation that I love
> Has fallen under attack
> A mighty sucker punch came flyin' in
> From somewhere in the back
> Soon as we could see clearly
> Through our big black eye
> Man, we lit up your world
> Like the Fourth of July

"Toby and Darryl both expressed to me what I think the country as a whole needs to feel. If you look at World War II, the majority of the country did not want to go to war until Pearl Harbor. But we couldn't *not* go to war. I think people think this is not a war, really, just a bunch of guys out there fooling around . . . But we all know this: These [terrorists] are very powerful, they take their time, and they do a lot of damage. All you have to do is get on a plane to know how much the world has changed. It's not right and it's not fair, and it's not something that I think the U.S. should put up with. If we're gonna stop these people, like our parents did in World War II, you do what it takes to win, or you stay home. That's a simple way of looking at it, but I'm a very simple person when it comes to my emotions, and I get very emotional when I see kids out there in uniform. Every time I see one at a restaurant or anywhere, the first thing I try to do is buy them lunch. I feel the same way toward the police. I have blinders on when it comes to supporting those who protect this country. We can argue about the Iraqi war, and I don't know if I would have supported us going over there the way we did. But now that we're there, it's just so important that we don't let these kids feel like it's Vietnam. It's like the Anheiser Busch commercial: when they walk through a foyer or whatever, you say 'Good job.' "

Stroud insists that Keith really didn't want to record "Courtesy" and did so only at the behest of the head of the USMC, "who told him, 'We *need* that song.' And Toby said, 'Well, it's a very personal thing about my father.' I told him that these soldiers want it and need it. I could talk for hours about what it did for those kids." Worley wasn't so hesitant. "Darryl cried and said, 'It's my responsibility as a communicator to the public . . . This needs to be heard. We don't need to forget those buildings crashing. And we are—we're getting soft.' And I supported him. But I'm also friends with Steve Earle and the Dixie Chicks, and I support them in what they say, too."

Steve Earle isn't quite as generous in return, as far as Keith and Worley go. "The people that control music are Republicans. But they want country music to be apolitical—unless it sells records. What Toby Keith is doing is not about patriotism, it's about selling records." He's got an analogy coming on. "Years ago, I was playing Billy Bob's in Fort Worth. I had a three-piece rockabilly band, a lot of skinny ties, and we were opening for Hank Williams Jr.—and the audience was just barely letting us live. So about three songs into the set, I said, 'Well, we played Dallas last night, and it sure is good to be back in Texas.' And the crowd went, *Yeahhhhhhhh!* And then I played 'Bad Moon Rising' and I had 'em for the rest of the set. That's all Toby Keith was doing with those songs, trying to get the crowd to go *Yeahhhhhhhh!*—and make a lot of money. I think it's pandering. That type of political statement is permissible in Nashville, not necessarily because it's a Republican viewpoint, but because it makes money."

Some executives and artists on Music Row weren't so thrilled with the songs, either. CMT head Brian Philips remembers, "There were music executives who wouldn't stand up when Darryl Worley got an ovation at our awards show for 'Have You Forgotten?' Bernie Taupin was in the audience that night, and I think he was one of the guys that didn't stand up." He laughs. "Maybe he was protesting the rhyme!" (Worley's pairing of "forgotten" and "bin Laden" proved almost as polarizing as the song's politics.)

Ronnie Dunn, not surprisingly, has a more charitable view. "I think the 'boot in your ass' *was* a knee-jerk reaction, but an honest one. It doesn't make Toby a mindless redneck ass. People gravitate to honesty as much as they do content, half the time. And good for Toby, for standing up and swinging back. Is it the next national anthem? Probably not. But it represented what was in people's minds at the time. I'm sure even the most liberal person, when those planes were going into the towers, thought, whoever it is, once we find out, yeah, *go get* 'em—under their breath. With his song Alan hit the nail on the head, too. That's probably the most universally well-written song that came out of here as a result of what happened."

Keith insists that "Courtesy" wasn't part of some profile-broadening strategy. "I didn't have any idea other Americans would accept the song like they have. But General Jones, the commandant of the Marine Corps, was very instrumental in me releasing that song, because he said, 'This is an opportunity for you to serve your country. Our military people travel on their morale as much as anything. You've just played it for all these Marines, and the ones who aren't goose-bumped-up are crying. And when you emotionally move people like this to go in and do their job, we can conquer anything.'

"I *didn't* say we were gonna attack the whole entire Middle East. I was talking to the people that flew those planes: 'Hey, you flew planes into these buildings. We're gonna come light your world up, buddy.' And, everything that the foreigners called us, I wanted to put in the song and say: You know what? We *are* the big dogs. This is when we put our foot down. Everything you say we are, okay, now we are that, so here we come. 'Courtesy' was written for our military, not for everybody else. But America allowed it to become a hit song, and I was grateful that most of the country felt the same way I did. I knew we were gonna get some opposition to it. There's nothing more dangerous than a liberal with a cause. You wouldn't believe some of the liberal crap I've gotten. But one little letter from a kid who's got a dad overseas will make up for all the bad letters you get."

Keith's follow-up was another military-themed song, "American Soldier." "Until the end of the song, it sounds like a workin' man song, because he talks about his day-to-day and what he's trying to do and how he's behind in his bills. At the very end, it lets the cat out of the bag that it's about a soldier, who's just like a guy getting up and going to work at a construction job." It would've been an even neater twist if the title weren't a complete spoiler. But anyhow, "I think when you look through the TV screen at our military, you see a fighting soldier who's trained to kill, and you don't understand that they have a wife and kid back home or a husband and daughter and son. That soldiering is just another occupation in our world where people try to provide for their family, and when they're called upon, they don't ask any questions. They deliver, and then they're frowned upon as baby killers and all kinds of stuff when they do their job that we pay and train 'em to do. The song is my attempt to lift that lid and show that they're just working people."

SheDaisy's Yellow-Ribbon Blues

In recent years, the demographics of country music has been subject to a stereotype—that its audience consists mainly of soccer moms. Since 9/11, with thousands of troops called into duty overseas, a sub-demo has come into focus: war brides.

John Michael Montgomery's "Letters from Home" hit No. 1 by expressing the point of view of a soldier sending missives back from the front. But the song that really represented those left behind was "Come Home Soon," by the sister trio SheDaisy. The group's singer and primary songwriter, Kristyn Osborne, was compelled to write it with her partner, John Shanks, after hearing about the husband of an old family friend who was being sent to Iraq. Since the song came out, the soldier whose MIA status with his family inspired the lyric *has* come home . . . and been redeployed. The simple, plaintive lyrics—"I walk alone, I cry alone / And I'll wait for you; don't want to die alone / So please, come home soon"—make this one topical country single that won't soon go out of style, as long as the military continues to be overextended and supposedly limited tours of duty keep seeming more like Bob Dylan's Never-Ending Tour.

"We didn't know what the political climate was going to be like in our country by the time the record came out," says Osborne. "When we were writing it, we thought, 'Well, if we're fortunate, the war will be over by then.' We didn't know how angry and bitter people were gonna get. I never would have imagined we'd be sitting where we are today." The song intentionally avoids making any overt references to war, and, Osborne explains, "it could be relatable to anybody who is separated from a loved one. But it *was* inspired by the circumstances of a soldier being taken away from his family and sent to do something he didn't really understand or want to do."

As the performers of an unambiguously "pro-troops" song, SheDaisy got a lot of requests from Republicans in 2004 to do political cal events. It shouldn't have been that hard a call, in some ways; the Osbornes hail from a very conservative family in Utah that would have been pleased as punch to see their girls on the GOP dais. Kristyn's sisters were inclined to take up some of the offers. But, she says, "I was vacillating on opinions of what we were doing and what was going on. I was against the war, then I was for it. And I was against it *and* for it. Either way, I didn't feel like I could stand up and make a statement about it. So we said the only thing we can say as artists about what we believe is going on, and it's just this: our hearts are breaking for you. I've never felt more nonpartisan in my life. If I could settle into one point of view I would, and I'd do it a hundred and fifty percent. I don't necessarily disbelieve what I'm being told; it's just that I feel torn. You just have to be firm about the fact that you don't know. My sisters feel a little bit more one direction than I do, and so I'm the one keeping them from representing a side. But we have to be of one voice or not do it."

The single's success opened up the door for some charity stuff; the group ended up partnering with the Red Cross to hawk "Come Home Soon" bracelets to benefit support services for military families. But Osborne felt particularly glad she didn't get involved in any publicly partisan efforts after an e-mail she got the other day from a new fan. It was from Eric Jenkins, a veteran in Oregon.

"I can't sleep," Jenkins's letter begins. "It's 1:30 a.m. and the pain in my joints is keeping me up. It's been like this for about a decade; ever since I came back from the Persian Gulf. I was in the Air Force for eight years, turning tankers during the Gulf War in 1991, and then working tank-busting A-10 Warthogs in Saudi Arabia and Kuwait in 1994–1995 during Vigilant Warrior. For the past few years songs like 'Have You Forgotten?,' 'Courtesy of the Red, White and Blue,' and 'American Soldier' have largely driven me away from country, because they're written by people who just don't understand what's going on over there. We fight wars so that the next guy doesn't have to. You sacrifice so that things change for the better. The fact that we're over there again, and then hearing these songs, makes me feel wasted, like it was all for nothing. Nobody learned anything. Nobody listened. These guys just don't get it and I doubt they ever will. However, tonight, 'Come Home Soon' is on CMT, and it struck me deeper than anything I've ever heard. Sometimes you can just tell when someone gets 'it.' There's a tone associated with understanding. It makes me feel that some of what I did was worthwhile, and that's something that I really need. Especially on nights like tonight."

Travis Tritt Bogarts the Peace Pipe

Travis Tritt . . . peacemaker? It's not exactly typecasting. But this is the role he's cast himself in with "What Say You," the can't-we-all-just-get-along song he shares with duet partner John Mellencamp.

Tritt can be a contentious guy, to say the least. He's well known for coming down on poppy, watered-down, or crossover-inclined country—or, as he puts it, "ABBA with a steel guitar." His stuff is as much Southern rock–influenced as it is strictly traditional, all the better to strut the cultural defiance he sometimes parades.

We're getting a little of that attitude today. "Political correctness is starting to have a tremendous effect on our society, and not necessarily always in a positive way," he says during a break in an NBC green room shortly before taking the *Tonight Show* stage to perform with Mellencamp. "We live in an age where it seems like everything is constantly under scrutiny. I saw a big article the other day about the word 'Christ' being in 'Christmas,' and people trying to be politically correct, saying 'Happy Holidays' rather than 'Merry Christmas.' They're actually taking polls now where they're interviewing people across the nation to determine whether they accept Christmas as Christmas. Really, it's wacked. It's hard for me to understand how we've come to analyze everything from a political-correctness standpoint. I think 'What Say You' is refreshing in that it says, just take things on face value. It is what it is."

You have to give Tritt credit: Perhaps only he could have recorded an ode to tolerance and mutual respect that still manages to sound slightly belligerent:

> Man, I don't talk no religion
> And I ain't gonna wave that flag
> But I love God and America
> And I fight for what I have
> What say you?

He didn't write "What Say You" but welcomed it when it was offered him. "To me, it was a song that said, 'Look, I've got my own views, they're very strong, and I don't mind telling you what they are. But at the same time, I'm not naive enough to believe that I've got all the answers or I'm the only person who has the right ideas about everything. And I'm not foolish enough to limit myself by not listening to an opposing view. And, between the two of us, can't we come together and find some common ground?' I thought this was a positive message, especially in an election year when people are more divided than we can ever remember. I thought, let's put partisan politics aside and come together as human beings."

This reconciliatory sentiment, from the guy who called the Dixie Chicks "cowardly"? But more on that in a minute.

"When I decided to record the song, I heard it as a duet, and when Mellencamp's name came up, it worked for a lot of reasons. He understands his brand very well, and I always admired that. And the fact that he and I are on opposite ends of the political spectrum, I thought us coming together would really illustrate what the song is talking about. I was aware that there were gonna be some people out there, especially at country radio, who were probably going to frown on the idea of having John on a song—either because of his politics or because some programmers resist having anybody, be it Uncle Kracker or Kid Rock or Sheryl Crow, come in from the pop world and 'invade' the country-music world. Fortunately, they're not a majority. Obviously, John being a vocal and outspoken guy, there's no question that we knew there was gonna be a certain amount of backlash. But that's been a very small part of the response we've had. When we play the song live, people put their fist in the air, and that lets you know you've hit the right spot."

But Mellencamp has less in common with Tritt than with Tritt's old nemeses, the Chicks, including, most obviously, the anti-Bush, pro-Kerry Vote for Change tour they both did different legs of in late 2004. Mellencamp even made a protest song available online ("To Washington," based on Charlie Poole's 1920s hillbilly hit, "White House Blues") that began with the words, "It's worse now since he came from Texas to Washington . . . And he wants to fight with many, and he says it's not for oil . . ." Why does Tritt applaud and even collaborate with one artist after dissing the other?

"You have to be smart enough to know that if you're going to make your political feelings known, you're gonna polarize some people," he explains. "The question is whether or not you're willing to deal with that backlash. If you're not, you should probably take your cue from Elvis Presley in the late sixties. When somebody asked him about Vietnam, he said, 'Hey, man, I'm just a musician. What do I know?'

Where I have a problem is when people put strong opinions out there and then have the nerve to act offended when there's a backlash. John's never done that. John's the kind of guy who, at least in public, says what he says, and damn the torpedos when it comes back, because he knows there's gonna be a backlash and expects it. That was the problem I had with Natalie Maines. With her, it was sort of like shooting yourself in the foot and then wondering why it hurts. If you're going to make your politics known, understand that this results in a certain amount of polarization in your audience, and some people will jump on your side and others will say 'You know what? You're an idiot.' Be willing to take the bad with the good, and if you're not, take the Elvis approach."

How far did Tritt and Mellencamp get into their different views, as they collaborated? Not much. "We broached the subject at the video shoot. He had just come off a situation where he had made some pretty strong comments in the media, and I think he was having some problems with the backlash from that. Any time you make strong statements, man, for every action there's a reaction, and the stronger the statement, the stronger the backlash. We talked about it briefly. I said, 'Well, John, with all due respect, what did you expect?' He said, 'But I didn't expect it *this* bad.' I said, 'I know. I grew up in a country where you could say what you wanted and not have people flip the finger at you when you go to the grocery store.' John and I are both aware that our political beliefs are totally different, but we never went any further than that, talking about it. Henry Fonda and Jimmy Stewart were the best of friends and could not have been more different politically and in their religious beliefs. But they never discussed politics and never discussed religion, and they got along famously right up till they passed away."

So is the key to bridging the gap in agreeing not to discuss the meat of the matter, then, or to have a real dialogue? That much isn't clear. But at least Tritt is trying to open some doors. "When I look at all those red states, that represents a lot of the people I play for on a day-to-day basis. When I first heard and recorded the song, it was never about 'God, I hope this is going to be a window for world peace.' But if this can play just a small part in ending some of the partisanship that we see existing now, then, man, that's a win/win all around."

It does end up being a smaller part than Tritt might have hoped. Popular on some country stations but completely ignored by others,

"What Say You" peaks at No. 21 on the *Billboard* country chart. Hey, Travis Tritt . . . you've been Dixie Chicked!

The Education of Chely Wright

The world's second-most-famous white SUV—lagging behind only O.J. Simpson's Ford Bronco—is parked outside a coffeehouse on Nashville's Demonbreun Avenue. Chely Wright's Isuzu Trooper is still emblazoned with the u.s.m.c. decal that instigated an altercation about a mile away from this location, an event recounted in the song "Bumper of My SUV."

"The war was a few months old," remembers Wright, "when this lady flipped me the bird and got me to pull over at the red light and mouthed 'Roll down your window!' I thought, okay, don't think I'm gonna get shot; she's in a minivan with a car seat in the back, and we're on West End, near Bowling Avenue, where rich people live. I rolled down my window and she said"—Wright drops her voice so her fellow java junkies can't hear—"'Your fucking war is wrong. You're a fucking killer!'

"I'm a mouthy person. Typically I would have something to say back. I don't know if you've ever been in a wreck, where your legs feel like Jell-O and you've got to pull over. But I had no response. As she pulled away, I was looking at her two bumper stickers; one was from a private school here in town, religious in nature, and one was a Bush sticker with a line drawn through it. It shocked me that she was so angry, but it didn't shock me that she had something to say. Because people at that time were being really, really outspoken, vocally and with stickers and banners reflecting which side they were on. They can both be American sides. You can be against this war and still be pro-American, don't get me wrong. Like I say in the song, 'Yes, I do have questions, but I get to ask them because I'm free.'"

> 'Cause I've been to Hiroshima
> And I've been to the DMZ
> I've walked on the sand in Baghdad
> Still don't have all of the answers I need
> But I guess I wanna know where she's been
> Before she judges and gestures to me

'Cause she don't like my sticker
For the U.S. Marines
On the bumper of my SUV
So I hope that lady in her minivan
Turns on her radio and hears this from me
As she picks up her kids from their private school
And drives home safely on our city streets
Or to the building where her church group meets

Wright's dad served in the navy in Vietnam from 1967 to 1971, on the USS *Nimitz*. Her granddad got a purple heart; he was in the army division that hit Normandy beach in WWII. Her marine brother is the one who sent her the sticker, recently promoted from staff sergeant to gunner. Wright herself grew up playing taps on the bugle at more than a hundred military funerals, and as a country star she's been entertaining the troops and visiting VA hospitals for ten years. But GI Jane she isn't, not quite.

"We typically think that if you sing about the military or if you have military in your family, you're a Republican. And I'm very much not. I'm very much not a Democrat either. I hate political parties. I told G. Gordon Liddy on his show, 'I think it's gang warfare at its finest—corporate-funded gang warfare." He said, 'Okay, explain yourself.' I said, 'Well, it's like you're a member of the Bloods out in east L.A. and you see a brother getting beat up by a Crip, and you'll go over and beat up the Crip to get him off the Blood, though you don't know what happened or what the fight's about. But you're gonna defend your brother because he's wearing the same do-rag on his head? That's retarded. Likewise, how can people go down a ticket and vote "Republican" in one fell swoop?' People may think my family sits around and says, 'Go, President Bush! Start a war! Kill people!' But I really love the fact that I grew up not knowing my parents' political affiliation. I never heard the words *Republican* or *Democrat* used in my house as one being the good one and one being the bad.

"I've been told by people, 'Hey, way to go, I'm glad you're pro-Bush.' And I tell them I've never endorsed a candidate. I'm a country singer who likes to support my troops. I was on Sean Hannity's show and he said, 'You're a good Republican girl. I like that.' I said, 'Ahhh, easy there, Sean! I did an event with Senator Clinton this morning.' I had been grand marshall of the Veterans Day parade in New York City.

He went, *uhhhhh*. I said 'She came out and shook my hand and said, "Thank you for all you've done for the troops," and she seemed very genuine to me.' He started to berate her. I said, 'That really bothers you that I touched a Democrat today, doesn't it?' He said, 'It really does. I feel like I need to go wash my hands. I feel dirty. Come on, you're a Republican. You've gotta be. Your brother's a gunnie! You've performed for the troops for ten years.' I said, 'I never reveal who I vote for. I have issues with both candidates.' He said, 'What are your issues with President Bush?' I said, 'Thank you for asking me that! I think his whole angle on amending the Constitution to preserve the sanctity of marriage between a man and a woman is just ludicrous, and just shy of a hate crime.' And a vein popped out in his neck and he said, 'Do you realize what show you're on?' I said, 'You wanted me to talk about my song, and when I say in the song that I'm not a Democrat or Republican, I'm not a liar.'" All good, clean broadcast fun. "He and I had a good banter back and forth, and we've remained friends via e-mail. But it's not some big secret I'm trying to keep, as if I really do have a political affiliation and you have to guess it. In high school and college, I was kind of a jock, kind of a scholar, kind of a band geek. I had subsets of friends. I never believed in cliques."

All those hospital visits have had a cumulative effect. She has tale after tale of the newly wounded and amputated and how each guy she visits requires a fresh emotional approach. "I've been visiting VA hospitals all my life, but there you're dealing with men who have had their legs gone for thirty years. It's a different emotional experience when you're going to Walter Reade in Bethesda and sitting with a kid nineteen years old on a body bed who's been missing his limb for twelve days, and he says 'Come sit by me' and goes to scoot over and move his leg and it's not there.

"With another guy, almost his whole torso was missing, and they had skin-grafted it and it was like a moon shape where they were able to shift all his organs. He lost his kidney and I think his spleen. But he said, 'Isn't it cool that they could fit all of my organs in half of my torso?' I said 'That's awesome!' and asked what kind of weapon did that to him. Mortar? He said, 'An RPG . . . and I saw it coming.' Told the whole story, and he just sobbed, and said he lost his best friend he'd trained with and been with for three years. He said another RPG went straight through his friend. He grabbed his friend and his hand went right through his back. His friend talked to him for about a minute before he expired. You always hear about chickens with their heads cut off, that they can run around for a while. And people really can clinically have all their organs gone, and the brain still functions for a while. I walked out of there and the chaplain was bawling. He said, 'That kid's been in here ten days and has never talked about what happened.' I asked him why he thought he told me. He said, 'I think he told you because he knows he probably won't see you again.'"

Because Chely has made so many trips to Iraq, everyone wants to know: Is what we're doing worth it?

"Had I not traveled over there, I would probably be of the mindset—because my grandfather always told me 'My brothers in arms died so you can have your freedoms,' and that's been welded into my brain—that it's worth it. A marine once told me that somebody came and cussed his wife out about his Marine Corps sticker and then pointed her finger at him and said, 'How many lives have to be lost?' And he said to her, 'As many as it takes to secure our freedom. As many as it takes.' When I hear that, I want to rally behind it. But then I know that if my brother were lost, that's gonna be one too many for me.

"But then I went to a school in Bilad, which is near Camp Anaconda, north of Baghdad. It took a convoy of seven armored vehicles to transport me, one person, to a school the coalition forces had built. I had on a Kevlar helmet and flak vest. The kids' teeth were rotting out of their heads, but they were so beautiful. The boys wanted to play with the toys I was giving out, but the girls were touching me all over and going 'Madam?' I thought, are they copping a feel? Are they little lesbian Iraqis? Finally I asked the colonel, who was a British national, 'Sir, why were the little girls pulling at my flak vest?' He laughed and said, 'They don't believe you're a girl because they have never seen a female walk parallel with males in their lives.' The women walk eight paces behind. So part of me says get the hell out of there, and part says a little girl should not have to marvel that a female gets to walk parallel with a man—or, worse, made to feel that she might be raped and killed in the city square while people watch.

"Some of the kids in that school were thirteen years old and this was the first day of schooling they'd had in their lives. That lady in the minivan who flipped me off, she's celebrating a whole host of freedoms in one moment, driving a gas-guzzling minivan—like my gas-guzzling SUV—safely on our infrastructure and amassing enough wealth to send her kids to the private school on her bumper sticker.

We have so many things in America that I would love to see other people around the world have too. But I also know America is America for a reason. It's because people with an ideology came here from different nations and we wanted a new plan. Part of me thinks that we will implode as a society at some point, because all these freedoms will bite us in the ass at some point. We ought to remember how young we are; we're a baby country, compared to Iraq. But we also have to remember why people want to come here, why people break laws and risk their lives to get within our borders. There's something they're coming for and something they're running from."

As a loyal military brat who's seen the worst that battle can do to combatants and innocents, Wright can articulate both sides of the debate about as well as anybody. She seems legitimately conflicted—a poster child for America's divided feelings about Iraq. Despite this balanced outlook, "Bumper of My SUV" has an uncanny power to enrage Nashville liberals for reasons that aren't always immediately clear, maybe even to themselves. Several said to me that it's not about any stand she's taking; "it's just a bad song." Yet it seems like the kind of effort that, if not for its perceived politics, these same types of country fans normally would applaud: an anecdote spontaneously translated into a long, raw, unpolished recording, it's the antithesis of what normally comes out of the Music Row song factory, and something that, as she points out, never would have been allowed on a major-label album coming out of the Nashville system. Again: a true modern folk ballad. So why does it piss people off so?

Wright is a more curious brand of country star than she first appeared when she came on the scene in the early nineties. *The Metropolitan Hotel* is her first indie-label album after a long streak with the majors, and its growth finds her in transition—halfway between conventional mainstream country and more idiosyncratic singer/songwriter material. She may be the first in the history of this unconditionally mama-loving genre to write a wrenching song about resentment toward a distant, estranged mom, as she does in "Between a Mother and a Child." A tune like that fits squarely into rock's confessional tradition—as does, in its fashion, "Bumper of My SUV." That the latter is perceived as right-leaning, though, creates a problem; conservative confessionalism is an unmined, uncoined subgenre. If she claims in the lyric to not be a Republican or Democrat, that may only exacerbate suspicions among the left, who, just like Hannity, can't believe she's serious about that. To the committed, public disavowal of party lines can come across as the disingenuousness of a wolf in moderate's clothing, trying to sneak some nefarious agenda past the other side.

Doubters kept insisting Wright must have concocted the road-rage anecdote, or at least exaggerated it, in search of a publicity-rich, career-advancing single. They finally got the "gotcha" they were looking for when a damning December 2004 story in the *Tennessean* indicated that some of the support for the song wasn't on the level. The president of Wright's fan club, a Wall Street worker named Chuck Wilson, was revealed to have encouraged core members of Wright's "street team" (volunteers who do local grunt work to promote their favorite singers) to call radio stations' request lines and pretend to be wives of overseas servicemen desperate to hear "Bumper." Upon being asked about this by a reporter, Wright fired Wilson from his unpaid position and claimed ignorance, saying she's too busy to keep track of fan-club and message-board activities. That disavowal seemed reasonable enough—but on the other hand, she'd previously referred to the fan club prexy as her best friend. One radio programmer speaking to the paper said that Wright actually had the "cleanest" record in the business at the moment, since there was none of the usual tainted radio promotion work being done for her single, just grassroots efforts, however misguided. But by now there was a taint on the song that devastated her. The brouhaha added up to one more chapter in the everlasting debate over music's relation to the military, and where the line between exhortation and exploitation lies.

In her mind, the "scandal"—she puts ironic quote marks around the word—ultimately can't take away from the organic origins of the song and, especially, what it meant to a kid named Josh Henry and his family after she previewed it in Iraq.

"We played Fort Summerall. It's very remote, and no one had visited the troops there. They scrubbed a port-o-potty for two weeks and didn't let anybody go in it so I could have a clean one." These are the privileges afforded a rare female civilian in this far removed an outpost. When she and her band performed, "the response from the troops was so subdued, it took me aback. Afterward the colonel said, 'This is the rowdiest I've seen them since they've been here. You have to understand, they've lost friends and their spirit is broken. It's bad, very bad, here.' Then, a kid came through the line and on his flak vest it said 'Henry.' I told him 'Dude, we could be cousins—my mom's maiden name is Henry.' He said, 'Damn! That means I can't ask you out!' I said, 'If we're in *Kentucky*, you can!' One of those in-breeding jokes we all love to make. He came through the autograph line three times, with his buddies all teasing him, and I started saying 'Hey, cousin!' His name was Josh Henry, and he ended up hanging out a lot with the band that night. The next morning we got word that Josh had been killed.

"For a few days after we got back, I thought, nah, I'm not gonna do it"—do a studio recording of the song the soldiers had loved so much. "Then I was able to talk to Josh Henry's mom, and she said 'I found myself going back to your website. I asked, 'Oh, you were looking for pictures maybe of us with Josh?' She said, 'No, I just kept looking at your picture.' I asked if she knew why. She said, 'I didn't until the other day. It's because you were the last woman to talk to my son.'"

George Wallace, who was once again governor of Alabama, helped induct Tammy Wynette into the Alabama Music Hall of Fame in 1985. Wynette sang "Stand by Your Man," a song she'd dedicated to Wallace and several other political candidates over the years. Later, the governor, a reformed former segregationist, also helped induct the Commodores. PHOTO BY ALAN MAYOR

Town & Country, Jungle & Trench

A Short History of Country in Wartime and Election Time

Country music was a hotbed of protest music in the late 1960s. Very little of it took issue with the Vietnam war: most of the protest was directed against the protesters. An entire subgenre, from Merle Haggard's "The Fightin' Side of Me" to Dave Dudley's "What We're Fighting For," from Stonewall Jackson's "The Minute Men (Are Turning in Their Graves)" to Ernest Tubb's "It's America (Love It or Leave It)," devoted itself to lyrical extremism in the defense of liberty.

A spirit of forgiveness and understanding would have us not judge too harshly or laugh too loudly when we look back on how some of the concerned singers of that time deigned to explain it all for us, à la Sister Mary Ignatius by way of Robert McNamara. Quaint as it may seem this long after the fall of the Berlin Wall, the domino theory did not seem so utterly ridiculous in the mid-sixties; heaven knows it wasn't just hillbillies who believed that entire regions and ultimately the world were at stake if America lost her way in the jungle. Anyway, a few of these Nashville hawks and badgerers of flower children ended up taking some unexpected career paths of their own.

Take the writer of what was arguably the kitschiest of all the singles to launch a counterattack against the counterculture. The lyrics of Autry Inman's infamous "Ballad of Two Brothers," which reached No. 14 on *Billboard*'s country chart in 1968, took the form of alternating pieces of mail from the titular siblings, the Goofus and Gallant of wartime youth. The first verse, set to a martial beat, is a recitative direct from the front:

> Seeing how close these people are to losing their freedom
> Makes me that much more determined to help win this war
> 'Cause if we don't, the next battlefield
> May be closer to home than Vietnam
> Must close for now, all my love
> Your son, Bud
> P.S. How is Tommy doing at State University?

Funny he should ask that, because suddenly, the beat loosens up and the music starts to swing, which in this culturally charged context is a sign of impending moral decay. In the second verse, Tommy, the wayward collegiate, is writing home to brag about how his parents should check the front page of the paper to see him marching for peace, though his dad might not recognize him behind his "groovy beard." Then Tommy lays into Bud, who's "murdering all those people overseas," and wonders how bad it could be if South Vietnam did fall, as his economics prof has been tooting the horn for communism as a perfectly far-out alternative lifestyle.

> I'm sorry dad, but this God and country bit just isn't my bag
> Gotta go dad, big rally tonight
> Your son, Tommy
> P.S. Dad, better send me an extra fifty bucks this week, dig?

A bittersweet ending is in store. The third letter is a "regret to inform"–type missive from Bud's sergeant, sent to the parents along with their late son's Medal of Honor. And then—here comes the twisteroo—the fourth and final verse is from Tommy, so moved by his brother's sacrifice and so convinced it couldn't have been for an unjust cause that he's given up his draft card-burning ways and is now signing off as . . . *Private* Tommy. The groovy beat slows back down to a rigid march, and everyone, reformed bad seed and befuddled drummer included, lives righteously ever after.

What were we just saying about not laughing at these dated efforts? OK, let's face it: this *is* funny stuff. A mention of this song brings a grimace to the face of the legendary tunesmith who cowrote it, Bobby

Braddock. We're talking at the Music Row offices of Sony ATV Tree Publishing, a house he helped build through smash hits like "He Stopped Loving Her Today," "D-I-V-O-R-C-E," and "I Wanna Talk About Me." But it's clear as we talk that there won't be any plaques to be found on the walls honoring "Two Brothers," even if it did establish him as a Nashville writer. Recently, Braddock has been one of the leading anti-war voices in a fledgling organization called Music Row Democrats, and this hawkish anthem to end all hawkish anthems is no feather in his cap.

"Politics aside, 'Ballad of Two Brothers' is one of the worst pieces of crap ever assembled by the human mind," Braddock boldly proclaims, taking a seat in the conference room. "What it says was one-dimensional, simple-minded, and right-wing cliché-ridden. The first time I voted in an election, my hero was Barry Goldwater. By the time that song was out, my views on Vietnam had already started to change, because of the My Lai massacre and the issue of *Life* magazine in which the week's war dead were displayed as though it were a high school annual . . . I have all of my BMI Awards displayed on my 'ego wall' except for that one. In fact, I had my name removed from the copyright many years ago."

A similar reversal of sentiment involves another hit of that era, "Talkin' Vietnam Blues," which went to No. 12 in 1966. It was performed by Dave Dudley, who, like Inman, had a good run with this kind of what's-the-matter-with-kids-today material. "Blues" has but one narrator, but he's a doubly disgusted one, a soldier who happens upon some demonstrators in Washington who are soliciting signatures for a "telegram of sympathy." At first he figures it's for the families of U.S. soldiers who've made the ultimate sacrifice, only to learn that the condolences are being sent to a certain foreigner whose monogram is HCM.

> I said, "Ho Chi who?" He said, "Ho Chi Minh
> People's Leader, North Vietnam"
> Well, I wasn't real sure I was hearin' him right
> But I thought we'd better remove before we got in a fight
> Because my eyes were smartin', and my pulse started hitting a lick
> I thought about another telegram I'd read
> Tellin' my buddy's wife that her husband was dead
> It wasn't too long till I was feelin' downright sick

"Talkin' Vietnam Blues" was the very first hit for a young song-writer fresh out of the army—Colonel Kris Kristofferson. Later, of course, Kristofferson went about as far left as it's possible to go, de-voting much of his career in the 1980s to excoriating American policy in Nicaragua and El Salvador. But, unlike Braddock, Kristofferson isn't embarrassed by *his* jingoistic entry into the hit-writer ranks.

"It wasn't so much pro-war as just pro-soldier," says Kristofferson, cutting his younger self a break, "because I was still in the army when I wrote it." He was about to go to West Point to teach English lit when he decided to head for Nashville instead. "Up until that time, all the information I got was in the *Stars and Stripes*, and it was a slow process of me changing my ideas. Over the next couple of years I started get-ting a lot of reports from my friends who were serving over there. I re-member a few years later listening to these pilots when I was flying down to the Gulf of Mexico. They had a warrant officer program where you only had to be a high school graduate, and they'd send you straight through flight school and over to Vietnam. These kids were talking about things that were just inhuman—pushing people out of helicopters—and I thought about all the shitty things people were do-ing in the name of duty that they were gonna have a hard time living with later. Anyway, within two or three years, I'd gone about a hun-dred eighty degrees, thinking that the war was wrong."

But he never regretted having penned "Talkin' Vietnam Blues," his entrée to the Row. "It was pretty well-written, I have to say!" Kristof-ferson says, laughing now. "And I remember how Harlan Howard liked the song so much."

He would have, because Howard was not only one of Nashville's most venerated songwriters ("I Fall to Pieces," "Heartaches by the Num-ber") but one of the town's most prolific hawks, though his penchant for writing anti-counterculture numbers isn't usually recounted on his ré-sumé. Though Howard mostly worked behind the scenes and rarely went into the recording studio himself, he felt strongly enough about the state of the world in 1968 to cut an album of his own, with a title that Nixon would have been proud of: *To the Silent Majority, With Love*.

This odd LP ends with a nonpolitical love song, "The Chokin' Kind," that had been a hit for Waylon and was destined to become one again decades later for white soul singer Joss Stone. But few of its other selections are likely to be revived. Several equate anti-war senti-ment with cowardice. In "Better Get Your Pride Back, Boy," Howard tells Vietnam's draft dodgers, "They're needin' you boy and you're sittin' in your coffeehouse / Whatcha gonna do when your woman begs you save her from a mouse?" A later verse goes so far as to invoke the image of the bodybuilder bully kicking sand in a weakling's face. "Three Cheers for the Good Guy" pays tribute to average hardworking joes who "lead a very normal life" and whose better attributes include the fact that "they don't march and they don't shout." One tune, "Mister Professor," became a minor hit for another singer, Leroy Van Dyke. It offers some trenchant advice to a prof at the local public university: "On the subject of God, if you have any doubts, don't discuss 'em . . . We sent you a good Christian boy and he knows right from wrong / Beware of the danger, don't send us a stranger back home . . . Just help them learnin', not marchin' and burnin', and we'll like you fine." (Not that Howard comes off as that much more orthodox in his Christian theology than the academics he lambastes: An odd tune titled "A Little More Time" pays homage to the unlikely trinity of Stephen Foster, John F. Kennedy, and Jesus Christ, each of whose premature deaths gets a separate verse of lament; the final chorus contends that if Christ had only lived longer, peace on earth might have been achieved, a heretical doctrine to most Christian moms and dads.)

Harlan Howard wasn't the only country figure releasing an actual pro-war concept album that year. The song Braddock penned for Autry Inman served as the title song and centerpiece of the latter's *Ballad of Two Brothers* LP, which also included Inman's version of Sgt. Barry Sadler's beyond-gung-ho pop hit, "Ballad of the Green Berets," Marty Robbins's left-baiting "Ain't I Right," Buffy Sainte-Marie's "Universal Soldier" (an antiwar song often mistaken by country singers of the time as pro-troops), a remake of the Dudley/Kristofferson hit "Vietnam Blues," and the most tellingly titled of all the counter-counterculture songs: "Must We Fight Two Wars." Inman was the country rapper of his day; nearly all his songs are spoken-word monologues, and "Must We Fight Two Wars" takes the form of a long rant against the enemy within:

> This great land of ours is fighting two wars
> Although it was never intended
> Were it not for the war we must wage here at home
> The one in Vietnam would be ended . . .
> They say we must lose, we're on the wrong side
> Our enemy? No, they're some of us . . .

Ho Chi Minh calls them comrade, and very well they might be
They've been helping kill our young men, not with bullets from guns,
They shout "we won't fight," but they tear down the foundation from
    within . . .

Needless to say, country music wasn't the anti-war left's music of choice in the late sixties. Yet by 1973, improbably enough, the largely depoliticized remnants of the counterculture were claiming country almost as their own. A host of rockers, from the Flying Burrito Brothers to the Eagles, were adopting the trappings of country, as Bob Dylan had done before them; within the country mainstream, the outlaw movement informally headed up by Willie Nelson, Waylon Jennings, Jessi Colter, and Tompall Glaser put the kibosh on countrypolitan politeness and brought a distinctly rock attitude into the mix.

How that shift occurred—and then reversed itself by the early Reagan era—is still a subject of fascination for many. In his book *Redefining Southern Culture*, James C. Cobb sets out the provocative and unflattering notion that the confluence of rednecks and hippies didn't represent a true spirit of mutual inclusion so much as one last post-sixties bacchanal, free enough of all those messy wartime politics that squares and jarheads could join in. Cobb says that Willie and Waylon "symbolized the 'outlaw' movement in country music, a curious phenomenon seemingly out of phase with prevailing trends toward conservatism and respect for 'law and order.' In fact, however, the appeal of the outlaw movement may well have been that it offered a brief nostalgia trip into the uninhibited lifestyles and flaunted traditions of the late 1960s without requiring any sort of ideological commitment."

There has to be some truth to that—everybody loves a party, or a Willie-sponsored Fourth of July picnic—but such a strict oversimplification doesn't account for the more thoughtful, war-doubting strains that had gradually crept into even non-"outlaw" country music in the late 1960s and early 1970s, fostering a greater sense of inclusion for the longhairs who for a few years had figured, probably correctly, that they'd gotten on the genre's fightin' side. Even if this drift was negligible compared to the anti-war rhetoric being cranked out on the rock side of the fence, the work of singer/songwriters like Tom T. Hall—who, like Kristofferson and Braddock, started out specializing in love-it-or-leave-it songs, but then underwent a profound transformation—made it easier for estranged youth-culture types to associate country with sophisticated pieces of cultural satire like Hall's "Watergate Blues" instead of the rural stereotype epitomized by Peter Fonda's and Dennis Hopper's pickup-driving antagonists.

In 1966, Hall wrote "What We're Fighting For" for Dave Dudley, from the point of view of a soldier writing home to his mom. (It was later adapted as Sara and Maybelle Carter's "I Told Them What You're Fighting For," to adopt the mother's point of view.) Young patriots lacking a sense of what the war was about may have eagerly looked to songs as promisingly titled as these: At last, Vietnam explained! But Hall's apologia consisted of a broad leap: "Tell them that we're fighting for the old red, white, and blue / Did they forget Pearl Harbor and Korea too? . . . the world must learn that we will fight, we will protect our shore." The domino theory was so taken for granted that the war's Nashville defenders didn't even have to lay it out: in the songs of the time, it's understood that as goes Saigon, so goes Saginaw.

A few years later, now into his own recording career, Hall was singing a different tune. His "Mama Bake a Pie (Daddy Kill a Chicken)" was far from the feel-good hit of the Vietnam-era summer:

People staring at me as they wheel me down the ramp toward my plane
The war is over for me, I've forgotten everything except the pain
Thank you sir, and yes sir, it was worth it for the ol' red, white,
   and blue
And since I won't be walking I suppose I'll save some money
   buying shoes

Even as country has endured as the most patriotic of all musical genres, there've been plenty of interesting variations of opinion on war, recovery, race, and justice even within those seemingly rigid, nationalist confines. Country music's pioneering recording artists ran the gamut in the attitudes they expressed toward social issues as far back as the World War I–era, the twenties, and the thirties, when it wasn't unusual to hear a performer play the race card one minute and espouse what today might be considered progressive politics the next.

"You found a lot of class consciousness in older country music, and a lot of resentment against the rich and privileged," says historian Bill C. Malone. "And occasionally those older songs will comment upon exploitation of workers, particularly in the textile mills. On the other hand, you also find some social conservatism in songs like 'Why Do

You Bob Your Hair, Girls' and 'Saved,' which comment on certain moral positions that were considered to be wrong. But politically, before the 1960s, there wasn't any explicit posture of Republicanism or *political* conservatism in the music. That's all pretty recent—if you consider the last thirty or forty years to be recent."

Over Thar: The Politics of World Wars I and II

Fiddlin' John Carson is the man some consider the first major hillbilly recording artist, which might make 1914's "I'm Glad My Wife's in Europe" the first real war-themed hit country record. And being pro-war it does set a trend. But its gung-ho sentiment is satirical, with Carson grateful for the outbreak of major combat because his spouse has been prevented from returning from her overseas vacation. The Great War didn't inspire a great deal of truly nationalist material in the nascent hillbilly music industry. What topical songs there were sometimes tended toward cynical reflections on the human cost of war, nostalgia for earlier, more easily defined conflicts, or outright comedy. Among Fiddlin' John's other hits was "Dixie Division," which lauded the Southern troops headed to the front—patriotic, of course, but also defining a Confederacy-über-alles standard for the rest of the republic to live up to.

It took World War II to gather momentum for the kind of go-get-'em material we're familiar with today. Anyone who supposes that somebody like Toby Keith or Darryl Worley has taken a careerist approach to these types of songs should get a load of Denver Darling or Carson Robison. Darling was so speedy in responding to current events that he had released "Cowards Over Pearl Harbor" as a single by Christmas 1941. Within the following six months, he recorded follow-ups like "The Devil and Mr. Hitler" and "When Mussolini Laid His Pistol Down." Robison, meanwhile, enjoyed an even longer and provocatively titled run of topical singles, including "We're Gonna Have to Slap the Dirty Little Jap (and Uncle Sam's the Guy Who Can Do It)," "Get Your Gun and Come Along (We're Fixing to Kill a Skunk)," "Mussolini's Letter to Hitler" and its B-side, "Hitler's Reply to Mussolini." But at that point theirs became careers built on sand—Iwo Jima's—and Darling and Robison faded from the public consciousness after the war.

The biggest WWII-themed hit song in any genre was "There's a Star-Spangled Banner Waving Somewhere," the tale of a handicapped lad champing at the bit to join the war effort, first recorded by Elton Britt. It went on to be cut so many times—by the Louvin Brothers, Dave Dudley, Autry Inman and many others—that in 2003 Germany's archival Bear Family label put together a CD containing eleven renditions of the tune, including versions rewritten to include events of the Cold War and Vietnam eras.

A wartime thirst for vengeance and country music's essential good-naturedness have always been slightly odd bedfellows. There's probably a good reason why Francis Coppola used the "Ride of the Valkyries" on the soundtrack of *Apocalypse Now* and not an agreeable shuffle by Bob Wills and His Texas Playboys. Such a reason will come to mind as you listen to any of three versions of the arguably bloodthirsty "Smoke on the Water" that reached the Top 10 in 1944–45, one of which was by Wills, and another of which, by Red Foley, reached No. 1. The music is jolly and two-step-friendly, almost to the point of preposterousness, while the bloodshed-anticipating lyrics might be better suited to a musical bed more akin to the one in Deep Purple's unrelated metal anthem of the same title:

> For there is a great destroyer made of fire and flesh and steel
> Rollin' towards the foes of freedom; they'll go down beneath
>   its wheels
> There'll be nothin' left but vultures to inhabit all that land
> When our modern ships and bombers made a graveyard of Japan

The unwieldy marriage of cheerful major chords and take-no-prisoners lyrical threats in "Smoke on the Water" seems to be promising a giant barn dance, to commence across the Nipponese wastelands immediately following total annihilation—where, presumably, any lingering survivors would be clogged to death.

Full Pedal-Steel Jacket: The Politics of Korea, the Cold War, and Vietnam

In the political songs of the Korean War and Cold War eras, humor, threats, and apocalyptic dread took turns at dominance. Hank Williams's "No, No, Joe"—an altogether rare moment of topicality in his catalog—featured music as benign as the chipper strains of "Smoke on the Water," but here it fit Williams's chidingly sarcastic tone, which, in addressing Stalin, included the assurance that hell-dwellers Hitler and Mussolini were "saving a spot by the fire" for the Soviet leader. Roy Acuff similarly offered threatening "Advice to Joe," and he didn't mean Joe McCarthy. Cactus Pryor's comedy record "Point of Order" *did* spoof the McCarthy hearings, rather bravely. But the duo Lulu Belle and Scotty didn't even have to be subpoened by Congress to make a joint oath in "I'm No Communist." "They Locked God Outside the Iron Curtain," complained Little Jimmy Dickens. Elton Britt returned with the wordy color-coding of "The Red We Want Is the Red We've Got in the Old Red, White, and Blue." In the musical equivalent of the infamous Dewey-beats-Truman headline, Jimmie Osborne had a wishful-thinking hit with "Thank God for Victory in Korea," released shortly before the Chinese Communists entered the war in 1950. Acuff's "Doug MacArthur" included a plea to not "let the Communists take over all creation." And Gene Autry advocated for keeping "The Bible on the Table and the Flag upon the Wall."

One of the most oft-recorded country military songs, "Deck of Cards," is, in its original form, the story of a soldier reprimanded by his superior after being caught with a forbidden set of cards. The enlistee goes on to testify how each card is a mnemonic device that, in lieu of the Bible he's not allowed to carry, reminds him of some theological principle. Modern cynics may wait for a concluding verse in which the soldier snickers at having pulled one over on the gullible brass, but no such capper comes in either of the versions, by T. Texas Tyler or Tex Ritter, that made the Top 10 in 1948, nor in Wink Martindale's 1959 cover, nor in Bill Anderson's Gulf War–era revival. In 1953, Ritter and Jimmy Wakely each recorded a rewritten version called "The Red Deck of Cards," in which the prescribed pack is no longer full of biblical reminders but is a Korean means of brainwashing POWs—a preview of *The Manchurian Candidate*.

The atom bomb also provided country with an entire subgenre of material. In the early fifties, the Sons of the Pioneers' "Old Man Atom" urged international cooperation to avoid a nuclear holocaust. Jimmy Dean's "Dear Ivan" had the star gently addressing a theoretical Russian farmer, assuring him that they both want peace and that, if they could only get together without any of their leaders around, everything could be worked out. The song is not that far from Sting's "I hope the Russians love their children too" lyric, three decades early and considerably less cloying.

Between 1965 and 1970, country entered its most militaristic era, starting with Johnny Wright's number-one hit, "Hello Vietnam" (immortalized for subsequent generations on the soundtrack to Stanley Kubrick's *Full Metal Jacket*). The verses of this smash (an early writing credit for Tom T. Hall) took a resignedly fatalistic tack ("I don't suppose that war will ever end / There's fighting that will break us up again"), but the chorus didn't leave much wiggle room for ambiguity or dissent, firmly establishing the idea that Vietnam was the first in a series of open doors the communists would walk through on their way to the California coast:

> I hope and pray someday the world will learn
> That fires we don't put out will bigger burn
> We must save freedom now, at any cost
> Or someday our own freedom will be lost

Anger at anti–Vietnam War demonstrators boiled over in the very titles of "The Minute Men are Turning in Their Graves"—you say you want a revolution, indeed—and "It's America (Love It or Leave It)." The latter, recorded by Ernest Tubb, was not his finest moment; he sounds at once cranky and too lazy to have done enough takes to master the meter. Johnny Sea's "Day for Decision," a Top 20 hit and title track of an entire LP of topical material, saw the decline of American morals and the possible rise of Hi Chi Minh as interwined. But with the tide beginning to turn even in middle America, these types of songs had mostly run their course by 1968, with the notable exception of the biggest anti-protest protest song of them all, Merle Haggard's "The Fightin' Side of Me," which lasted at No. 1 for three weeks in 1970.

Buffs would remind you that it would be a mistake to characterize as Republican country music or its audience at this time on the basis of overwhelming support for any military effort. "Remember, LBJ was the person who really got us involved in Vietnam," says Malone, "and if Kennedy had lived, he probably would have, too. I don't think those anti-protest songs were Republican, but those attitudes *became* Republican later, after 1968."

Indeed, JFK shows up as an iconic touchstone in some of these same songs. In "Where Have All the Heroes Gone?," Opry stalwart Bill Anderson takes aim at the flower children, but also defies easy stereotypes, in a ballad positioned as a reaction to coming across some kids he finds admiring a figure in a magazine, a "hero" of theirs who turns out to be "a folk singer who proudly claims to be both a member of a party alien to our government and a non-tax-payin' citizen." The song's narrator can barely contain his disgust and starts waxing nostalgic for "Winston Churchill, whose two fingers raised together meant victory, not just a let-your-enemy-have-it-all kind of artificial peace." But Anderson doesn't just take on hippies, he draws a bead on sports figures who indulge in gambling, girls, and good times instead of being role models. In the end, his list of suitable heroes is an inclusive one that runs the gamut from Charles Lindbergh, Ike, MacArthur, Gary Cooper, and Joe DiMaggio to the Kennedys, Martin Luther King, and Jesse Owens. And in "A Little More Time," hippie-maligning Harlan Howard could devote a whole verse to the divine mission of JFK, "a man loved and respected by I guess just about everyone"; Howard even presages Alan Jackson's "Where Were You" by a few decades when he sings about November 11, 1961: "As we gathered around our radios that afternoon, the whole world stopped a little while."

Guy Drake, who specialized in monologues of comic disgust, tried to follow up his anti-assistance hit song "Welfare Cadillac" with a pro-war 45 called "The Marching Hippies": "I think the thing that bugged me most was the rollers he had in his hair," he chides a protester, and, upon seeing a MAKE LOVE, NOT WAR sign, Drake mutters, "How he'd qualify for either one, man, is a sure enough mystery to me." But "Marching Hippies" was a flop, as was another of Drake's attempts to pander to the far right, "School Busin'." Even country music's most steadfast patriots were tiring of the fight, both abroad and on AM.

Bring the Foggy Mountain Boys Back Home:
The Politics of War as Hell

In the latter years of both the Korean and Vietnam conflicts, mournful singles began to appear, songs whose overwhelming sense of melancholy would be unthinkable as wartime expression in today's mainstream industry. When even anti-war activists are compelled to reaffirm support for the troops, as they are today, songs that are downers about the war dead would be considered unrecordable, major-league buzz-kills. In this time of callout research and unrelenting positivity, it may be difficult even to fathom that there was a time when folks went to town and eagerly spent their hard-earned cash on 45-rpm singles that could only be described as feel-bad hits of the summer, if not the stuff of pathological morbidity or sedition.

So consider the anachronistic oddity of the Louvin Brothers' remarkable 1961 album *Weapon of Prayer*. The siblings' re-recording of their apocalyptic fifties hit "Great Atomic Power" was a launching point for this patriotic-religious concept album, and if ever an LP was the complete antithesis of "we'll put a boot in your ass," to an almost perversely fatalistic degree, this was it. God forbid that any actual troops near the front were unlucky enough to find a turntable and slap on a war-themed album in which death looms or strikes in nearly every song. The cheery title track suggests that folks on the homefront can do their part for the war effort by becoming prayer warriors, but after that, it's all downhill toward that final landing spot under the daisies. These are songs in which soldiers warn their loved ones that they may have a "one-way ticket" to the front, and just such a fate is confirmed by the letters their families inevitably receive. The only good news for grunts who might have heard this morale-crushing stuff was that the Louvins seemed convinced all of us, not just soldiers, were about to meet our maker: "Great Atomic Power" seems to accept as a given that America will suffer a nuclear holocaust.

> When a terrible explosion may rain down on our land
> Leaving horrible destruction blotting out the works of man . . .
> There is one way to escape and be prepared to meet the Lord
> When the mushroom of destruction falls there is a shielding
>   sword . . .
> Will you shout or will you cry
> When the fire rains from on high
> Are you ready for that great atomic power

Radiation sunburns notwithstanding, the tone of this death-drenched album can very nearly be described as upbeat, as the underlying idea is that, for believers in Christ, heaven is just a grenade or nuclear blast away.

Some other less-than-jingoistic material also began to appear late in the Korean conflict, though not everyone saw the silver lining of eternal life in it that the Louvins did. "A Brother in Korea," sung by another pair of famous siblings, the Osborne Brothers, was written by their sister, Louise, about the enlistment of yet another brother, Bobby, in terms that can be described alternately as mournful ("He may never come home"), resentful (she describes "drunkards loafing around" in barrooms who haven't answered the call to war), and borderline-cynical ("It's sad, it's sad but it's true / He had to report over there / The people aren't happy unless they're fighting in a battle somewhere").

The era's oft-recorded "Rotation Blues" dealt with the misery of soldiers repeatedly sent back into action; draw your own contemporary parallels. In "Dear John Letter," first recorded by Ferlin Husky and Jean Shepard, a soldier learns that his fiancée is marrying someone else back home in his absence; in the final grim twist, the new groom turns out to be the soldier's own brother. This downer did not become a staple of USO shows, needless to add, though it did inspire a mildly spiteful "answer" song, "Dear Joan," as well as a happily-ever-after sequel in which the wife and her new husband agree to split up and let the original engagement resume when Johnny comes marching home.

The same emerging pattern of ruefulness became evident in the Vietnam years, as even mission-supportive country couldn't stay the nation's emotions as anti-war sentiment was crossing over from the demonstration lines to middle America. Loretta Lynn had the first jingoism-free war-themed smash of the Vietnam years with "Dear Uncle Sam," which hit No. 4 in 1966. The theme was a mother's loss, later also reflected in Wanda Jackson's "Little Boy Soldier," in which a mom takes her unwitting tot to meet his daddy's casket at the train station, and Jan Howard's heartfelt "My Son."

The most chilling and unlikely hit to appear while the war was still in progress was Arlene Harden's "Congratulations (You Sure Made a Man Out of Him)"; although obscure (it remains unissued on CD), this remains one of the finest anti-war records ever made, and more akin to Dusty Springfield covering Randy Newman than much else in the genre at the time. Harden's countrypolitan ballad shifts uneasily between major and minor chords as a wife or mother—it's not clear—details a close-to-home case of post-traumatic stress disorder: "Although he takes me to church every Sunday / He sits there but he doesn't pray / He keeps things inside like there's something to hide / And he gave up root beer for gin / Congratulations, you sure made a man out of him." With a title that mocked a ubiquitous military recruiting motto, and strikingly bitter admonitions like "It's no use to pretend / I admit it, you did it, you win," Harden's cynicism is clearly directed at the army itself. That the single made it only to No. 49 is less surprising than the fact that it was released and charted at all.

Another slightly bizarre entry in this subgenre was the Wilburn Brothers' "Little Johnny from Down the Street," which served as the title song for a 1969 LP whose cover pictures the brothers leaning against a white picket fence, gazing somewhat wistfully at a smiling, freckle-faced cherub of a boy. Nowadays, pedophilia might be the first thing the cover art brings to mind, but what the Wilburns really are is in this picture is Western-styled angels of death, because the song itself, otherwise an utterly zesty paean to small-town youth and innocence, ends almost incongruously with the title lad having "died in a foreign land . . . He made the biggest sacrifice, never had a chance to make Janey his wife." When even some of country's happy, uptempo dance numbers, like this one, were climaxing in the ugly and meaningless slaughter of America's innocents, it was safe to say something was up.

The biggest hit by far along these lines was "Ruby, Don't Take Your Love to Town," about a handicapped veteran who begs his able-bodied and apparently openly mocking wife not to go looking for love in all the wrong places, reminding her that if his legs don't work, his gun still does. Mel Tillis said he wrote it about a WWII veteran and never meant it to be an anti-war song, but it was widely and reasonably interpreted as just that. Johnny Darrell's original version had the greater impact in the country world, reaching No. 9 in 1967, though it was Kenny Rogers's 1969 remake, which was only a minor country radio hit, that had a huge impact on the pop chart. Lee Andresen, a noted collector and curator of Vietnam-related popular music, writes in his book *Battle Notes* that "although it was far from a favorite of the anti-war movement, 'Ruby' is regarded as the song that finally turned the public against the war." Kenny Rogers—tipping point for war sentiment? An arguable assertion, but stranger things were happening, in Hanoi, if not Hendersonville.

That Tennessee city's most famous resident, Johnny Cash, got bolder as the conflict dragged on, though he never explicitly came out against the war. Cash once remarked that anyone who didn't want to stand by

President Nixon should get out of the way so that *he* could stand behind him. But by the time he recorded "What Is Truth?," a No. 3 hit in 1970 that was equally inspired by the Christ-baiting biblical words of Pontius Pilate and the anti-war movement, there were cracks in his America-first façade. "Singing in Vietnam Talking Blues," a Top 20 hit in 1971, related an unnervingly shell-filled trip he and wife June Carter took to a "livin' hell" in order to entertain the boys. It firmly established country's pro-troops-even-if-we're-wrong mantra once and for all: "Whether we belong over there or not / Somebody over here loves 'em and needs 'em." The same year saw the arrival of Cash's signature song, "Man in Black," in which he spoke in nearly messianic terms, reminiscent of Tom Joad's concluding promises of benevolent omnipresence in the film version of *The Grapes of Wrath*. His renunciation of color, Cash declared, stood for every incurable social ill, with 'Nam the primary culprit for his limited wardrobe:

> I wear it for the sick and lonely old
> For the reckless ones whose bad trip left them cold
> I wear the black for mournin' for the lives that could have been
> Each week we lose a hundred fine young men

High-mindedness aside, Cash could also be heard to admit what any woman with a little black dress knows—that charcoal just looks cooler than baby blue—but this bit of self-mythologizing further ingratiated him with the urban folk crowd as well as his rural base. The Man in Black used his dual mandate to build all sorts of cross-cultural bridges, starting with his 1969–71 TV variety show, which found a lot of diehard country fans being exposed to the likes of Dylan, Joni Mitchell, and "Fortunate Son." Toward the end of his life, he recorded a Vietnam veteran–themed song, "Drive On," full of ambivalence both political and mortal ("Took 'em twenty-five years to welcome me back / But it's better than not coming back at all"), pragmatic acknowledgement of emotional irresolution ("My children love me, but they don't understand") and a sensible, no-nonsense joie de vivre. "Drive On" was a hit only within the closed circles of the Americana genre, but that very special episode of polarization in the United States known as the Vietnam era couldn't have had a better belated epilogue, even as a new chapter in the war song book was aborning.

Bootstrap City: The Politics of Money

Cash liked to joke that he "grew up under socialism," because his family back in Arkansas got a land tract under the terms of the New Deal. Through the mid-1960s, any references by country artists to the aid programs set in place by Roosevelt tended to be more favorable than not.

One prominent exception came from Roy Acuff, with his satirical song "Old Age Pension." For decades, while the South and the genre tended to lean Democratic, Acuff was the music's most renowned Republican. He was ahead of his time; his several runs for Tennessee governor as a GOP candidate were unsuccessful, though he occupied an arguably greater position, as unofficial king of the Opry, for decades. Acuff kept the politics offstage, except for this 1939 bit of whimsy that spoofed Social Security by picturing geriatric types too old to benefit from the dough they'd been compelled to invest in their youth:

> Grow a flowing long white beard and use a cane
> 'Cause you're in your second childhood, don't complain
> Life will just begin at sixty
> We'll all feel very frisky
> When our old age pension check comes to our door

In an era when Republicans are urging privatization, that song might be ripe for a remake, at least on the PAC circuit.

In recent years, most references country made to governmental aid have been derogatory. But for a time, country had sympathy even for those on the dole and railed against the feds only when farm foreclosure was imminent, as in Fiddlin' John Carson's "The Farmer Is the Man Who Feeds Them All." Blind Alfred Reed was one of the earliest hillbilly recording stars—despite the decidedly blues-sounding name—and the song generally considered to be his masterpiece is "How Can a Poor Man Stand Such Times and Live?," a 1929 track (memorably revived as roots-rock twice in the 1980s by Ry Cooder and the Del-Lords). Reed's lyrics are full of choice down-on-his-luck couplets like: "When we pay our grocery bill / We just feel like making our will . . ." Reed presented idyllic visions of heaven in some of his other songs, but in this one the church seemed less a universalist ideal than yet another place for the flock to get fleeced: "Most all preachers preach for gold and not for souls / That's what keeps a poor man always in a hole / We can hardly get our breath / Taxed and schooled and preached to death."

Blind Alfred's career was short-lived, quite unlike that of Uncle Dave Macon, who started singing professionally in 1917, when he was already in his thirties, and continued till his death in 1953, when he was the Grand Ole Opry's most beloved geezer. Macon sympathized with the downtrodden in early songs like "All In and Down and Out Blues" ("They'll take you to jail and if you can't make bond / Content yourself there, why you're certainly at home / I've got no silver and I've got no gold / I'm almost naked and it's done turned cold").

Cut to the late 1960s, and the emphasis has shifted radically when economic issues are raised; poverty is rarely the focus, except in the occasional Merle Haggard song like "They're Tearing the Labor Camps Down." Eyes are now trained on the bootstraps everyone is pulling themselves up by, and woe to those who milk the government for milk money. The most famous attack on the nonworking poor was one-hit-wonder Guy Drake's infamously snarky—some said nasty, or even racist—recitative, "Welfare Cadillac" ("Every Wednesday I get commodities / Sometimes four or five sacks / Pick 'em up down at the Welfare Office / Driving that new Cadillac").

Even Haggard, no scold when it comes to the destitute, has the bedraggled narrator of his "Workin' Man Blues"—a guy with nine kids!—boast that, no matter how bad things get, "I ain't never been on welfare—that's one place I won't be." By 2005, the prevailing attitude in mainstream country was largely the same: freshman artist Ray Scott, a traditionalist with an obvious liking for both Waylon Jennings's vocal style and conservatism, devoted a verse to that same kind of pointed self-sufficience: "You know, there's a whole lot of able-bodied takers out there in that welfare line / But you can bet old Uncle Sam ain't wipin' this boy's behind / Ain't no government cheese on this plate / I'm makin' my way."

That's pride, all right, but is it prejudice? You don't hear many songs in country anymore about the very bottom rung, which may be a result of country radio's increasingly mercenary need to target a middle-class, middle-aged female demographic that doesn't necessarily want to get spooked by songs describing desperate men one step away from the breadline. The men of country can sing in a general way about struggling to get by, but the spectre of unemployment is rarely if ever raised in the twenty-first century, rendering songs as desperate and heartbreaking as Haggard's "If We Make It Through December" strictly the stuff of nostalgia. For country stars who deal with real destitution, you almost have to go back to the mid-1970s, when Tom T. Hall recorded "America the Ugly," which made the then daring—and still daring—assertion that, until the United States gets its act together and takes real steps toward eradicating poverty, it may deserve some of the bad rap it gets overseas:

> There were some folks had plenty and some had none at all
> The enemy knows when a heart gets hard the country is bound to fall
> If we get hearts and heads together we won't have to hear them say
> America the ugly today

In 1975, Bobby Bare released an almost foolhardily brave concept album, *Hard Time Hungrys*, billed as "a concept by Shel Silverstein," who wrote most of the songs. The back cover is a stark black-and-white portrait of a homeless man digging through garbage cans. Interspersed among the songs are snippets of real-life interviews with down-and-outers, conducted by Bare and Silverstein in the style of Studs Terkel. It's a lively and often funny LP, but every one of its dozen tunes deals with economic hardship—not just those suffered by farmer types who then might still have been presumed to be country's core audience, though there was that ("A Mississippi farmer he's watchin' the sky wondering if it's gonna rain / The payment's due on the tractor, Lord, and the subsidy's been taken away"), but also the suburban moms who would later be recognized as the genre's target audience ("There's a Tennessee housewife shoppin' in the market wearin' her last used jeans / She picks up a roast then changes her mind, puts it back down and buys some more beans"). Despite having something for everyone—or everyone who's broke—Bare's recessionary song suite sold poorly, even despite coming right on the heels of the most successful album of his career; needless to say, this remarkable song cycle has never been reissued on CD. A lesson here for the country stars of the future: It's fine to allude to financial limitations, but don't go on too much and too long about seriously hard times unless you want to experience them yourself.

Running with the Devil: The Politics of the Campaign Trail

If we were to propose a pop-quiz question about the biggest country hit ever designed expressly to endorse a political candidate, we might field some guesses along the lines of Huey Long or, more recently, any given GOP candidate. Not so: Uncle Dave Macon's "Governor Al Smith" was a musical tract supporting a Roman Catholic from New York who ran for president on the Democratic ticket. It may not have hurt that the endorsee was running on an anti-Prohibition platform; with the song's calls for legal booze instead of moonshine ("many a good man's been poisoned to death") and its favorable references to rum, "Al Smith" was not just a political broadside but a classic country drinkin' song, too. Maybe because the end of Prohibition made it more difficult to reasonably combine those two genres, the list of recognizable country songs openly endorsing candidates is short. Rare further examples included Jimmie Osborne's "Ballad of Robert A. Taft," which sang the praises of a conservative Republican senator. And Lawton Williams had what was certainly the last national hit single ever to support a Democratic president, with "Everything's OK on the LBJ," which reached No. 40 in 1964.

The 1968 election saw a turn of the tide, with a good number of country stars coming out for Nixon or George Wallace, but none for Hubert Humphrey. Carter won back the genre, only to have the Democrats lose it in a big way thereafter. Loretta Lynn had stumped for Democrats before, but there was no question whose camp she was in after the Reagan years. "I can't even say that other guy's name," said Lynn, referring to Michael Dukakis as she thumped the tub for George Bush at a Republican rally in El Paso in 1988.

The 1992 GOP convention was filled with Nashville luminaries. A New York *Newsday* article had a field day pointing out their personal peccadilloes. "The actors and artists assembled to entertain the Grand Old Party in Houston are some of the finest in the land. But most of them would also seem to be at variance with what the Republicans consider to be a traditional lifestyle . . . Last April, [Lee] Greenwood married for the fifth time . . . On Family Night at the convention, Greenwood will be followed by Wynonna Judd, who broke up with her live-in boyfriend, Tony King, a few months ago . . . And then there's whisky-voiced country singer [Tanya] Tucker. She's a single mother of two with a lifestyle that should make Vice President Dan Quayle blanch . . . Tucker, who has two children out of wedlock, has been treated for alcohol and drug abuse and . . . has driven a car with a license plate reading, Ms. BAD ASS." Alert the media, indeed. The reporter even dug up a statement Tucker had made about Dan Quayle after the *Murphy Brown* brouhaha: "Who is he to call single mothers tramps?"

Bill Clinton didn't seem to care much about country, but that was okay with a lot of Southerners—he *was* country, to his core, sax-noodling Kenny G wannabe or not. But Gore's inability to connect with the main industry of his campaign base in Nashville (a *New Yorker* story said he needed directions to Opryland after having lived in town for a decade—not a good sign) seemed to signal the true extinguishing of whatever embers might have been left over from the late and lamented alliance between hillbilly music and the Democratic party.

Sadly, at least for fans of truly colorful political campaigns, the days are gone when candidates might do their own crooning—the ultimate crossover artists. We won't again see the likes of Opry legend Roy Acuff, well known for running for Tennessee governor; though unsuccessful, he did pick up more votes in his 1948 campaign than had any Republican in the state in any previous election.

Wilbert Lee "Pappy" O'Daniel helped pioneer the crossbreeding of country and politics. He was the radio announcer, emcee, and occasional lyricist for the well-known western swing group the Light Crust Doughboys in the 1930s before putting together a new band, the Hillbilly Boys, that made barnstorming campaign appearances with him when he ran for Texas governor in 1938. His run was successful—maybe it was the "Flour, Not Pork" slogan—and he became known as "the hillbilly governor." He went on to become a hillbilly senator when he defeated Lyndon Johnson in 1941, at which point he became known for being strangely, virulently anti-Roosevelt, despite earlier having penned the Doughboys' "On to Victory Mr. Roosevelt."

Perhaps the most famous crossover artist in this regard, seeming to give equal weight to music and governmental service throughout his life, was Jimmie Davis, the Louisiana governor and putative writer of "You Are My Sunshine." It's highly debatable whether Davis really wrote "Sunshine" or just affixed his name to a copyright he'd picked up for a few hundred dollars, as was his wont. But tunes like this and other hits for the singing cowboy-turned-actor helped keep the coffers full and ensured the treasure chest for his many campaigns was never empty. His music career was a target for opponents, who were among the first to learn that attacking country music isn't necessarily a winning proposition. "How you gonna debate a clown like that?" complained fellow Louisiana politico Earl Long. "All he gives them is music." One opponent, congressman Jimmy Morgan, is said to have held a rally of outrage at which he played "Red Nightgown Blues," a racy Davis tune from 1932 (sample lyrics: "We bought the license / Went to see Parson Brown / Corrine couldn't wait / And she throwed me down"). The addendum to this story—that Morgan's followers started dancing to the offending record—is probably apocryphal. As late as 1960, another foe, New Orleans mayor Chep Morrison, was complaining of songs in Davis's catalog that were "too filthy to quote in public." But it was hard to get the best of a singer-politico whose self-aggrandizement was so sharp that he was able to go to Hollywood and star in a heavily glamorized movie of his own life story, *Louisiana*, in 1947. Ironically, though Davis was known as one of the first hillbilly singers to have black musicians playing in his band, and he even recorded a duet with an African American bluesman in the 1920s, he went on to be known as an anti-busing segregationist in his last term in office in the 1960s.

Many politicos have tried their hands at songwriting or even making records. Senator Everett McKinley Dirksen's "Gallant Men" charted in 1967. West Virginia Senator Robert Byrd, a prominent Democrat, issued an album of fiddle music in 1978. Utah Senator Orrin G. Hatch, a Republican, has been the most noted dabbler in recent years, releasing patriotic and/or Mormon-themed records of his own like *Morning Breaks on Arlington*. Hatch is affiliated with the Sony Tree publishing house on Music Row and, among other covers, his "Everyday Heroes" was recorded by Brooks & Dunn for the soundtrack of the movie *Joshua*. Hatch's website (www.hatchmusic.com/songs.html) advertises no fewer than nine CDs, including such song titles as "America Rocks!" and "You Gotta Love This Country." His music isn't strictly aimed at fellow Republicans: he wrote a song especially for Vicki and Ted Kennedy called "Souls Along the Way."

In 1998, Emmylou Harris and Steve Earle visited House majority leader Dick Armey to lobby for greater copyright protections. Their reward, according to news reports, was getting to hear the Republican Texas congressman recite some lyrics he'd just written, for a song called "The Beamer Man." The tune was apparently a protest song against the titular type of driver, since Armey favors pickups. (Sample

Armey lyrics: "I'm the beep, beep Beamer man / I only give a damn about me, myself and my 320i.")

One of the great mysteries in political-musical crossover is whatever happened to an album recorded by a quartet that was alternately known as the Singing Senators and the Vocal Majority. The group consisted of four GOP senators: majority leader Trent Lott, John Ashcroft of Missouri, Idaho's Larry Craig, and Jim Jeffords of Vermont. On December 12, 1998, they went to Nashville and spent two days recording a ten-song album that has, from all indications or lack thereof, never seen the light of day. Fans of the quartet have to rest on their memories of the group's many public appearances, like the 1997 occasion when they joined the Oak Ridge Boys on stage in Branson, following a *Today Show* appearance in which the senators had covered the Boys' hit "Elvira." ("Seeing Senate Majority Leader Trent Lott singing 'oom-pa-pa-mau-mau'—it freaked us right out," said Oak Ridger Joe Bansall, no doubt speaking for millions.) At least collectors can keep hoarding the three albums released earlier by future Bush administration stalwart Ashcroft, dating back to a 1970s solo effort cut when he was Missouri's attorney general.

Most candidates, of course, have been content to merely let country songs blast out of the PA system, not their own Marshall stacks. Both presidential aspirant George Wallace and Georgia senator Zell Miller were serenaded by Tammy Wynette crooning "Stand By Your Man"—a questionable choice, given the lyrical inferences about the scoundrel of the title. Speaking of questionable theme songs, independent Ross Perot used Patsy Cline's "Crazy" as his, meant as ironic reference to the supposed nuttiness of his campaign.

This and other campaigns harked back, for some, to Robert Altman's 1975 film *Nashville*, which loosely revolved around an unseen populist presidential candidate trying to pick up support in the country community during a Tennessee primary. "In my opinion, the character of the political candidate predicted Jimmy Carter and, later, Ross Perot," the director said many years later. Altman wasn't entirely original in making celluloid hay out of the idea that country folk might be used for cynical political purposes: Elia Kazan's 1957 *A Face in the Crowd* had Andy Griffith as a contemptible guitar-wielding bumpkin who puts on a humble face and becomes a star while developing his own civil-service aspirations.

Accidental Feminists: The Politics of Sex and Gender

Blind Alfred Reed was progressive on some counts, but no one would accuse him on the basis of his 1920s recordings of a feminist agenda. For one thing, he seemed obsessed with the length of women's hair on a level shared by only the most ardent biblical literalists, to the point of repeatedly doubting that flappers would make it past the pearly gates. His "Why Do You Bob Your Hair, Girls," an indulgence in gender politics, was a treatise on the morality of hair length, admonishing women that "it is an awful shame, to rob the head God gave you and bear the flapper's name." (The recording of this song was so popular it merited a sequel titled "Why Don't You Bob Your Hair, Girls No. 2"—the switch from "do" to "don't" representing not a change of theology but merely a misprint.) Some charitable types believe that Reed must have had his tongue in his sexist cheek when he envisioned the heavenly wheat being separated from the chaff: "When before the judgment, you meet your Lord up there / He'll say, 'Well done—for one thing, you never bobbed your hair.'" However, judging from the earnestness and religious severity of some of Reed's other songs, he probably wasn't kidding—though some of his 1920s listeners may have been swayed toward iniquity, figuring a hell full of Louise Brooks look-alikes was an all-right place.

Five decades later, this attitude was still alive, if not entirely well. In 1975, Johnny Paycheck told women to take their feminism and shove it with "All-American Man," possibly the boldest anti–women's lib anthem ever to make any hit countdown this side of Saudi Arabia. Paycheck baited the same fundamentalist instincts Blind Alfred had appealed to five decades earlier ("God made man for himself / But he made you for me"), though he probably got more traction by adding a sort of ERA=fewer female orgasms sub-argument ("I guess you won't be satisfied / Till you're workin' 9 to 5 / So you can say you're bringin' home the bacon / Well, of all the tragic things in life / It's a woman who don't want to be a wife / Missin' all the love we could be makin'").

But country has always had a soft spot for strong women—more so than any other genre, on a consistent basis. Call it steel magnolia syndrome if you will. But supposedly progressive rock & roll was so slow on the grrl power uptake that the femme-led group Heart was still considered a novelty act well into the 1980s. After a period in the early

nineties in which alternative rock was taken over by the Alanis and
Courtney brigades, female rock in Y2K had retrogressed to the point
that months went by without a single woman appearing on *Billboard*'s
mainstream or modern-rock airplay charts. Hip-hop also seemed to
back away from its brief flirtation with real feminists in favor of Lil'
Kim types. But country has almost always had some tough cookies entering and sometimes leading the fray, whether they spoke in words of
empowerment or not. With the possible exception of Joni Mitchell,
there may have been no more crucial female singer/songwriter in the
twentieth century than Loretta Lynn.

"Loretta's songs are fascinating because she has taken what were
basically personal sentiments and made them culturally pervasive
and significant political statements," says Chet Flippo. "'The Pill' was
a very radical song for its audience, and many country-radio stations
banned it, but I think it was accepted by women country fans because
it was a message addressed especially to them, it was coming from
one of their own, and it hit home. With that and other songs of
strength and empowerment, Loretta was pretty much the one-woman
women's-liberation movement in country music. No one else talked to
the stay-at-home-moms, to the blue-collar women, and Loretta never
pondered the consequences of taking a stand."

Here's the most fascinating irony of all: Loretta insists that she
made the country world safe for aggressive feminism in order to . . .
please her husband.

"Mercy!" says Lynn. "I was right in the middle of that"—the feminist movement of the 1960s—"and I didn't understand why. All of the
women lib people was coming to my shows, getting interviews, and
they'd say, 'You're breaking ground as a singer. What do you think
about that?' But I hadn't thought of it until they reminded me—
'You're the first woman to do it this way or say that.' Well, I might
have been, but I didn't think so. I was just doing what I could do. I *had*
to. Doolittle believed in me, and I had to make him proud of me."

Lynn says she didn't encounter much overt chauvinism as a rising
star in the early sixties; the resistance came mainly in the form of cat-
tiness from other female singers, not the menfolk. But occasionally a
kind of sexism did rear its old-school head.

"You know, I had this song called 'Don't Tell Me You're Sorry, Because I Know How Sorry You Are.' Me and Ernest Tubb was recording [duets], so I wrote that for us. Ernest looked at me and he said, 'I'm

not singing that.' I asked him why. He said, 'I'm not saying I'm sorry!' So that kind of jolted me a little." She put it in the drawer till it was time to change partners. "And when Conway Twitty started recording with me, he said, 'I like the song—*I'll* do it.'"

Today, songs that could reasonably be described as feminist, like Amy Dalley's "Men Don't Change" and Terri Clark's "Girls Lie Too," regularly appear on country radio without much flak. The tone of Clark's song almost borders on the emasculating at times, with its utterly sarcastic assertions that male-pattern baldness is pleasing to your average gal and that—gulp—"size don't matter anyway." It would be interesting to see how far a lyric that bold would go on pop radio.

One song that did briefly raise a ruckus was Garth Brooks's "We Shall Be Free," one line of which was widely viewed—correctly, it would seem—as pro–gay rights. "When we're free to love anyone we choose / When this world's big enough for all different views / When we all can worship from our own kind of pew / Then we shall be free," Brooks sang, in slightly stilted, well-meaning, protest-era-invoking language. There was grumbling in the not always gay-friendly South, but he got away with it because he was Garth, the thousand-pound gorilla in the room. As another superhero once said, with great power comes great responsibility . . . as well as a free pass to say something moderately controversial once every few years.

Surprisingly—or not, depending on your take on Southern justice as well as feminism—country is the form of music that's been most approving of a practice not always smiled upon in polite society: murdering an abusive husband. The Chicks' Earl is far from the only one who's had to say good-bye in this genre: Garth let a woman let her husband have it with a shotgun in "The Thunder Rolls," and even meek Martina McBride sang not altogether disapprovingly of a wife-beater going down in a burning house in "Independence Day." (Yes, the chorus of that Martina tune *is* Sean Hannity's theme music, and yes, he knows it's not about the Fourth of July.)

Xenophobia-philia: The Politics of Exclusion and Détente

The Carter Family's "No Depression in Heaven," a song that the alt-country movement of the 1990s would take one of its many names from, represented the Depression as a fulfillment of biblical prophecy.

The tribulation would be followed by an afterlife in which there would be "no orphan children cryin' for bread; no weeping widows, toil or struggle." Which was not to preclude the coming storms that would "sweep lost millions to their doom." The title notwithstanding, to those who might want their depression relieved without additional doomsaying, this wasn't exactly musical Prozac.

More encouraging, for some, would have been the startlingly inclusive vision of heaven in the Carter Family's 1940 recording of "There'll Be No Distinction There," a cover of a 1929 tune by Blind Alfred Reed. The Carters and Reed painted a portrait that could have inspired the final scene of the film *Places in the Heart*, which similarly takes place in the kind of egalitarian country chapel that could only be found in the afterworld:

> In the same kind of raiment and the same kind of shoes,
> We'll all sit together in the same kind of pews,
> The whites and the colored folks, the gentiles and the Jews,
> We'll praise the Lord together and there'll be no drinking booze,
> There'll be no distinction there

Flash-forward to the early seventies when the anti-protester climate had abated and, for a few brief moments, the nexus of country music seemed to be one big summit meeting where the bikers in *Easy Rider* and the hillbillies in that truck quit exchanging middle fingers and buckshot, and just broke bread instead. Nixon's downfall was something most parties could agree on, and in "Watergate Blues," Tom T. Hall managed the impossible task of creating a fun talking-blues hit that dropped names like McGovern, Muskie, and Eagleton. It was, if anything, very nearly open season on hawks, as Jerry Jeff Walker cut "Up Against the Wall, Redneck Mother," which invoked Haggard's name on a list of ignorant bubba-isms. Détente between hippies and rednecks was further established in Bobby Bare's "Redneck Hippie Romance," about a marriage between representatives of the formerly warring factions:

> Because I realize you'll never love Hank Williams
> And I don't like the Rolling Stones a bit
> And all my friends have short hair and smoke Luckys
> And all your friends have long hair and smoke shit

> So go and roll yourself another reefer
> And I'll go pour myself another beer
> And please don't ask me why we can't give it one more try
> Because I'm too drunk to tell you baby
> And you're too stoned to hear

Haggard had his own paean to generation-gap-transcending love, not quite as vivid or profane as Bare's, but still fun, and maybe less doomed: "We don't agree on nothin', but I'll be danged if we don't make a pair / My friends call her 'hippie' and her friends call me Big Time Annie's square."

The 1970s "outlaw" movement, which included Willie Nelson, Waylon Jennings, Tompall Glaser, and Jessi Colter, wasn't particularly political in nature—Willie's and Waylon's politics were very different, for starters—except perhaps in its ecumenical spirit. But think "politics and country" in the eighties and nineties and that road inevitably leads to the whisky-spattered door of another would-be outlaw, Hank Williams Jr. His reign seemed to signify an end to the days of openness to liberal ideas—though most country partisans like to blame the early eighties *Urban Cowboy* fad, and its attendant bull-riding and line-dancing, for ruining the genre for a decade or two. The music was getting slicker and blander, and Hank Jr. would have seemed like just the kind of rounder who could keep it tethered to its rough-and-ready origins and still produce hits. But for all his booze-swilling swagger, Hank Jr. was as much an in-law as an outlaw when it came to toeing a certain kind of conservative—some would say reactionary—line. Bocephus's lyrics increasingly relied on shtick, the production more on shlock. And all of a sudden, "outlaw" music consisted of extreme-right vigilante bravado, backed by bad electronic drums.

Some years later, Trent Lott would be forced to resign as senate majority leader for suggesting that the country would have been better off under a Strom Thurmond presidency, but Hank Jr. received no such censure for "If the South Woulda Won," which avoided some of the stickier issues of a Confederacy-victorious alternate universe but did address some benefits:

> If the south woulda won we woulda had it made
> I'd make my Supreme Court down in Texas and we wouldn't have
>   no killers getting off free

> If they were proven guilty then they would swing quickly,
> instead of writin' books and smilin' on TV
> We'd all learn Cajun cookin' in Louisiana
> and I'd put that capital back in Alabama
> We'd put Florida on the right track, 'cause we'd take Miami back
> and throw all them pushers in the slammer

The Cajun part sounded good—and who'd want to risk whatever the singer's penalty might be for not partaking? Thus emboldened, Williams Jr. embarked on a series of far-right songs, such as "I Got Rights," in which the narrator exercises his Second Amendment duty by killing the scoundrel who murdered his family and was set free on a technicality by some pantywaist judge. "A Country Boy Can Survive" mourned the death of a friend who was mugged in New York City, suggesting again that vigilantism and cultural separation are the twin safeguards against such evil. After 9/11, Hank Jr. rewrote the song as "America Can Survive," redirected at terrorists instead of street thugs.

Perhaps his best remembered war anthem—possibly thanks to the most creative use ever of the word "sassafras" in a song—is "Don't Give Us a Reason," released during the first Gulf War and directed at Saddam Hussein:

> Yeah we've heard all your threats and you're gonna fret yourself to
>   death
> My advice is, don't give us a reason
> You can take that poison gas, and stick it in your sassaphras
> Don't give us a reason
> Yeah I'd like to find out, just for fun, just how fast those camels run
> I'll tell you son, don't give us a reason
> No the desert ain't Vietnam
> And there ain't nowhere to run
> And we got the real top guns

After a while, you may get the impression that Hank Jr. never needed much of a reason. This 1990 smash wasn't often revived during the second Gulf War, maybe because the urban landscapes of Iraq *did* provide insurgents with places to run, rendering moot Williams's mockery of the enemy landscape.

Hank Jr.'s attitude lives on, to a less chest-thumping degree, in aggressively toned songs like Travis Tritt's "When in Rome," which tells a visiting city slicker what's what, with the warning that "when you're at the courthouse before Judge McCall / You'd best not say a word 'bout them commandments on his wall—naw." The duo Montgomery Gentry's 2004 hit "You Do Your Thing" represents an interesting case of trying to have it both ways. Its libertarian-sounding title promotes mutual tolerance, but the lyrics clearly suggest that citified, sissified liberals will never tolerate conservative Southern values, which may mean that all bets are off. This message is particularly pronounced in the video for the song, which portrays the singers driving back into town from a hunt with a deer on the hood, returning the stares of tony al fresco diners with their own looks of disgust.

"I think it's part of the broad mosaic of country," says CMT's Brian Philips, who aired the video. "At any given time there will always be a macho 'don't mess with me' song, which is kind of what the Montgomery Gentry is. It's like 'A Country Boy Can Survive,' which talks about the evils of the big city, and which in the early eighties probably made a lot of people in Tennessee and Georgia and Alabama in small towns think, 'I ain't never goin' to one of those big cities. They got all kinds of bad things happening there.' But that's a legitimate point of view. It's a little scary sometimes, if it starts to border on the survivalist."

Philips agrees that the message of the Montgomery Gentry song may be slightly confusing, given its ominous tone. "Are we really a country where I'll do my thing, you do yours? I feel like that may mean one thing if we're talking about gay marriage and a different thing if it means you want to take my gun away. I think what it really means is more 'my way or the highway,' in context. Do they really want to leave you alone if you live a life that somehow messes with their ideals? If you had a few drinks with 'em, would they really want you to go your own way and live in a peaceful world? Maybe, I don't know. But you've got to wonder. I don't think 'you do your thing and I'll do mine' means quite the same thing it did in the sixties," he laughs.

Already Gone: The Politics of the Expats

In the Bush Sr. years, Lee Greenwood's "God Bless the USA" became a new national anthem, forever to be heard as the soundtrack to fireworks displays directly before or after Neil Diamond's equally overexposed "They Come to America." Randy Travis helped make country safe for neotraditionalism again in the mid-1980s, but as a big Bush supporter, his contributions to the war effort—"Points of Light" and "America Will Always Stand"—rank among his least appealing or enduring recordings. Waylon Jennings's "The Eagle," recorded in 1986, came into popularity a few years after its initial release, when it was embraced as a prescient back-to-war anthem ("Lately I've heard rumors that the eagle may be lame / Just because I've been idle don't mean that I'm tame").

Meanwhile, a steady stream of more liberal-minded folks were getting the hell out of Dodge and quitting mainstream country. Ironically, an inordinate number of them had been signed to their deals by Tony Brown, a notorious conservative and, as one of the most revered execs in Nashville, someone with an ear for strong, independent artistic sensibilities. Steve Earle, Nanci Griffith, Allison Moorer, the Mavericks, and Lyle Lovett were all MCA artists who had their brief time in the mainstream and drifted to the alt world. Canada's k.d. lang—a Warner act who'd once worn old-school cowgirl outfits, worked with Owen Bradley, and claimed to be literally the reincarnation of Patsy Cline—abandoned the shtick and got out right after pissing off the beef industry with her pro-vegan stance, but before coming out as a lesbian.

It wasn't only the fresh crop of eighties signings who found themselves in political hot water. Kris Kristofferson, who'd been accepted as part of the Nashville firmament since the late sixties, became an extraordinarily political and polarizing figure in the eighties and early nineties thanks to his sentiments on American involvement in Central America. Although he'd once written that hit country song, "Vietnam Blues," about a soldier who stands back in disgust as he watches antiwar protesters, by 1990, he was writing tunes that seemed to accuse American collaborators, the Nicaraguan contras, if not the U.S. airpower that protected them, of being like the "baby killers" of My Lai. Imagine the unsuspecting concertgoer who came to hear "Help Me Make It Through the Night" only to be surprised by verses like: "I heard there was a baby / Somebody heard her crying weaker through the night / They beat her mama bloody / And shot her with her daddy / It was the terror from above / El Aguila del Norte."

Ironically, Kristofferson's transformation happened at about the same time that the heads of his new label were attempting to strengthen his position as a country artist, partly because he was finding new notoriety as one fourth of the Highwaymen, an occasional supergroup that also included Willie, Waylon, and Johnny. Just when he thinks he's out, they drag him back in, offensive politics and all.

"When I first started performing, it was in rock & roll folk clubs like the Bitter End and the Troubadour," Kristofferson recalls. "But eventually I was working in places where I *was* getting a mostly country audience. I just felt it was my duty to tell the truth as I saw it, and in some places it didn't go over very well. I can remember one time down in Atlanta—which I had always considered a friendly town because they had made such a big hit out of 'Why Me,' being the first ones to start playing that on the radio—about three hundred people asked for their money back at a show I did. I was talking about Oliver North and the contras and what we were doing around the world.

"I remember Jackson Browne telling me years ago, 'Listen, man, you're taking a lot more chances than we are, because your audience is so much more conservative.' And that may be true. I guess I first started speaking out back in the eighties or at the end of the seventies. But I have a much more receptive audience today, because I think more people have had the experience that I had—they love their country and want to believe in it, but it's hard to accept that we're doing those people in Iraq any good. If you look at the pictures of what we've done to Iraq, for Christ's sake, there's no way we can ever repay those people for flattening their cities and killing their kids—and we're not even trying to."

Bringing this sort of stuff up at a Highwaymen gig didn't always end in backstage kudos. "I mentioned the bombing in Iraq or something in the middle of one of the songs I was singing. And Waylon really got mad, because Colin Powell was in the audience. I didn't know that when I sang it," he laughs. "I probably would have sung it anyway. But that was Waylon—always upset about something with somebody. Nevertheless, he was also backing your play, you know. He was like a brother."

The traditional country audience has finally deserted Kristofferson, for the most part, and now he attracts crowds whose younger members sometimes only know him for his character roles in such recent movies as the *Blade* trilogy. "I was doing a show in Sweden about a year ago, and somebody backstage said, 'There's all these kids out there saying "Geez, Whistler sings?"' If you're realistic about it, some of these kids weren't even born when I was better known for the songwriting."

Kristofferson realizes now that some of his angriest albums of the late eighties and nineties might have been a little over the top, and he's striving to find a more palatable balance in his live shows, but you won't find him apologizing for his drift over the years. "Everything is political," he insists. "It just sounds worse if you call it political. I mean, we're talking about life and death and the things that matter."

Different Drums: The Politics of Stage Banter

Here is Kristofferson's initial benefactor, Johnny Cash, introducing another lefty-to-be to an unsuspecting public, back in the late sixties:

"Right now I'd like you to meet a young lady, a very lovely young lady, that I really think has what it takes to be around for a long, long time to come," Cash tells the studio audience on the third episode of his network variety series, *The Johnny Cash Show*, broadcast June 21, 1969. "Enjoy with me a very pretty sight, because she sings just as pretty as she looks. The exciting sounds of Miss Linda Ronstadt!"

In her television debut, Ronstadt sings a gender-switched version of a Waylon Jennings tune, "Only Mama That'll Walk the Line," then is joined for a chat by the show's host, who says, "You sure sing pretty. That's R-O-N-S-T-A-D-T. I'm sure you're gonna be hearing a lot more of that name from now on. Where you from, Linda?" Arizona, she says. "I used to go out there in my jeep huntin'," says Cash. "You ever go jackrabbit huntin'?" "I never could pull the trigger," she giggles. Enough talk: "Let's do an old Carter Family song," he suggests, and they duet on "I Never Will Marry."

Cut to 2004. Ronstadt never did wed, though she famously dated a Democratic California governor, Jerry Brown. As I reach her on the phone in Phoenix, it's a few days before the election, and she's taking a break from doing door-to-door canvassing with Arizona's Democratic governor. That peculiar name, the one Cash tried so hard to imprint on his viewers' minds, has been on country fans' minds thirty-five years later though it's one that might go down in infamy for some of them. She, too, has gotten herself Dixie Chicked.

"We're determined to get Arizona to vote for Kerry," she says, explaining that she's going to help drive people to the polls. "If this country reelects George Bush, I'm gonna be deeply disappointed in what that means for the culture. We're gonna have to throw up our hands. Because the first time he stole the election, but if they turn around and elect him, what it really means is, they love this war. And then what? Everybody I know is saying 'Maybe we should move to Canada, maybe we should move to Spain.' But unfortunately, everything everywhere is tied to the American economy, which is about ready to fall on its face. And George Bush is racking up debt like crazy to the Chinese to finance this war. He's turning around and giving all the power to people who are a bigger threat to us than the Iraqis ever were."

It's been so long since Linda Ronstadt was considered one of the leading lights of country-rock that it's not always easy to remember she was considered a star in that format, producing number-one country singles throughout the seventies. Still, she still has enough of a following that her recent controversies have been covered in publications like *Country Weekly* magazine. It's safe to say that conservative country fans still comprise a share of her fan base. She's not overly concerned with keeping them, her interests having drifted since those days of Carter, Waylon, and Hank covers toward traditional Mexican music and pre-rock pop standards.

"Growing up in Arizona, I heard a lot of country music and obviously have great respect for it. But there isn't country music anymore, really," says Ronstadt. "It's mall-crawler music. Because there barely exists an agrarian lifestyle. I grew up in it, on the last ten acres of my grandfather's cattle ranch, where our neighbors were all farmers and ranchers. I didn't even have a path to put a bicycle on—I had a pony. You had to have hooves if you wanted to get around in those days. And I have great respect for the music that comes out of those agrarian traditions. I love it dearly. But really, that's not what country music is anymore. Country music is suburb music. And there's some wonderfully talented people that do it, and they're entitled to do it. But I don't feel like I'm part of that Nashville thing. I didn't grow up down there, I'm from the Southwest, and I'm a Mexican American. I do Mexican American agrarian music now!"

In 2004, it was widely reported that Ronstadt had been kicked out of a Las Vegas casino. Each night on tour, she put in a plug for Michael

Moore's film *Fahrenheit 9/11* just prior to closing the encore segment with "Desperado," which she'd decided would be her small way of contributing to the discourse without making quite as polarizing a statement as she might like to. Supposedly, this dedication to Moore had gotten her boos, walk-outs, and even some tossed cocktails before she was escorted off the premises at the casino owner's request. She remembers it a bit differently than the legend that got printed as news, saying she never heard any adverse reaction and didn't learn she'd been "thrown out" until days later.

"I was leaving, and some woman came up to me and said, 'I'm sorry, you can't leave. I'm told to keep you here till the owner of the Aladdin gets here. He wants to talk to you.' Every time I've ever played at the Aladdin, there's been a fight, because those guys run those hotels like little city-states. If they've got some rich gambler who's gonna lose a lot of money, in order to encourage them to continue on in the great myth of Las Vegas they take him around backstage and introduce him to the people performing there. I said, 'He's not on my backstage list. I'm not talking to anybody.' But she said, 'Well, I won't let the car leave until he gets here.' So my assistant and I took the suitcases out, hopped on the bus with the band, and that was the end of that. I didn't even know they were mad. I thought she wanted me to stay because he was bringing some fool gamblers around! I'm not a TV watcher, so I didn't even know this was in the news until forty-eight hours after it had been cooked up. They didn't throw me out, but what they gave me inadvertently—and I'm very grateful to whoever the fellow was that wanted to meet me at the Aladdin—was a bigger audience to recommend Michael Moore's movie."

Her most recent album at this time brings her full circle, in a way: she sings "Never Will I Marry"—not the Carter Family tune she did for Johnny Cash thirty-five years earlier, but the Frank Loesser show tune. It's a running theme, obviously. She has adopted children, and insists the difficulty of packing them up is the only reason she won't be fleeing for Canada or Spain if Bush's star remains ascendant.

The question remains: Can't the audience rightfully count it as a broadside if a pointed, partisan comment pops up at the end of an evening otherwise devoted to pre-rock standards and romantic pop? Martha Hume's commentary on the ferocity directed at the Dixie Chicks—if they'd been remotely political up to that moment, like a

Cash or Haggard, their jibe might have gone unreported—may apply here. Setup and context are everything: If Barbra Streisand knocks Bush, it goes with the territory; if Barney the Dinosaur does it, hell will break loose. But Ronstadt says her fans should have seen it coming.

"My politics were always there from the beginning, with all the No Nukes concerts that Jackson Browne, James Taylor, Bonnie Raitt, and I did. It *is* a hard one, because you don't want to stand up there preaching too much. Jackson took a stand with the business that was going on in El Salvador in the 1980s, but it really cost him. And then you have a smaller audience to speak to, you know? I didn't want to get up and make the whole show about the election. I had made one remark early on in the tour in the middle of a show about George Bush, and the audience, instead of getting mad at me, started getting mad at each other. So I thought, what positive thing can I do that's at the end of the show, so people don't have to get in a big fistfight with the guy across the aisle in the middle of the show? That's when I decided to give my 'Atta boy' to Michael Moore each night before the final encore. The only place we got a truly nasty response was at Wolftrap, outside of D.C. There were a lot of Republicans there, including some people from Bush's cabinet. Republicans are notorious pottymouths, as Dick Cheney has proven on the floor of the Senate. So that's where I got 'You bitch!' But it was generally very good-spirited everywhere else— even in Las Vegas. I just felt, as a citizen, it was irresponsible of me to not try to do something, because this could be the most important election we'll have in our lifetime. I think it's comparable to the Weimar Republic in Germany, before the Nazis took over."

The "I Love the Eighties!" Party: The Politics of Nostalgia

No form of politics is quite so pervasive in contemporary country as the politics of looking backward. During times of trial, like the Vietnam era, this took the form of songs like "God Bless America Again," originally written and recorded by Bobby Bare and later remade as a duet by Loretta Lynn and Conway Twitty. Rather than partisanship, the song pleaded an earnest kind of prayerful ignorance: "You know I don't understand everything I'm readin' here about what's wrong with America / And if you don't have a lotta book learnin', I guess there's a lotta things you don't understand," they sang, prefiguring Alan Jackson and his "simple man" "Iraq and Iran" confession by a few decades. "But let me say this, God, she's like a mother to me . . ." The upshot: a troubled nation needs the Almighty to step in, "like you did way back when it all began."

Here's a strange but true political split: if you spend very much time pining for the good old days, chances are you're a conservative. If you spend time trying to get laws enacted to keep business from ruining what little is left from the good old days, chances are you're a liberal. Bobby Bare straddled that divide in an early concept album, the nostalgia-themed *A Bird Named Yesterday*, released in 1967—which actually shared some themes with the Kinks' *Village Green Preservation Society* but beat it by a year. Song titles tell the tale: "Somebody Bought My Old Hometown," "The Day the Saw Mill Closed Down," "They Covered Up the Old Swimmin' Hole"—with corporations shouldering some of the blame in the lyrics, mostly penned by Cowboy Jack Clement. The most poignant number, "The Air Conditioner Song," credits the onset of AC for the downfall of community civility once mandated by life lived out on the front porch.

Move forward to the 1990s and 2000s, and country singers are still pining for the past, as ever; see Rascal Flatts' boomer-baiting smash, "Mayberry." In contemporary country, though, in place of truly heartfelt paeans for a better time, we mostly get list-making, or lyrics as trivia contests. Probably no song in the early years of the twenty-first century was more irritating in this regard than a Mark Wills smash called "19-Somethin'." It makes Billy Joel's "We Didn't Start the Fire" look like the very model of trenchant narrative analysis as Wills simply reels off everything the writer thought was cool in the seventies and eighties, from Farrah Fawcett-Majors and *Star Wars* to Daisy Duke and parachute pants. Even those details, he can't get completely right: Pacman, which debuted in 1980, is placed in the verse enshrining seventies junk culture.

There's probably a reason they're country singers and not history profs. Keith Anderson's 2005 song, "Three Chord Country and Rock & Roll," mentions the singer's grandfather reminiscing about how "he kicked Hitler's butt in 1942," but the more relevant lines venerate old Bocephus and Aerosmith songs. When most young country stars think of God bestowing his blessing on America, they think of the 1970s and 1980s. The amount of country tunes that have actually name-checked classic-rock hits and artists of that era in the last few years is staggering. The standard setter remains Kenny Chesney's "I Go Back," which directly cites "Jack and Diane," "Keep on Rockin' Me Baby," and "Only the Good Die Young." (Though the tune commemorates a dead friend, "Don't Fear the Reaper" missed the cut.) Tom Petty and John Mellencamp are the real gods of this new generation of country, with the Boss running third, if lyrical citations and encore choices are any indication. In the course of one month, I saw both Keith Urban and Andy Griggs cover "Free Fallin'" in concert, while Chesney's nightly set recently included "Hurts So Good," just to scratch the surface. It must flatter and alarm Mellencamp, a legendary rock liberal, to know he's now a symbol of country conservatism too.

The Race Is On: The Politics of Color

Uncle Dave Macon is one of the most important figures in the development of country music and the Opry in particular. If he isn't as heralded today as some of his contemporaries, this may have to do with ditties like an old perennial he once popularized, "Run Nigger Run." An argument is sometimes made that, for its time, the song wasn't really racist—after all, it's advising an escaped slave to hurry, not stumble and get caught, right?—but other songs in Macon's catalog, like "New Coon in Town" and "The Coon That Had a Razor," suggest that he might not have been first to join the desegregation marches had he lived into the sixties.

Macon was hardly alone in performing this type of material. A recent major-label boxed set of recordings by proto-bluegrass pioneer Charlie Poole was obliged, for the sake of history, to include a golden oldie called "Coon from Tennessee." Happily, race-baiting—which was encouraged by the Northern labels that recorded these Southern crooners—was mostly a thing of the past by the 1930s. It did live on, overtly, in underground recordings made by the likes of the pseudonymous Johnny Reb, whose outrightly ugly tracks continue to be widely disseminated on the Internet by collectors who are post-modern aficionados of transgressive material, or racists, or both.

Yet country music has proven remarkably open, at the right times, to songs and personalities that address race in provocative ways. "There's no way the world will understand that love is color-blind / That's why Irma Jackson can't be mine," Merle Haggard sang, in an ode to thwarted interracial love named for the song's black romantic interest. In "The Ballad of Ira Hayes," which reached No. 3 in 1964, Cash made a particular point of addressing Native American themes and issues, and later that same year recorded an entire concept album, *Bitter Tears*, about the treatment of Indian cultures, cleverly using it as an opportunity to address civil rights in general. Waylon Jennings took an almost confrontational tack in the chorus of his 1980s hit "America": "The red man is right to expect a little from you / Promise and then follow through, America."

In 1975, Tanya Tucker had a hit with "I Believe the South Is Gonna Rise Again," one of the few successful country singles ever to address the racial divide head-on.

> Our neighbors in the big house called us redneck
> 'Cause we lived in a poor sharecroppers shack
> The Jacksons down the road were poor like we were
> But our skin was white and theirs was black
>
> But I believe the South is gonna rise again
> But not the way we thought it would back then
> I mean everybody hand in hand
> I believe the south is gonna rise again

Its writer was Bobby Braddock. Asked if he still feels that hopeful now, he observes, "Things are both better and worse than I thought they would be. In many ways, there is a familiarity between Southern whites and blacks, far more intimate than the relationship between the races in other regions; this was evident in the special kind of rapport Clinton had with African Americans. Yet, there is an underlying prejudice so embedded that it will take more than a few laws and a generation to erase; for instance, today few self-respecting Southern whites will overtly display race prejudice when blacks are around, but many still use the word 'nigger' behind their backs. Opposition to integration was the first issue to start the Republicanization of the South."

Charley Pride and his producer, Cowboy Jack Clement, have said that Pride met with almost across-the-board acceptance and little or no overt racism as a black country singer when he arrived on the scene in the mid-sixties. His first single was sent out with no picture, to test radio's acceptance of a black cowboy, but once programmers and DJs learned the truth behind the tease, most seemed to have no problem with him. Pride had a run of more than a dozen number-one hits, starting at a time when much of the South was still in freak-out mode over segregation, and he was named Entertainer of the Year by the CMA in 1971. Given that triumphal reign during a theoretically less enlightened era, why hasn't a second Charley Pride come along in the last forty years? Are blacks in country music on a quota system, and, if so, is there a way to bump it up from one per century?

Big & Rich are determined to make Cowboy Troy, the rapper who made a guest appearance on their debut album, the first black country star since Pride. Their shows already take on a P-Funk aura, with six-foot-four Troy holding down one end of the stage and a three-foot dwarf named Two-Foot Fred anchoring the other, in their attempt either to live out their MUSIC WITHOUT PREJUDICE motto . . . or maybe just be a little freaky.

"There's enough prejudice in the world already, man," says Big Kenny, the first half of Big & Rich. "The one place that there shouldn't be prejudice is in music. I mean, we have prejudice in religion, we have prejudice in color, we have prejudice in the workplace, we have prejudice against handicaps. There are so many prejudices in the world that it's like splitting hairs finding 'em all. But if there's one thing, by God, where prejudice should never exist it's music, because music is the universal language of love and tolerance and acceptance. It's the greatest cathedral in the world . . . In the second verse of 'Live This Life,' we sing, 'I met a girl in a chair with wheels but no one else would see her.' Do you know how many people would have actually approached Two-Foot Fred last night if Two-Foot Fred wasn't part of our world? They'd think 'Oh gosh, that's weird, I can't be near that.' But put him on stage, hand him a beer, and put your arm around him, and now everybody wants to get his autograph."

"We like to take our stage and force people to look at things," says John Rich, the duo's other half. "We got your attention, right? Good. Because now we're gonna force you to look at this: a black rapping cowboy." The terminology is deliberate. "I didn't call him an African American. Troy says, 'I ain't never been to Africa, doubt I'll ever go. I'm an American, by God, and I'm a black American guy,' But people say, 'He just called him a black guy! Oh my God, is that okay, to call him that? Oh, okay.' He calls himself a blackneck.

"We are believing that a lot of country radio stations are going to at least play it once or twice, just to see what happens, because it makes great radio—just to stir up the debate. I don't expect them all to play it. They're not all even playing Big & Rich, so how can you expect 'em all to play Troy? But Troy, the thing is, country is so devoid of color and of racial integration in its music that people like the CMT network, the Academy of Country Music, the Country Music Association, the ACMs and the CMAs, are already wanting to put him on their shows doing his first single. Because first of all, the music kicks ass. Second of all, it's important that country start joining the rest of the world in the year 2005 here. We're acclimated to a red and yellow, black and white world, man." The phrase "red and yellow, black and white" comes from the gospel chorus "Jesus Loves the Little Children of the World"; it shows up again in Troy's multilingual anthem, "Wrap Around the World," and was adopted in acronym form as the name of Big & Rich's new label, RAYBAW Records.

Before Big & Rich became famous or even released their first album, I went to see them do a promotional show at a nightclub in the middle of nowhere in central Texas. It was as true a country bar as you could find: every man there had a hat, and any man who didn't felt profoundly naked. There was a lot of two-stepping, and just a little line dancing, for an hour and a half straight. It was like a scene right out of an imagined 1950s. And then, out of nowhere, "Baby's Got Back" came out of the sound system, and suddenly every Joe Bob in the joint and his girl were grinding like it was 1999. Yet when Big & Rich came out, marrying those two sensibilities, there was great befuddlement in the land.

"Country people like to shake their asses too. They're not sure they like hearing a rap on our record, but they'll sure as hell dance to it," says Rich. "Yeah, they'll dance to a 'Baby's Got Back,' but Kenny does a spoken-word passage in 'Save a Horse (Ride a Cowboy)' and they're saying, 'Keep rap out of country,' and shit like that on the message boards. Those are the same people who are out bangin', bouncing up and down to Nelly records."

Speak of the devil . . .

We have Nelly on the line. Tim McGraw is joining us on a conference call. It's two days after the presidential election. The people of America have made their choice: "Over and Over," a duet between hip-hop superstar Nelly and country superstar Tim McGraw, is probably the fastest-rising single in recent American Top 40 history.

"Who would have ever thought it would work?" says McGraw about this wholly unexpected crossover success. It's not receiving any country radio airplay, but CMT is showing the video on a regular basis, making "Over and Over" arguably the first real joint R&B–country hit since Ray Charles conquered both charts in the 1960s. "The only reason it works is because Nelly and I are the same guy, really, in a lot of ways. We grew up in different areas and around different people, but we love our family, we love our business, and we treat people well."

Ironically, McGraw has a separate song topping the country chart at this very moment, and it's "Back When," a humorously nostalgic ditty in which the narrator laments, "They put pop in my country / I'm reading *Street Slang for Dummies*." So maybe someone on the hip-hop side should do a similar song in the wake of the Nelly hit, complaining, "They put country in my hip-hop."

"I think Nelly should do that: 'They came in and fucked up hip-hop, put country in it'," laughs McGraw.

"But I think that's why it works," Nelly says, "because everybody knows hip-hop was born within the inner city and the urban community, and we've been able to branch it out and expand it so much that it's become one of the most popular forms of music on the planet. And country's the same way—they both come from those kind of poverty-stricken communities and expand out. So putting those together, it's gonna work—it just has to be done right."

Speaking of the unexpected: I mention to McGraw how people have been putting two and two together on his political inclinations: First, he said he was an admirer of Bill Clinton, which suggests that maybe he missed the memo about all country stars being Republicans; then, he said he was interested in running for office someday. So, maybe, *he's* the one who could turn the South Democratic again.

McGraw laughs. "I would hope. But you know, the only thing I have to say about the election now is that it's time for everybody to come together and do the best thing for our country, the best thing for individuals, and let's pull some people up. That's what I want to do. That's what I'm all about—pulling people up."

Nelly chimes in: "I think we made a difference in that we were able to get so many people out to vote. I know that the outcome may not have been the way a lot of people expected—definitely not to my liking . . ."

"Mine, either," says McGraw.

"But it is what it is," continues Nelly, laughing. "I think we had to take steps, and the first step was to get many people in urban music community registered to vote who weren't registered before. We got the hip-hop community involved in this election, and for many elections to come. You've got to look at that and see the beauty in *something*." Another bittersweet chuckle.

"I agree that we got people out to vote and that's the biggest deal," says McGraw. "Now a whole generation of people are gonna be involved in politics that might not have been before. And also, we've got a president. We might have wanted a different president, but he's our president and deserves our respect, and now let's go forward and see if we can get some things done."

No immediate McGraw for President campaign plans? (His equally famous wife launched the Faith Hill Family Literacy Project back in 1996; if ever anyone was born to be First Lady . . .)

"Tim, you gotta run for office," Nelly pleads.

"Nelly, that would be a good ticket, don't you think, man? You and me?"

"If you'd let me handle the paper. Let me be the secretary of the Treasury."

Not counting the Dixie Chicks and Nelson, McGraw is the only major country star in recent years who's been willing to admit he's a Democrat in good standing. Even that has come about slowly, in baby steps. The fledgling organization called Music Row Democrats tried to get him publicly on board, but he wasn't down with that. There had also been some hope in the Vote for Change organization of putting together an all-country bill that would have hit the road before the election, independent of what the Chicks were doing. One female freshman artist told me she'd been approached by her agents in L.A. and asked if she would go out on such a tour, headlined by McGraw. She was still weighing whether this would help or sabotage her fledgling career when word came back that McGraw had decided not to do it. Which doesn't make him a coward by any means, any admission at all is a brave thing these days.

A week later, during CMA Week in Nashville, I sit in on a press conference for radio DJs held jointly by McGraw and Kristofferson. Organizers had gingerly inquired ahead of time whether Kristofferson would stay off politics; naturally, his reps balked at that request. Surprisingly, it's McGraw who broaches the verboten subject, briefly. In a

spirit of fun, a jock points out that McGraw had made disparaging remarks about Southern California in the past, then asks if there's any
hypocrisy in the fact that he and his wife have purchased a second
home in L.A., since they've both taken up acting.

"Aw, you just want to hear a Democrat flip-flop," he quips, getting
a big laugh.

A programmer in front of me starts grumbling about the indignity
of having to hear a couple of Democrats spout off, even though this is
the only remotely political remark of the evening. His comrades josh
with him, tell him to calm down and buck up. It'll all be over in a few
minutes, and they can get back in their car and get some rest before
the following night's CMA Awards show, which will feature a more re-
assuring array of Bush-backers, including Sara Evans, Montgomery
Gentry, Darryl Worley, Toby Keith, and your hosts, Brooks & Dunn.

Ain't No Rag, It's a Designer Piece: The Politics of the Flag

In the 1990s and on into the new century, flag-burning was epidemic
in America. At least in the imaginations of a handful of country music
alarmists.

Merle Haggard continued to have his conservative moments in the
years that followed "Fightin'," his 1970 hawk anthem, and in 1989, he
recorded a lament over the Supreme Court's decision to allow protesters
to destroy the flag under free-speech protections. "Today they ruled
to burn Old Glory down," he sang, "and only me and crippled soldiers
give a damn." Johnny Cash had his own anti-flag-burning number, the
Marty Robbins–penned "Song of the Patriot," which may represent
the low point of his career, as he halfheartedly croons: "I'm a flag-
wavin' patriotic nephew of my Uncle Sam / A rough-ridin' fightin'
Yankee man . . . / When I see Old Glory burnin', my blood begins to
churnin' / And I could do some fightin' of my own." Johnny joined his
brother Tommy Cash on "Thoughts on the Flag," written by Tom T.
Hall as a somewhat more thoughtful response to flag desecration.
Charlie Daniels's "Ain't No Rag, It's a Flag" spoke for itself.

On the red carpet at the 2004 CMAs, both members of Montgomery Gentry are approaching, and as much as one might always be
inclined to get out of the way of the crazy-eyed, linebacker-sized Eddie Montgomery, that instinct is even more pronounced now. He's

wearing a black designer jacket with a glittering flag embroidered on the back, along with a message that is a not-so-open invitation: TRY AND BURN THIS ONE, it reads. He's a regular rhinestone commie-baiter.

The previous day, I'd visited the shop of Manuel, the legendary designer of celebrity Western wear, who has costumed everyone from Elvis to Dwight Yoakam to John Lennon to Emmylou Harris. (He did those famous jackets worn by the Flying Burrito Brothers of yore, including Gram Parsons's legendary marijuana leaf jacket.) A visitor raised the subject of the TRY AND BURN THIS ONE jacket he'd just finished for Montgomery. Why work on something that . . . inflammatory? "Because I'm a fucking whore," the famously blunt Manuel explained, shrugging his shoulders.

It's just a few days after the presidential election, and the CMA red carpet *does* seem a bit like a valedictory receiving line with Bill Frist on hand, as well as some members of the White House staff. I act as a defensive block just long enough to ask Montgomery if he's happy with the results of the electoral process. He does a slight dodge.

"Man, in America now, what I want more than anything is everybody to be united. In fact, that's what it's all about," he says—meaning the war effort, apparently—"so everybody across the whole world can have parties like this everywhere. Maybe, hell, we can have the CMAs over there [in Iraq]—who knows? I think it would rock."

It's controversial enough that the 2005 CMAs have been scheduled for Manhattan instead of Nashville, but he'd like to go even farther afield and hold 'em all the way over in the Middle East? "Hey, you know what," says Montgomery, "if it's good enough for our heroes over there, it's good enough for me."

Tennessee-based ex-VP Al Gore was one of several major political figures to address the newly formed Music Row Democrats, founded by country music executives in anticipation of the 2004 election. AP PHOTO/JOHN RUSSELL

6

The Donkey Under the Elephant
in the Room

Music Row Democrats Come Out

Music Row Democrats. It has a ring to it, no? Kind of like Skid Row Neocons or the Savile Row Riflemen's Association or Log Cabin Republicans—it has the weird inevitability of anything so inherently oxymoronic.

For years, it was assumed that the business behind country music was as conservative as the public face some of its Republican activist artists put on it. In this regard, plenty of people on either side of the political spectrum will tell you that nothing has changed. "I think if you were to run it down, there are sixty-some-odd people on the CMA board of directors. It's probably 70 to 80 percent Republican, if not more," says Universal Music Group Nashville cochairman Luke Lewis. "The rest of us are a pretty serious minority at this point. For someone to have a perception that the industry leaders were all Democrats or liberals, I think they're way, way off."

But others beg to differ on the executive imbalance. "Seems to me like it's pretty split," figures Lee Ann Womack. "I would say right down the middle. Saw *huge* support for the left in Nashville this time around."

By "this time," Womack means the lead-up to the 2004 election, which found Music Row Democrats making the leap from theoretical self-contradiction to organized reality; head honchos at four out of five of the town's major labels coming out as Dems; a large turnout of worker drones as well as bigwigs for beat-Bush events; and . . . almost no major radio-friendly country artists fessing up to being Kerry supporters.

Tim DuBois is the cofounder and copresident of Universal South Records. He looks and sounds like a good old boy, which is why so many young Democrats were surprised to see him at the MRD meetings, though the fact that his partner, Tony Brown, is a known conservative, may have something to do with that, too. "One of the things that got me involved in the Music Row Democrats was the way that country radio treated the Dixie Chicks," DuBois says, "and the fact that nobody who had a forum within our community—including myself—stood up and said, 'Wait a minute. I might not exactly agree with what she said or how she said it, but she certainly had a right to say it, and to start having CD-burning parties really is out of place.' As a result, some of the best music that's been made in this format got pushed off of our radio dial in a lot of places. My involvement came from that, and from the fact that I was opposed to this war from the beginning. I saw it coming, and I felt like it was a war of choice for America, which I don't believe in. That's what got me up off of my chair and made me politically active for the first time since my early twenties."

MRD founder Bob Titley, the former comanager of Brooks and Dunn, sees a trifold purpose in the org's origins. "Certainly the Dixie Chicks were a big thing at our first two meetings—what happened to them and that nobody in the community stepped up in their defense. That carried us forward to the election, since it was the Chicks' concerns about Bush's policies that got them in trouble." That was their second, and for a time biggest, focus. "But thirdly, I believe that the impact the 1996 telecommunications bill had on our industry brought home in a graphic way how profoundly one piece of legislation can affect our world . . . Most people live in a world where government policy feels a little bit disconnected from the real world and kind of abstract. But for the country-music industry, deregulation was a real, concrete connection"—and a disaster. In a nutshell, the corporate consolidation of radio that resulted from relaxation of ownership rules led to ever more restricted playlists, thanks to the conglomerates' tendency to rely on callout research instead of local programmers' gut instincts, not to mention zeroing in on even narrower demographics to sell more targeted ads and provide the all-important "shareholder value."

But wait. Wasn't it Bill Clinton who signed the deregulation bill? Yes, and his name is mud even among many Democrats in Nashville, who believe he helped precipitate the ruination of the country radio format with a single signature. Every time a mediocre song goes to No. 1 because Clear Channel, Cox, and Cumulus thought it would hit undiscriminating soccer moms right where they live, someone on Music Row is using Slick Willie's photo as a dartboard.

At the time Music Row Democrats was first organized, some of its members felt a twinge of paranoia, wondering whether anyone associated with it might face being Dixie Chicked themselves. "I think at the first few meetings, people were looking over their shoulders," remembers Fletcher Foster, marketing VP at Capitol Nashville. "They thought 'Okay, if I run real quick from my car to the building, nobody will see me.' But after the first three meetings, when we opened it up to all of Music Row and all of a sudden there were a thousand people at the Belcourt Theatre, seeing that strength in numbers, people started to get energized."

Not everyone felt trepidations about coming out, as it were. "I never felt any of that paranoia," says Sony Nashville head John Grady, dismissing talk of early nervousness among the ranks. "It's just about freedom of expression. I never had that kind of conversation with anybody, and I went to a few meetings."

On the other hand, while Luke Lewis is not usually the yellow type—he's more likely to go down as the most candid label head in the history of the industry—he'll admit to a moment or two of hesitation. "For a while I felt kind of oppressed, that I couldn't speak my mind or it would have been harmful to the people who work with me and the artists I represent," says Lewis. "And so I couldn't take a position publicly, or even very discreetly in a private way, on how I felt about the war and what was happening to the Dixie Chicks. Because what happened to them was terrifying to me. Having been in Nashville for twelve years, I realized full well that the mainstream country business was populated by—and I'm talking about industry and artists both—conservative-leaning Republicans. But their political viewpoint didn't manifest itself in any sort of an ugly way, where it felt like it was impacting your life in a personal way, until the Chicks' thing happened.

"Until this group formed, we had been pretty underground. My peers who are leaders in the industry and also Democrats had felt stifled and kept quiet for a while, because it would have been harmful to our business." But after Music Row Democrats' membership rolls went public, Lewis says he "never felt any retribution. And maybe I had been misreading the climate. *Possibly.* But all of us had our radar up pretty high to see whether somebody might try to retaliate in some way, by not being right by our artists. And I didn't sense that."

Paul Worley is the chief creative officer of Warner Nashville, and a producer of recent records by Martina McBride, Sara Evans, Cowboy Troy, and Big & Rich, as well as the first two major-label Dixie Chicks albums. His activism was actually just starting to cool down when the Music Row Democrats were starting to ramp up. "Early on, I was out marching, and when the president came to do a family-values conference, I stood out in the snow with my wife, carrying a sign that said WAR IS NOT A FAMILY VALUE. It got on TV. Then I felt conflicted, because in this job I represent the business interests of a lot of people who don't agree with my political philosophies. And it would be a shame if their careers were impaired because of my public display of my beliefs. So I rethought what I was gonna do, and found a less public way to share my resources and help the causes that I believe in. And that didn't always feel good. I had to talk with Natalie one day and I told her that I wanted her to know that although I've always supported her and that I agree with her, I felt shame for pulling back publicly, and I told her why. I'm not sure if I know exactly how she felt about all that, but we did have a conversation about it."

But at least one other exec in the organization delights in being on TV, if only to tweak some of his old pals. "I'm the guy who put Brooks & Dunn together," brags Tim DuBois. At least it *sounds* like a boast. "Their music has been played by the GOP so many times, it makes me wish I hadn't put 'em together . . ." Um . . . "Just joking. But to show you the light-hearted back and forth that goes on around here, Music Row Democrats had a get-out-the-vote event down in front of Shoney's where we had a bunch of press people. It was a rainy morning, and I went down to the garage to get my raincoat, and there was a Brooks & Dunn umbrella. So I took it and had it up in the rain all day down there—because I knew it would irritate Ronnie!

"I don't have a problem with Kix and Ronnie. They hold strong convictions. It's not like they're doing it for additional exposure. They truly want to see those ideas win. I disagree, but I don't have any problem with it. Anyway, some publication ran lists of which musical artists supported which political side. You had John Mellencamp and the Boss and P. Diddy and all these people on the Democratic side. On the other side you had Brooks & Dunn and Charlie Daniels and then Pat Boone and some real pablum. I sent it to Ronnie and said, 'Hey, they forgot to put Lee Greenwood on your side!' My message was, which side of this do you want to be on?"

With most of the top label presidents on Music Row having come out as Democrats, the perception persists among some artists in the industry that, although they themselves are conservative, the fan base is conservative, and radio is conservative, the liberal middleman, in the form of top-label brass, is resistant to putting out their kind of messages.

Joe Nichols is one of the relative young 'uns who helped usher in a welcome new wave of neo-traditionalism shortly after the turn of the decade. With those traditional sounds came some traditional values. For his second album, *Revelation*, Nichols cut a song called "If Nobody Believed in You," one of several to be released around the same time that mixed God-talk with everyday anecdotalism. In the first verse, a Little League player gives up because his angry dad lacks faith in him. In the second, an elderly man decides to forgo his driver's test because of his own children's disdain for his efforts. In the concluding verse, which takes quite a broad leap, the singer wonders if God might just give up, too, in the face of humanity's indifference toward Him. This is preceded by a middle-eight in which the disappearance of prayer from public schools is decried.

"There's a message in that song that probably not a whole lot of artists or record labels are gonna touch," says Nichols. "But a lot more people out there share that opinion than Nashville thinks. The whole song is great, but it's that message in the third verse, that knockout punch, that *makes* it." He chuckles over how people tend to perceive Music Row, as opposed to the reality. "If you live outside of Nashville, you might think it's the conservative capital, full of old country boys running the show. But they're not."

DuBois, cochair of Nichols's label, responds: "Well, I don't think he's that far off the mark. I certainly didn't agree totally politically with that song, but at the same time, it was a statement that he wanted to make, and something that he wanted as a single, and there were people within this building obviously that wanted it to be a single. So I wasn't going to stand up and go, 'I don't think so.' It certainly wasn't a statement that I was bothered by Joe making at all." But as for the split between artists' sensibilities and execs' sensibilities, "I think he's probably right on."

For Worley, working so closely with Sara Evans was "very stretching. I love Sara and her husband, Craig Schelske. Disagree with 'em on just about everything, but I find them to be kind people. We worked through our differences, but, yeah, we had some doozies of discussions, until we finally just quit talking about it." When Schelske made his unsuccessful run for Congress in Oregon, Worley made an early donation, "which I regret only because it put me on the Republican mailing list. Jesus Christ, I just gave the guy a little money! Anyway, Craig thanked me, and I said 'Look, you know that I don't agree with a lot of what you stand for, but I know that you are a kind and good man, and I respect your desire to give your life to public service. I also believe that once you get elected and start representing a constituency, it's gonna stretch you, and you're gonna realize that your point of view is not the only one that has validity. You're gonna grow to understand what it is that people think that's different.' And we kind of agreed to go along that way. And since then, I can't tell you how many times I've written to the Republicans saying 'Don't send me any more of this shit!' I got a signed picture of President Bush that was just the biggest joke around my house."

Dangerous Learning Curves on Chet Atkins Drive

Songwriter Marcus Hummon, who also tilts left, has his own set of personal ironies. "The humor of it for me is that Dick Cheney was introduced at the Republican national convention with Sara Evans singing 'Born to Fly.' That's a song that I cowrote with her and Darrell Scott, who's also sort of a rabid Democrat/left guy. That's sort of a synthesis of what working in this town is like if you're on the left."

Hummon used to record for Sony, though now his concerts are pretty much restricted to writers' nights. "Sometimes when I'm performing, I'll do a couple of the things I wrote with the Chicks, 'Cowboy Take Me Away' and 'Ready to Run.' I tell about how my kids never have made the differentiation between the artists and myself. To them, those are my songs, and the Chicks just happen to be singing them. I remember one morning my eight-year-old saying 'Daddy, they're burning your records.' I picked up the *Tennessean*, and there on the front page was somebody in South Carolina holding up the *Fly* record and, with his children, burning it. I have to say, I found it amazing, amusing, and sad."

In Nashville, Hummon is an institution, married to a fellow local institution, the Reverend Becca Stevens, chaplain of St. Augustine's Episcopal Church on the Vanderbilt University campus and a well-known social justice activist. They're not liberal isolationists, by any means; Hummon and Stevens do charity work together alongside socially minded conservatives in town like Tony Brown and his *Nashville Star*–judging wife Anastasia. But Hummon had his culture-shock years.

"I grew up thinking conservatives were just nuts—you know, really not well!" he laughs. "That's an ism, too, and I've had to throw off the shackles of a lot of that." Because Hummon's father was in the State Department, he grew up moving around overseas, assimilating into different cultures, with the pictures on the walls of moderate-to-liberal family heroes like Martin Luther King, Bobby Kennedy, and Lyndon Johnson being the main constant.

Upon his on arrival in Nashville, in his late twenties, "the first wave where I realized that I wasn't in Oz anymore was when I was signed by a company that had a large contingent of evangelical Christians. And I had been brought up by parents who were Christian but also in a multicultural context. For example, while we lived in Saudi Arabia, during the Carter administration, Christian services were illegal, but it was a tradeoff to the American government, in order to have a presence there. We didn't have the luxury of having separate places to worship, so it became a remarkable ecumenical experience. For me, it also transferred into a sense not only of ecumenicism within Christianity, but also a multi-religious experience. I grew up with Christian parents who talked about how beautiful Islam is. Suddenly I was in Nashville, and they said songwriters should go to a Christian prayer meeting, and I thought, 'Well, that would be a great idea.' I didn't know anything about Christian music, or how evangelical Christendom differs from mainline denominations. We'd talk about our writing and our experiences, and it was fascinating—again, like a new culture. People would pray in a certain way, and it was invigorating. But I remember we got talking about Buddhism, and I was recalling that when I was at Williams College I really loved Thomas Merton, that I'd gone to a Trappist monastery, and that I thought

Buddhism was beautiful and instructive. I remember this absolute dead calm after making that comment. It may seem funny now, like 'Of course, you idiot, you don't talk about Buddhism in Nashville, Tennessee, at an evangelical Christian writers' meeting!' Anyway, a couple folks said, 'Well, that's all fine and good, but of course, these individuals, if they don't profess Christ in their life, they're gonna roast in hell, basically.'" Hummon laughs at his own naivete. "And so things come to you in waves, and you begin to understand. There's the surface, and there's this strong undertow of sentiment that relates to politics and religion. And the South is unique and exciting and scary at times, too," he laughs.

He's not the only lefty in town farming out songs to artists on the right. "If I could point to one group that's the most Democratic or slightly culturally left, however you want to call it, it would probably be the writing community, to some degree," Hummon says. But even there, he says, folks are sometimes afraid to speak their minds. "You have to remember, people are genuinely afraid. They're vocationally frightened, after seeing what happened to the Chicks."

But in terms of the messages it's able to communicate, country is a mixed bag. Some messages are clearly not allowable under any circumstances, like "Fuck tha police," or "I got ninety-nine problems and a bitch ain't one," or "Just so you know, we're ashamed that the president [fill in the blank]." But then, there are messages that aren't allowable in any other popular-music genre that flourish here, such as: *I wish I'd been there when my mama died. I miss my husband in Iraq. Babies and old people rule. If I die, take care of my kids for me.*

"One of the things I love about country is that we don't have to finesse saying 'I love you'—we just say it. We don't have to apologize for how we feel about family," says Hummon. "And in that sense, I feel terribly comfortable here. Whereas sometimes in New York or L.A., there is that sense of the latest, hippest thing we have to cater to, and I'm just not interested in that at all. That's one of the reasons why a place like Nashville is a great home for a guy like me.

"I cowrote Rascal Flatts's new single, 'Bless the Broken Road,' which is the fastest-moving song right now in country music, and it actually has a sort of God component. Those guys have joked with me about being liberal, and I know at least a couple of 'em are very, very conservative, and we just try to leave it at that. But I can imagine people hearing the song Rascal Flatts has done and thinking, 'Oh, the writer of that is obviously this wild Christian evangelical, very much a part of that world.' And I'm not." (Rascal Flatts member Jay Demarcus acknowledges the political gulf between the band and Hummon, but adds, "Politics aside, I know that he does have a heart for God.")

"It says at the end, 'God bless the broken road that led me to you.' The line comes from a talk I had with a guy in a bar who had been through a terrible divorce and had made a lot of mistakes, and he was very candid about it. But he looked at his life and, he told me, what came out of that experience was that he met a woman and fell deeply in love. And so he began to look back on his life, not as if God had literally manipulated all these events to lead him to his own moral malaise . . . but sometimes you have to look back on events and simply take a position of, if you believe that God is somehow making all things right—if this is somehow an essential Christian belief, which I would argue it is—then brokenness takes on this other component."

Hummon considers Sara Evans "a dear, dear friend," and he describes their friendship warmly. "I have stayed up late at night with her husband, who is sometimes on *The 700 Club*, talking about these very issues. She still befriends me, still writes with me, still cuts my songs, and I still adore her and her family. But I have real strong feelings about, for example, how the Christian right can feel comfortable about the idea of a preemptive strike without clear evidence of eminent threat. How they think that that is a Jesus position . . . I don't believe in literal biblical inerrancy, but I know that my brothers and sisters on the right claim to be about biblical literalism. How they're able to pull the militant response of the United States out of the gospels is an absolute riddle. I would love to have it explained to me. I don't like Christianity being hijacked." The evangelical position on gays tests his patience, too.

Hummon has lately been writing theater pieces that have been produced in Nashville and off-Broadway (one is a musical drama about a fictional Charley Pride–type of black country star). He says he encounters a different kind of resistance in New York. "You have to be candid about who you are, even if, when you're working the coasts, it's not always appropriate to talk about God. Working in pop music or theater, I have found that people respond to me sometimes by saying, 'Well, why do you want to bring the God thing into it?' And I might say, 'Well, because God's in my life.' People then immediately tag you as, oh, you're the right-wing Christian agenda. And I'm like, 'No, actually, I'm a Christian man who is adamantly opposed to that position.

And let me tell you why.' And then, you know, all the fun's gone," he laughs.

Political Code Words and Punchlines

Tracy Gershon has a picture on her office door of kitties romping in a field. Next to it is the caption EVERY TIME YOU VOTE REPUBLICAN, GOD KILLS A KITTEN. Abandon all hope, ye overly sensitive conservatives who enter here. Gershon is A&R director at Sony Nashville, and familiar to many TV viewers as a judge on the first two seasons of the USA Network's *Nashville Star*. She was stunned when she went to her first Music Row Democrats meeting, "because I thought it'd be ten people. I kept looking at people going, 'I could've sworn they were Republicans!' I thought 'Tim DuBois? Really?' You start feeling better, because it is almost like your dirty little secret here." Then she points toward the exit. "Well, you see my door? Obviously not *my* dirty little secret," she laughs. Plastered there next to the divine threat to cats is a Kerry/Edwards sticker, plus a fake *Time* magazine cover that circulated for a while after the election, featuring the headline WE'RE FUCKED. "Mark Wright [the second-in-command at the label] and I have door wars," Gershon adds. "I'd put something on his, and then there'd be an anti-Kerry thing on my door." She says she feels a degree of safety knowing that John Grady, who's boss over both of them, is a Democrat. "Because if he wasn't, maybe I couldn't do this stuff."

If you examine the top two positions at several of the Nashville labels, you notice a coincidentally bipartisan pattern. Sony has Democrat Grady on top and Republican Mark Wright right under him; the Universal Music Group has liberal Luke Lewis and conservative James Stroud in the top spots; Universal South has its own guys on either side of the aisle, Tim DuBois and Tony Brown, as cochairs; and so on . . . As for the political breakdown among the actual ranks of these or other music-related companies, it's hard to tell. Lewis is on the board of the Country Music Association and figures that its members are 70 to 80 percent conservative, maybe more. On the other hand, CMT's Brian Philips says that most of the cable channel's management-level staff were "heartbroken" the day after the 2004 election—but as a Viacom company that's been known to import people from sister channels like MTV and VH1, that skew may be the exception, not the rule. At Sony

Tree Publishing, which is headed by Republican activist Donna Hilley, the makeup of the company is mostly GOP, according to tunesmith Bobby Braddock, who figures he's well in the minority there.

What's clear is that Music Row has been revealed as a true melting pot of the kind rarely found in American residential or employment life anymore. It makes for many a tense moment as folks try to feel each other out—as well as some exciting ones as people who respect each other sometimes discover they're ideologically at odds and end up having substantive debates from across party lines, something you don't often find on the Upper West Side or in Birmingham.

"There still exists a sort of code approach language that people here have," says Paul Worley. "As you're sitting with somebody, maybe getting to know 'em for the first time, there's a little dance that people do to figure out whether to go there or not, probing ways of talking and looking that you can use to subtly let somebody know where you stand, that if they want to pull out, it's okay, and that if they go in, they may not like what they hear."

The Devil Went Down to GAC

These meetings of the minds don't always end with pleasantries and politeness. There was the locally famous case of Tamara Saviano, who, the week right before the Dixie Chicks controversy blew up, was fired from her job as operations manager at the Great American Country cable channel—CMT's competition—over a tiff that had to do with Charlie Daniels.

"The truth is, I wasn't very happy at GAC," Saviano says now. "Everybody else in the Nashville office reported to me, and after the election of 2000, it became very clear that I was the token Democrat in the office, and I lost the respect of everybody who works for me because they are such hardcore right-wing Christians. I was the crazy liberal. Two weeks before I got fired, we had an Iranian woman calling from L.A. to request a song, and she had a very unusual but beautiful Persian name. So during the show I had to tell my host several times how to pronounce her name so she would get it right when she was on the air. And after the show was over, the host said 'What kind of a name was that?' I said 'A Persian name, she's Iranian.' And the whole staff, including the host, started using derogatory terms like 'towelhead.'

And I stopped the show and said 'You know what? We're done for the day. We're gonna do a rerun. I'm not working on any of this.' And then I went and called my boss in Denver, who's a Democrat, too, and he said 'You know what, Tamara? You're running the place, and if they don't like it, they can find other jobs.' And then, two weeks later . . ."

Publicist Kirt Webster had sent out an editorial Daniels had written for his website, titled "Open Letter to the Hollywood Bunch," that was openly contemptuous of Sean Penn and others who were expressing resistance to the imminent invasion of Iraq. Saviano says she received the e-mail three times from Webster, ignored it the first time, said "Please take me off your list" the second, and got angry enough the third time to send out her own open letter to a bunch of like-minded friends, copying it to Webster. In it, she suggested that perhaps Daniels was due for a taste of his own medicine, including boycotting. It was clearly not an official GAC statement, but her company signature did appear on the e-mail, so Webster wrote to higher-ups at the channel, to ask whether a TV special they were embarking on with Daniels was in danger.

After Webster contacted her bosses, Saviano complained to Webster, who, she says, further complained to GAC, claiming intimidation. "It just got out of hand," says Saviano. "It got down to the point where my boss said to me, 'Look, Tamara, you know I'm on the same page as you. But the new company policy is, you can't be involved in politics. You can't go to anti-war rallies. You can't discuss politics with anyone in the music industry.' I said 'Well, I'm not willing to do that.' I could have saved my job there if I would have agreed to those conditions, and I just wasn't willing to do that, because to me, it's not about politics, it's about a way of life as Americans. I can't separate the two.

"So they came in the next day and they had a gag order they wanted me to sign, that I would never talk about what happened—and for that they were gonna give me two weeks' severance. I told them to keep it. And I left, and it just so happens that all my friends are either in the media or they're publicists, because that's the world I live in, so then it just exploded . . ."

The week after Saviano was fired, the Dixie Chicks' controversy flared, and Saviano well remembers her feelings as she saw the CD smashings on TV. "People were bringing kids to watch. It did change the way I felt about the country-music industry and those artists and the fans. I thought, You know what? I can work in the Americana world, which is more in line with my musical tastes and politics. And they do go hand in hand for me. Because with me, it's not just politics. It is my philosophy on life."

Saviano ended up changing careers and becoming a publicist, concentrating on Americana acts with a left-of-center bent, like Kristofferson. "By choice, I don't work with any major record labels, because I don't want to work with big corporations. I don't want to work with—with all due respect—the Darryl Worleys of the world that are so philosophically different from me." Her own story ended happily enough: she won a Grammy in 2005 for producing a Stephen Foster tribute album. She even had a sort of rapprochement with GAC, which has gone through a change of ownership she describes in positive terms, and which picked up rights to an Americana Awards show she produces. But she doesn't expect any mainstream country artists sharing her convictions to enjoy such a safe landing. "I think it's very dangerous for a country artist to come out and admit they're a Democrat. The Dixie Chicks thing proved that."

Preaching to the Karaoke Choir

The roster of executives involved with Music Row Democrats includes the biggest names at the biggest companies. As for the artists who signed on with their support, it's a roster of such highly esteemed singer/songwriters as Emmylou Harris, Rodney Crowell, Nanci Griffith, Raul Malo, Kathy Mattea, Pam Tillis, Matraca Berg, Maura O'Connell, Allison Moorer—

"But not any mainstream, top-of-the-heap artists, huh?" interrupts Crowell, beating me to the punch. "Just those of us who have nothing to lose."

I wasn't going to be quite that uncharitable. But, as DuBois says, "If you'll notice, very few of the people who have been outspoken on the music side of the business have careers that are dependent upon radio right now. That's something that I think a lot of people dismiss, but it's a fact. People like Rodney and Emmylou, who have been great spokespersons for us, are wonderful artists who happen to not be dependent upon mainstream radio for their careers."

Indeed, the MRD lineup consists almost exclusively of former mainstream types who might echo Crowell when he says, "My audience is a fairly thoughtful audience nowadays. The audience that was there because of my radio accessibility in the late eighties and early nineties has drifted away, and the audiences today are more into having an ongoing relationship with the words and music I deliver. I still make a good living on occasion when somebody in the mainstream records one of my songs and the radio plays it up to the top of my charts, but I always think I could be jeopardizing that."

Malo adds, "We operate under the mainstream radar, and so we don't have a lot at stake. I can afford to speak my mind and join Music Row Democrats. If Toby Keith were to join Music Row Democrats—not that he would, but if he did—he'd probably lose half his fans. So I understand why the big stars don't get involved."

MRD founder Bob Titley observes, "Once or twice, people have had their nerves shaken a little bit when the Freepers mentioned them on their website"—that is, the online right-wing activists at freerepublic.com who so bedeviled the Dixie Chicks. "One mid-level artist who I'm a friend of, a very solid artist who's a liberal, told me, 'I just can't take the risk of doing anything after watching what happened with the Chicks.' Merle Haggard, after what happened to him when he put out his last album [which included the cynically war-themed "That's the News"], said 'I don't want to step forward.' Tim McGraw is a Democrat, but he doesn't want to step out there just now—although he's kind of done it, in the press, talking about Clinton and his ambition to run for office someday." Titley thinks they have nothing to fear but fear itself—and maybe retribution from overwhelmingly conservative-owned radio outlets, but not from the majority of fans. Titley points to a survey done in 2002 for country radio broadcasters by Seacrest and Associates, a research firm in Washington, D.C., which identified people who consider themselves partisan country fans as approximately one-third Democrat, one-third Republican, and one-third independent. "Among females, there was a five-point edge for Democrats, and among single females, a double-digit edge." There's a reason he points that out, since country radio has pursued a primarily female demographic in recent years. "So this notion that our listeners are all Republicans is false."

RCA's Joe Galante says: "I honestly don't believe that there are more Republicans at every single show than Democrats, because I think it depends largely on the states where they take place, and whether or not they're union towns or non-union towns. I think that, on balance, these folks are pretty much law-abiding citizens who love and want to support their country, who have a belief in a higher power, and for whom the important things are their family, their religion, their country, and keeping their economic level so that they can take care of the people that they have to take care of. It's not about being trendy. We've gone out and talked to the audience, and many times you hear people say, 'You know, I feel like I could sit down and have a beer with that person.' It's the relatability. Kerry never spent time really listening to some of those people. That's the danger that you have regardless of who you are. You could be the CEO of a company or you could be the president of the United States. Who do you surround yourself with, and what information do they let you see or hear? So, depending on your advisers . . . Because even with the Music Row Democrats, we would have arguments—Bob Titley and myself. He kept saying, 'Who are you voting for? Who are you voting for?' 'I haven't made up my mind yet. But tell me why I should vote for your guy'"—meaning Kerry. "And we'd argue back and forth and I'd go, 'He hasn't articulated that yet! The other guy hasn't articulated it, either, but you're convinced *your guy* has! So, what's up?'"

But something's not matching up here. If the base is really as diverse as Titley and Galante claim, how can it be that the stars of the genre are almost all bunched up at stage right? "The only artist I work with that I know is a Democrat is Mary Chapin Carpenter," says Sony's Tracy Gershon. "All my other artists, I think, are Republicans. I'd wear my Kerry button into the studio sometimes, and they'd laugh and I'd laugh. My favorite new artist, Miranda Lambert, wore a T-shirt in the studio that read: FRIENDS DON'T LET FRIENDS VOTE DEMOCRAT. I had to laugh. That's her belief, and it's okay. Her father is a Texas cop, totally red, and I adore him. You know who the Warren Brothers are? Diehard Republicans. I did *Nashville Star* with them last year, and I would always joke with them and say, 'It doesn't go with anything else about you. You're too cool to be Republicans!'"

Gershon obviously didn't talk the Warrens into joining her for "Kerry-oke." That was the Music Row Democrats' main contribution to fund-raising, if not consciousness-raising, in 2004. Putting her TV fame to work, Gershon hosted events at which artists would sing karaoke for cash contributions, ranging from Maura O'Connell performing an uncharacteristic cover of "I Think I Love You" to Crowell,

Griffith, and Hal Ketchum doing "If I Had a Hammer" Peter Paul & Mary–style.

Getting Emmylou Harris to do karaoke counted as a big accomplishment, as did getting her to stump for a Democratic candidate at all, despite past commitments to nonpartisan causes. "She's basically a military brat," says Steve Earle. "That's a tough thing for Emmy, remember that. Emmy was very quiet, hanging out with Gram Parsons and Chris Hillman and all those people during the Vietnam War, because her father was a marine officer, and so it was a tough thing for her. She felt she was being disloyal to him. But she got to a point with this election that it became important to her, and it was a huge step for her to do that, especially in wartime."

In the days after Bush's win, artists associated with MRD have mixed feelings about whether anything was accomplished. "I wasn't a member, but I did two Kerry-oke benefits," says Allison Moorer, "and I do think that just the fact that Music Row Democrats exists is a big step for the Nashville music industry. The public thinks we're all sittin' barefoot with our guns in our laps and still ride a horse and buggy to work, that we're all flag-waving people who think like Charlie Daniels. So the very formation of the organization is a great thing."

Raul Malo, who came up with the Kerry-oke concept, is more glum. "At the time, I felt like I was maybe doing something. But the truth is, we weren't doing anything. Preaching to the choir."

Crowell sounds even more downbeat. "Unfortunately, the Music Row Democrats are sort of a microcosm of the Democratic party, which is pretty friggin' ineffectual. We had some meetings, and I get what I call the preaching-to-the-choir e-mails. I get all these e-mails about something Michael Moore says, and it's all just the liberals circulating this crap, and I'm going, 'Do you have anybody's e-mail address who's on the other side? Send this to them!' It was some pretty good back-slapping, and we tried a few things, but we didn't really make much of a difference. All of the artists together didn't have enough clout to speak to the mainstream. We each spoke to our own audiences. But even if John [Cash] was still alive, and you got Kristofferson and Willie up there with me and Steve and all the people who were involved, Clear Channel still would not have given us anything. Those who have the forum to speak are in line with the present administration, and more power to 'em."

Capitol's Fletcher Foster will admit to still being confused by the imbalance among artists. "I look back on the time when the Willies and the Merles really spoke out politically for the common man, and I really and truly don't know where country music got this shift all of a sudden, or the perception of a shift. It just came upon us in the last six or eight years."

Surely things seemed conservative before that? "It did seem like a conservative format when I got into the music business in the mid-to-late eighties, but it didn't seem conservative in a moralistic way. And I don't know how to explain it. It was still God and country, but it seemed like a *different* God and country. You know what I mean?"

Closing the Tent Flaps

Music Row Democrats did make another small musical contribution to the culture-war effort, beyond mere karaoke. The group commissioned a theme song, "Takin' My Country Back," which was capably performed by session players and singers dubbed "Honky Tonkers for Truth" after some closeted Democratic stars declined to give it a croon; this theme song was widely disseminated as a free MP3. The lyrics focus on the national deficit and the war in Iraq: "You took our jobs and sent 'em overseas / Now we owe billions to the Red Chinese / You blew the budget and you botched Iraq / So I'm takin' my country back." Unlike Darryl Worley, the song's writers did not burden themselves with coming up with a rhyme for bin Laden.

It's a crafty, surprisingly catchy, even stein-friendly song. But besides avoiding any mention of what America should do about Iraq, it also neatly eschews anything that the other side would say falls under the rubric of "moral values." Should the call to reclaim these United States include the demand for more rights for gays and abortion providers? On issues like these, members of Music Row Democrats are split, much like the party as a whole in the South. For a hardliner like Raul Malo, those are points of simple tolerance and are nonnegotiable. Others think the party can't survive without finding a way to let moral conservatives feel welcome again at the table.

And here you find one of the great ironies of the reversal of fortune: the Republican party, in a way, has successfully repositioned itself as the bigger tent, the party of inclusion, inasmuch as it allows for small pockets of apparent liberalism or dissent in a way that doesn't find corresponding pockets of conservatism on the other side of the aisle. Along with the GOP's pro-life plank, there's a small but healthy strain of pro-choice sentiment. The religious right might want to ban gay marriage for all time, but the Log Cabin Republicans, a group of gay conservatives, are tolerated, at least for now. Meanwhile, moral conservatives—who make up the vast majority of voters in the heartland and the South, without some of whose electoral votes a national election can't be won—find themselves forced outside the Democratic party's shrinking tepee. The loss of the most conservative Dems is inevitable, a Steve Earle will tell you, and better just to let the Deep South go its separate way and focus instead on further shoring up the progressive wing in the Northeast that will drop out if any quarter is given on an issue like abortion. Meanwhile, not willing to write the heartland off, even Hillary Clinton is talking up conservate inclusion, which raises the hackles of some of the most faithful multimillionaire party backers who tend toward the "ultra" side of liberalism. And with every bit of infighting, a Bill Frist presidency seems that much closer.

Still, there are those in Nashville who think that country music can play a crucial role in coming elections on the Democratic side, reintroducing traditional values into the equation without the uneasy smarm that typically results when a John Kerry tries to get religion.

The writer of "D-I-V-O-R-C-E" has some ideas about what might be required for remarriage between the Democrats and his home region. "Thirty-five years ago, I don't think there was anything politically attached to people's religious beliefs," says Bobby Braddock. "That's a lot of the problem now, and that's why I think people in country music can do some good. You're not gonna win over evangelicals on the abortion issue or gay rights, but on economic issues—I mean, Christian people have children that get sick. And I can't see that it's such a hard sell to convince Christians to follow the prince of peace, to convince Christians that it's wrong to kill a bunch of innocent people in a war that those people did nothing to provoke. I'd like to see some progressive Christian populists get out there over the next few years and talk to the people. Being a Christian, I read the New Testament as a message for tolerance, for lifting people up and taking care of the poor and underprivileged. I cannot find the biblical justification for trickle-down economics. It just doesn't exist.

"I mean, if somebody gave me a litmus test, I'd probably be just really liberal right down the line on just about every issue. But even I have problems with third-trimester abortions, so I see where a lot of the people who are against abortions are coming from. I'm against the death penalty. I'm against innocent people getting killed in war. I even pick up spiders in little pieces of paper and put 'em outside rather than flush 'em down the commode. So I sort of feel the same way about fetuses. And I'm not saying overturn *Roe v. Wade*. But I think there's room to allow for different beliefs. There was a time when members of the Democratic party ranged all the way from right-wing Southern Democrats to the left, and the Republican party had people like Nelson Rockefeller who were very liberal on the social issues."

That particular America—the one in which a two-party system didn't force the entire population into picking one of two strict yet somehow arbitrarily assembled worldviews—may be beyond reclamation. But, with Music Row Democrats and others trying to envisage country music becoming visionary instead of reactionist, it's interesting to imagine a theoretical coalition of moderate stars or the independent-minded twang trust that could give it the old electoral college try.

Steve Earle's pointedly topical album *The Revolution Starts Now* included a spirited rocker called "F the CC." When the alt-country icon and his band got caught up in the song in concert, as at this 2005 Oregon show, fingers were known to fly. PHOTO BY TIM LABARGE

Steve Earle's Mouth Is Gonna Rise Again

Alt Country and the Loyal Opposition

The outcome of the 2004 election didn't do anything to mellow Steve Earle's famously fearless heart. "I'm from an awful fucking place called Texas," he tells the crowd midway through a February 2005 show at Hollywood's Music Box Theatre.

Natalie Maines, eat your comparatively Bush-coddlin', Alamo-rememberin', Lone Star–lackey heart out.

There will be no demonstrations, no breathless *Drudge Report* headlines, no record smashings, no repercussions of any sort as a result of Earle's proclamation that he's ashamed to be from the same state as the president, too. As far as most of the mainstream country fans who even remember him are concerned, Earle went to the dark side a long time ago, as disfellowshipped as a transsexual ex-Mormon. In the middle and late 1980s, he had Top 10 country hits and looked to become Nashville's own Bruce Springsteen. Not everyone turned on him, certainly, when he took his more politically and stylistically left turns. In Music Row circles, Earle is still well known and well liked, even by a good number of the conservative executives and musicians. But to the general, radio-reliant country fan base, it's as if he never existed.

In alternative-country circles, of course, it's a different story. Some in that camp find him too polemical for comfort, but for the most part he's their patron saint, poster boy, mascot, and mouthpiece—Sam Houston and General Antonio López de Santa Anna rolled into one conquering hometown hero. The loose grouping of subgenres known variously as alt country, Americana, insurgent country, or y'allternative music is often defined by what it's in opposition to, and nothing shouts "oppositional" like Earle, somebody who coulda been—well, was—a country contender and then struck out on his own path.

But is there a natural equation that follows that abandonment of the musical mainstream: alt country = alt politics?

No Depression is the bible of this movement and probably the best all-around music magazine in America. But even if there'd clearly been a tilt in the tone of their coverage's political overtones, it was still a bit surprising to see the mag publishing a front-of-the-book editorial against Bush and in favor of Kerry's candidacy during the fall of 2004. This struck some readers as a natural outgrowth of the progressive nature of the music the magazine covers. Other subscribers took the stance as an outrageous breach of their trust in what they believed was a bimonthly devoted to a set of genres and not a collection of ideologies. Grant Alden, one of *No Depression*'s cofounders and coeditors, was surprised by the backlash against the editorial, which played itself out on the letters page in subsequent issues.

Alden says, "We serve two distinct audiences: post–punk-rock fans coming to country and roots music because rock no longer serves their needs, or because it's always been a texture in their lives, or both; and classic country fans, disenfranchised by nineties pop-country, and cut loose, perhaps, by the demise of *Country Music* magazine. I know they're smart, and I assume they're independent-minded. That's the linkage. And because I felt they were independent-minded, I thought it reasonable and worth the risk to make the endorsement. Because I thought they might listen; because I actually believed we might change a few minds. I was struck by how often letters argued that we should be good boys and keep to what we knew. I did respond that I had far more formal education in politics than in music, but it didn't help."

For Alden, the maxim that mainstream country runs red and alt-country leans blue seems like a natural outgrowth of their respective creative processes. "The road to riches does not run often through the underground, any underground. The road to riches runs through conformity. I would turn this into an aesthetic argument: most mainstream country singers—who are not songwriters, in the main—want to be *stars*. The people I am drawn to write about, the performers who typically grace the pages of *No Depression*, are *artists*. One is not better than the other, though I prefer the latter. They have different motivations. The artists I like create art—visual, musical, whatever—because they *have* to, not because they think it will sell. A singer understands that, by signing a major-label deal in Nashville, he or she is consenting to be shaped, framed, and marketed, and that his or her individual identity is important only insofar as it creates a story for initial publicity, or a story that must be shielded from the press. That said, if a singer succeeds, he or she then becomes rich, and the rich vote Republican. By tradition, anyhow."

Steve Fishell tends to agree. He has had plenty of experience in the mainstream; after playing guitar in Emmylou Harris's Hot Band, he quit to help found the nineties group McBride & the Ride. But more recently he's been A&R director for the Americana label Sugar Hill and hasn't looked back at the more commercial arena he left behind. "When the label hired me, they said, 'We will never release a single to country radio. Don't even think about it.' And I loved that. I thought, 'Oh, great! This is wonderful!' Nickel Creek was a CMT phenomenon, and that's about as close to country radio as we've gotten.

"I would say that the people who follow indie-label music—Rounder, Sugar Hill, Vanguard—are generally open-minded, if they're interested in Americana music, if they're interested in singer/songwriters. Our artists do tend to be progressives. The mainstream audience in our world tends to be country radio, and that tends to be very Republican. This means that if you're a country music fan and you're a Democrat, you might stray into the alt world more often. There is a lot to be said about country artists with mainstream deals being chained to their work. They're highly controlled. When you sign a deal, you basically say 'Take me and mold me and do whatever you want with me. I'll do any song you ask me to do.' Very seldom have I seen situations where artists battled with an executive. Generally, they acquiesce and do as they're told, because they're insecure and they don't really know what's gonna be accepted or not on the radio, and they trust their labels to be their key to that world.

"A more conservative person will obey more readily than a free thinker who questions and challenges authority, not necessarily just for the sake of it, but maybe for the right reasons. Freethinkers are going to be more difficult artists in this environment, because they're going to find out that the road to success is probably gonna be very uninspiring, because there's a lot of money at stake. It's $600–700,000 to break a new artist. If you've just come out of the service and you just came and got yourself a record deal in Nashville, you're probably gonna say 'Yes, sir' an awful lot. God forbid I indulge in stereotypes, as the other side does, but I've seen a lot of young hats get their deals and give themselves up and shut the hell up."

On the other hand, a sizable minority of those who work in the alt-country world, or are its fans, find the genre's apparent bent toward liberal politics presumptuous or oppressive, as much as progressives feel oppressed in the mainstream world. Some are fearful of coming out as Republicans because of the scorn or disbelief they'd face.

"There is no upside to talking about being a conservative on this side of the industry," says one prominent player in the Americana biz who prefers to stay in the closet. "It could damage my relationship with a lot of the artists I work with. I was placed on the Music Row Democrats' mailing list because it was assumed that anybody who does what I do, works with the people I work with, and has the musical tastes I have would have to be on that side. They talk about tolerance, but when it comes to being tolerant of somebody who voted for Bush, I'm not sure you see that."

To locate the ultimate example of a fan who loves alt country or Americana in spite of the music's progressive leanings, not because of them, look no farther than Mike Long. Formerly a regular contributor to *National Review*, Long is a longtime Republican speechwriter who formed the White House Writers Group, which hires himself and his fellow GOP wordsmiths out for speaking engagements. Against all stereotypes, he hates mainstream country and counts the insurgent Drive-by Truckers as his favorite band, that group's flagrant hostility toward Bush notwithstanding. He and another conservative buddy often go to concerts where they assume they're the only two people leaning remotely to the right for any other reason other than alcohol-induced wobbliness.

Of course, even a musically open-minded conservative has to draw the line somewhere, and Long draws it at Steve Earle, or the post–*Copperhead Road* Earle, anyway. "You can't argue with certain kinds of talent," Long says. "Earle wrote 'The Devil's Right Hand' when he was fourteen, I believe. How can you not be interested in what a guy like that has to say for the rest of his life? But just as Al Franken used to be a really funny guy, and he's still funny once in a while, Steve's a lot less interested these days in making music than he is in hurting the people he disagrees with. Listen to that bluegrass record he made with the Del McCoury Band four years ago—that's a fine record, and he was already politically active, but he didn't feel like he had to say 'If you like Bush, you're going to hell.' Listen, if you've got a sweet musical way to say 'If you like Bush, you're going to hell,' I'll listen to it and appreciate it, but I just cannot see how somebody who's so overwhelmed with hostility toward his political opponents can make good music. Steve Earle was a great musician until he decided to become the pet monkey of the New York cocktail scene."

Ultimately, Long is in a distinct minority, a fan of *No Depression*–style music who isn't depressed by Republican governmental dominance. For all the flak over his magazine's position, Grant Alden says that only eight subscriptions were canceled. (One cancellation was from the presumably Republican mother of genre mainstay Jay Farrar.) The brief bout of conservatism or nonpartisanship on the letters page was replaced by another round of letters from readers firmly of the opinion that music and politics go together like white on rice.

It may be a truism that country and alt country serve completely different audiences, one of them appreciably more minuscule. There's an old joke, after all, about alt country being the one form of music where the musicians outnumber the fans. And to the extent that a good deal of alt-country musicians survive by farming their songs out to the mainstream, leaving conservative stars to sing the words written by liberal writers, it can almost start to seem too close to *The Front* for comfort. But Chet Flippo, who's been chronicling the music in all of its variations since the early 1970s, refuses to accept that these are now completely separate forms. "There's a huge amount of overlap in country-music audiences. It's always seemed to me that the notion of country-music Balkanization, that there is one huge monolithic mainstream country audience and one small alt-country audience, has been propagated by mainstream radio, some music critics, and music snobs. There are overlapping circles of country fans and artists and alt-country fans and artists, and that's always been the case. Kinky Friedman was alt country in 1975—but no such term existed then, so he was just considered a failed mainstream artist. But he still found his audience, which included some mainstream fans. That is still the case with artists and audiences today. I know many country fans who would be considered mainstream because they like Toby Keith or Sara Evans, but they're also listening to Outlaw Radio on Sirius and turning on to what are considered alt-country artists. It's a matter of what people are exposed to. Mainstream radio is still the main country delivery system, although satellite radio and TV are making dramatic inroads. The impact of downloads on country is still being assessed."

Still, there are indisputably thousands upon thousands of fans in the South and heartland who wouldn't turn on country radio under threat of death but who *do* live for the culturally despairing provocations of the Drive-by Truckers, the Zen introspection of Rodney Crowell, or Earle's most optimistic pep talks. For many of these locally disenfranchised musos, blue souls trapped in red electoral bodies, alt country may feel like the only lifeline that gets them through the daily harassment at the water cooler or alienation at the dinner table in the "awful fucking place" they call home sweet home.

Rodney Crowell: John the Baptist of the Suburbs

To find Rodney Crowell's home you have to drive through a neatly tended roundabout, in the middle of which is an obelisk that he laughingly describes in his directions to a visitor as "a monument to itself." Sure enough, there's the promised stone pillar, a Kubrickian talisman plopped into suburbia, proudly bearing the inscription FOUNDED 2003. Presumably, future generations of upper-middle-class middle Tennesseans will steer around it and look back fondly on these, the good old days.

Crowell answers the door in a bathrobe, having just sent the kids to school. It really is a *Father Knows Best* vibe out here in Williamson County, except for the occasional expletive, like the one uttered when he gets upstairs and finds out that the family's new puppy has chewed up a good deal of the foam soundproofing in his home studio. His best headphones are completely shredded, too. "Shit! I'm gonna kill that dog!" It's morning in America.

Crowell realizes that the scene is not what you're expecting from a guy who's gone from being a centrist Nashville star to one of left-leaning alt-country's most reflective singer/songwriters. It's not what he was expecting, either. "I'm surprised that we live here. As you can see, it's a Republican enclave. My wife, Claudia, and I and our family are kind of bohemians. At first, I said 'Let's get out of here.' Then I started thinking, well, it'll further define for us who we are. My daughter, a New York City kid, is going to a real right-wing, conservative public school. An excellent school, but remember, this is Williamson County—'Red County.' And I've never been prouder of my kid. Her name's Carrie, and she made her own T-shirt that said 'Carrie for Kerry' and wore it three days out of five, risking the ridicule."

There's conservatism within the Nashville city limits he left behind, to be sure, but "the kind of insecure wealth is out here" on the outskirts, Crowell says, helpfully mapping it all out. "The old, secure, and kind of decadent wealth is over in Belle Meade and that part of Nashville, and that's conservative, *way back* conservative. This is the career conservatives out here, you know, the ones dedicated to that upward climb. As my friends call it, start-up wealth."

He has a little present for his new neighbors. He's wrapping up his new album, *The Outsider*, which, after his severely introspective last two albums, moves the focus outward and aims to take the temperature of the culture. "Most of it is more forgiving, which is my tendency." But a couple of songs are less so. "During the election year, I was touring in Europe, and had a lot of pub conversations. I came back and wrote this song called 'Don't Get Me Started,' which I can play for you, if you want to hear it."

He fires up a rough mix of the freshly recorded track:

> It's the roofers and truckers and working-class suckers
> The firemen and nurses the soldiers and teachers
> Who shoulder the blows while it comes and it goes
> When it's a six-trillion-dollar debt you pay through the nose
>
> Don't get me started
> I'm a drag when I've had a few drinks
> Don't get me started
> I don't care what anyone thinks
> It makes me angry

"After I came back, the first gig I had was in Houston, so I thought, here's a good place to try it out. From the stage, I said, 'I don't understand our foreign policy at all. This is a song that I've written, trying to figure it out, out loud, for myself.' I played the song, and I felt like Moses parting the Red Sea, because it was palpable that I'd just polarized the whole audience. Half of 'em went to this side of the room, half of 'em went to that side. One half was yelling, and the other half was scowling. It was so well-defined. I really didn't want to contribute to the polarization, but I suppose I have. Or I am."

And since he got started, he didn't stop there. He switches over to another newly minted song, "The Obscenity Prayer."

> Give to me my tax-cut outsource
> Build me my own private golf course
> The Dixie Chicks can kiss my ass
> But I still need that backstage pass

You can't help but wonder how Crowell gets along with Vince Gill, one of Nashville's most notorious Republicans. The two of them came up through the ranks together, and in 2004 they reunited their pre-stardom band, the Notorious Cherry Bombs, for a thoroughly charming, if commercially negligible, supergroup-type collaborative album.

"I laugh at Vince and say, 'Vince, you're too rich. You play too much golf with rich guys. Because you really are a liberal soul. If you thought this out, you'd be on my team.' Vince travels in a different circle than I do, and I understand that. But I also know how much charity work he does and how compassionate and generous he is. He's Christlike, himself. He told me, 'You know, you can't just give people the way out. You've gotta help 'em find their way to climb out.' And I said, 'Vince, you do more than me, just giving people stuff! I don't advocate that we simply hand our money to people, either. We have to find a way to empower them. But you're actually more liberal than I am!' But he's also got his image, too. I'm telling you, though—that boy's a liberal! He didn't tell me who he voted for, but I suspect I know," Crowell says, smiling. "He may be a Republican, but I know that boy, and I've known him since he was nineteen. I know who he is through and through."

Crowell was crushed, but not surprised, by the election results. "We've sunk to a low, because you and I would have to conclude that George Bush was the most inspiring candidate. But I'm just romantic enough to think that if we get this all screwed up and we're on the brink, then God will send the delivery boy. It's gonna take a visionary. It's gonna take Gandhi," he laughs, "or Martin Luther King, with that kind of dedication to changing things by uplifting spirits. Maybe Bono will become an American citizen and actually step into that Christlike aura he has and wage a campaign. I still hold out for that kind of thing. For me, that's far more poetic and powerful than manufacturing some CEO to run all of this. Probably somebody really sarcastically intelligent of a conservative mindset would look at me and say I'm as bullshit as you could possibly be, that I'm indulging in some kind of stupid, liberal dreaming. But it's happened, historically, that kind of visionary breakthrough.

"It's hard for me to defend my kind of liberalism, because it's not intellectual. As an artist, I think there's no more articulate pathway than to speak from the heart. But in the political arena, there's no more articulate pathway than the intellect. Real hard-line conservatism is intellectual; somebody really smart, who knows their stuff, can whip me in a debate right on the spot, because the things that I try to introduce into that conversation are hard to defend, because it comes from faith. My spirituality is based on my understanding of a higher power, of God, that informs who I am and what I do.

"My response to 9/11 was definitely 'Let's go find who did this and let's take 'em out.' But I want my president to say, 'Okay, everybody, hold on. Let's take stock of ourselves. Let's see who we are in this global community and how we might have brought this on ourselves. Let's learn from that, and *then* let's go get 'em.' The guy who cocks a gun and says, 'We're gonna go blow those motherfuckers away,' that's not my president. But I understand that he's a lot of people's. There's three of me to seven of them. That's what I've learned to live with out here in Williamson County."

Quittin' Time Down South for Steve Earle

Steve Earle is headed in exactly the opposite direction from Rodney Crowell, strictly geographically speaking. He just turned fifty, and "Go north, young man" is the advice he's following for his second half-century. His migration will be more severe than Crowell's.

On behalf of his fans in the red states, the questions that have been posed to Earle are these: Since Texas pride, Southern pride, and heartland pride are so ingrained in anyone who grows up in those areas, how do you, as a "blue" person, keep that pride alive when you look around and see how red your surroundings have become? Do you embrace that political loneliness and wear it as a badge of ever-more-idiosyncratic pride, like some kind of leftist Confederate? Do you simply reconnect with your like-minded friends and hold them that much closer than before? Do you go on an anti-imperialist imperial crusade to change whatever minds you can?

Most of us can only imagine what it might be like to be a liberal music-lover living in Knoxville, having the Steve Earle tour come to town and, just for one night, not feeling like a bastard child of the South. I expect he'll have some encouraging words to pass along to his fans in these areas, as their stand-in, reconciling the stranger-in-a-strange-land dynamic for himself as well as them.

"Well, in my case, you're dealing with somebody that's just finally *done*," he declares, calling from a tour stop in Jacksonville. "I quit being proud of being from Texas a long time ago. I found Tennessee to be an easier place to live, and I've been there for thirty years. But the truth of the matter is, I spend a lot of time in New York, and I'm in the process of moving there, because I feel like a fucking Martian in Tennessee at this point."

Oh. "You know, I think I do my bit in the middle of the country. I spend two hundred days a year out here, so I don't think I'm in danger of losing touch by being in New York, because I was never in Nashville much anyway. The little bit of time that I am home, I'd like to be able to see any movie and get any book and see good theater. Those things are a part of the shortcomings of living in the middle of the country. In Nashville, when it comes to the movies you can see, you'll have a choice between whether you want to see stuff blow up or whether you want to see *big* stuff blow up. I'm done, and right now I'm not that proud of where I'm from. It's not because I think the people are stupid, but I don't want to be identified with it, and I don't want it to affect my life on a day-in, day-out basis. I don't want to live in one of the states where, in just a few years, you're not gonna legally be able to get an abortion. I'd love to live in a state that didn't have the death penalty, but at least New York qualifies as a state that hasn't executed anybody yet, and I don't think it ever will."

Given his current attitude, you might guess that Earle is not of a mind to go along with those Democrats who think the party has to find a way to talk about God or morality or whatever it takes to coax a few middle-American states back into the fold. You would be right.

"I think that's one of the huge mistakes the Democratic party is making," he says. "Fuck James Carville. Fuck people who think like that. The truth of the matter is, populations have shifted. There's still a lot of people in the heartland, but this obsession right now with the heartland . . . The truth is, the vanguard of thinking and social issues in this country has always been on either coast, and probably always will be. The coasts are exposed to more of the world than the heartland— the West Coast to the Pacific Rim, the East Coast to Europe—and that's the way it's always been. And this idea of winning an election for what passes for a left in this country by courting the middle is danger- ous. The 2004 election was still close, and I think if the Democratic party hadn't alienated the left, they might have had a much better chance of winning the election than trying to court these people in the middle of the country."

Earle almost sounds ready to cover the Talking Heads' old flyover- avoidance anthem, "Big Country" ("I wouldn't live there if you paid me / I couldn't live like that, no siree"). It's not that he's stopped caring about his heartland brethren. "You know, I only got through the eighth grade, but at least I could have gone to college if I wanted to. I was exposed to literature and art and things that make me see the world differently than most people who grew up where I did. Those of us who got lucky, in that sense, have a responsibility. We won't get anywhere by telling people how stupid they are, because that's not what the problem is. The problem is, they're being lied to, by very, very efficient, expert, straight-faced liars.

"Does a guy who grew up with money, who was handed absolutely everything he's ever had, really give a fuck about people who have to go to work every day and figure out how to send their kids to college? Do they even give a fuck about whether your kids go to college? This society is becoming more exclusive every single day. As tuitions go up, opportunities for scholarships shrink. Banks are collecting on student loans now. It's not like the seventies and most of the eighties, when you could default on your student loan and nobody did anything about it. The money's just not there anymore. Working people in this coun- try long ago lost track of where their interests lie. The idea that a union is going to cost you your job, that a union's going to exclude you from being able to work, the whole concept of a right-to-work state—that stuff's tough to go up against. Educated and progressive people have to learn how to talk to working people again."

Funny that, earlier, I should have mentioned Knoxville. "The only negative thing I heard out on the road this time was in Knoxville," Earle says. "When I was talking about unions at one part in the show, I said what I always say, that unions are the only power that working people have ever had. And somebody yelled, 'Bullshit!' A lot of people in the South have fought that idea, and what they don't realize is that a long time ago the South became a third-world country that jobs were shipped to. And now those jobs are being shipped away from them to places even farther south."

Earle's 2004 album, *The Revolution Starts . . . Now*, was about as agit-prop as popular music gets. It was written in a hurry, on an assignment—from himself. If you don't like the fact that the album includes only one of the great forlorn love ballads that Earle used to crank out with regularity, and that one tucked away toward the end of the album, too bad.

"It's harder to write chick songs in this political climate than it normally is. And there's other stuff that commands my attention. I wrote this last album because of two songs, 'The Revolution Starts Now' and 'Rich Man's War,' that I'd already written and decided I wanted out before the election. Because the election for me was about the war." A Kerry enthusiast? Hardly, but he helped raise money for the candidate anyway, "because creating any other scenario than Bush being in office would have created a climate that would make it easier to end this war."

If ever song titles were guaranteed to turn away propaganda-phobic customers at the door, it's a set with phrases like "revolution" and "rich man's war." He might as well have titled one "Blood for Oil" while he was at it. Too bad, then, that *The Revolution Starts . . . Now* scared away so many unnecessarily, because it's a much lighter album than its conceptual art, song titles, and other signifiers would suggest. The half-realized heavy-handedness of his previous album's Drudge- and Fox-baiting "John Walker Blues" is history. The title track is lyrically vague and sufficiently rockin' enough in its call to overthrow something or another that it could serve as an anthem for anybody's revolution—even Reagan's or Gingrich's. "Rich Man's War" is more character-driven and less polemical than expected, with a concluding verse in which a Palestinian kid wonders whether his call to arms is really just serving the purposes of some unseen manipulator. "F the CC" is just good old garage-rock, complete with a mid-song homage to the Ramones' spelling-bee breaks of old.

The CD's most countrified song, and possibly its best, is "Home to Houston." Earle is clearly a fan of Dave Dudley–type truck-driving songs, having previously covered "Six Days on the Road," and "Houston" represented his chance to write a rousing eighteen-wheel barn-burner himself with distinctly un-Dudleyesque politics. The Bandit is working for Smokey now, having turned U.S. contractor:

> When I pulled out of Basra they all wished me luck
> Like they always did before
> With a bulletproof screen on the hood of my truck
> And a Bradley on my back door
> And I wound her up and I shifted her down
> And I offered this prayer to the Lord
> I said, "God get me back home to Houston alive
> And I won't drive a truck anymore"

Certainly the album's comic highlight, and, in a weird way, its warmest song, is "Condi Condi," a reggaefied appeal to a certain secretary of state for some good lovin'. It'd be easy, and maybe even correct, to see the song as patronizing or insulting. Isolated from its politics, though, it's just a fun boy-from-wrong-side-of-tracks-beseeches-Juliet tune, in the tradition of pop songs like "Uptown Girl."

> Got no money but everybody knows
> I love you, Condi, and I'll never let you go
> Sweet and dandy, pretty as can be
> You be the flower and I'll be the bumble bee
> Oh she loves me, oops she loves me not
> People say you're cold but I think you're hot

As we speak, the Rice confirmation hearings are going on, and I have to wonder if Earle has been glued to the TV with lust in his heart. "Well, I mean, it's the gap," he explains, sort of. "I kind of dig the gap." It's not clear if he means the cultural gulf or, literally, her sexy teeth. "That's one of those things . . . I'm not sure . . . I spend a lot of time on stage going on ad nauseam about why I wrote songs, but in that particular case, I have no explanation," he finally laughs. "None whatsoever." More seriously, he adds, "Condoleezza Rice just fascinates me. She's my age, she grew up the same time in the same country

I did, she's black, she's a woman, and she's such a willing team player in this administration. That's pretty fascinating, any way you look at it. Colin Powell was an odd man out in this administration from day one, but Bush has got his gal in there now, so he won't be getting any more lip out of the State Department."

If anyone wishes to lodge a complaint that *Revolution* lacks subtlety, Earle isn't offering apologies. "Sometimes I do communicate in generalities, because my view of the world is pretty simple. I believe it's absolutely fucking criminal for anyone to go hungry in the richest country in the world—period. I believe it's criminal to attack other countries that haven't attacked you—period. Those are pretty general beliefs. And they're real black-and-white to me."

He realizes that the track record for dissent in popular music is a tricky one to chart, since its best-known practitioner disavowed ever having been political in the first place. "When Bob Dylan decided that he didn't want to be a protest singer, I understood why. He was twenty-three years old, and his record sales were the best-kept secret in the music business, and he was very ambitious. He made it hip for other artists to be at Columbia, but he really didn't sell that many records. I'm at a point where I'm fifty years old and I make a comfortable living selling a couple hundred thousand records worldwide every time I put one out, and I'm willing to work a lot, so it's a different situation. I can make a bluegrass record if I want to; I did a few years ago, and probably I alienated some people, but I didn't alienate anywhere close to everybody, and for the most part, my audience has been willing to hang in there with me."

Anyway, Music Row and environs won't have Steve Earle to kick around anymore. Not that the town did that much kicking; even the conservatives seemed to enjoy having him around, as a gadfly or sort of repellant bellwether. It's sad to imagine a Nashville where the possible scenarios for a Steve Earle to run into a Ronnie Dunn are severely diminished.

Speaking of whom, Earle offers his own account of a soon-to-be-legendary standoff. "I got assaulted by a very drunk Ronnie Dunn at a New Year's Eve party at Tony Brown's. He came all the way across the room to tell me that he had a *W* on his Hummer, and he was just the kind of obnoxious that people who have had too much tequila are. I didn't hit him, so I consider myself enlightened." Dunn's version of this exchange, readers may recall, had something to do with Wahhabism. "Yeah, he was trying to engage me in a bunch of really cultish, anti-Islamic ideas that he subscribes to. Really out-there, borderline Rosicrucian shit," Earle recounts. "But he was so hammered that he couldn't make himself clear about it. He's decided that it's evil and that's what the problem is. He totally agrees with the president. He really believes that we've got God on our side, and that however it turns out, we've got to do this." Now he's curious. "What *his* opinion of how that confrontation turned out the other night?"

Essentially, I tell him, that Earle was too uninformed about Islam and world events to even engage in the issues. "That's interesting," Earle remarks, "because basically, what I did was try to prevent him from getting his ass whipped at a friend of mine's New Year's Eve party, so I walked away. Believe me, Allison and I were the only sober people at that party. I don't drink." (Long story there, which you may or may not have heard, on Earle's sobriety.)

"So," Earle demands, "are you gonna believe me, or are you gonna believe Ronnie Dunn?" An eternal question.

Allison Moorer's Post-Alabama Song

The similarly sober bystander in Earle's tale is velvet-voiced Allison Moorer. She is yet another in a long line of mercurial artists who were signed by Tony Brown to a mainstream country deal before ultimately flipping to the alt side. While she's been out on the road touring for a few months with Earle, love has blossomed alongside respect.

"He's a real, live, bad-ass activist and works his ass off doing what he can to change the world," Moorer says. "What I'm seeing on our tour is people energized by the music and the hope he gives them. I could only hope to be half the inspiration to those people that he is. I haven't really delved into doing political songs, or what I like to call reflections of our culture, nearly as much as he has, though I hope to." Earle is planning to produce her next album, so all bets for that are on.

Her current album, *The Duel*, wasn't so much about the battle between red and blue as a duel between woman and God. The title track was as heavy a meditation on death and agnosticism as you'll ever hear in a putative pop lyric, making a song merely about politics seem almost like escapism. But *The Duel* did have one such pointedly topical number, "All Aboard."

> A team of old white studs
> Pulls this rolling country club
> Climb right on in and take a seat
> Down the beaten path we'll run
> High stepping to the drummer's drum
> And if you don't love it you can leave
> All aboard

Moorer credits Butch Primm, at the time her cowriter and spouse, for bringing in the idea for the song. "It came out of a sort of knee-jerk reaction to all the love-it-or-leave-it patriotism that was rampant around late 2003. A lot of people in the Nashville music scene had started exploiting 9/11 and the Iraq war for what we felt was their own personal gain. Toby Keith's song pissed me off so badly, I can't even tell you. It horrified me to think that someone overseas would hear it and think that's what we all thought. 'We'll put a boot in your ass, it's the American way'? *Excuse* me? Because I felt, maybe it's your redneck way but it's not mine. I have nothing against the guy personally, but I felt like he was banging on the drum to put money in his own pockets.

"There were several of those songs that I felt went for a kind of sucker-punch thing that I just personally hate. That's one of the things I hate about current mainstream country music, how it plays on people's emotions in a cheap-shot way. If you're jumping on the parade float and waving a flag and saying 'Let's go kick some ass' because you've given it some thought and that's what you really think, then go right ahead, because this is a democracy. But if you're doing it because you're just too stupid to find out anything else, fuck off."

Her feelings about how blue people in red states maintain regional pride is akin to Earle's, maybe not surprisingly. "When I was growing up in south Alabama my parents voted Republican. I don't know anybody in my whole extended family who ever voted for a Democrat. My parents were close to poor, so I think about it a lot—what were they thinking was gonna happen if they voted for Reagan? They're both passed away, so I can't ask them.

"There are great things about Alabama but I'm *not* really that proud of it right now. I think it's a good place to be from, but a cultural hot spot it ain't. I'm thankful I get to do what I do, because I see how the world works and how people outside of south Alabama live, and it's a real blessing. I don't want to ever live there again. Maybe when I get old, I will. That doesn't mean I don't love my family and friends there, but you know what? It's kind of the armpit, and I don't want to live in the armpit."

She's happy to have moved up to what she clearly considers to be a higher class of tourmate than she had in her early days on a mainstream country label. "One artist in particular, who I won't mention by name, we did a short little German tour, and the war in Bosnia was happening at the time. It was on TV in the hotel lobby, and he said, 'I don't know why we need to be involved in all that. Why can't we just take care of ourselves?' I said, 'Okay, would you *like* for me to tell you why?' It pissed me off so bad. I guess some people really think that's the way things ought to be, and the people who can't take care of themselves, well, fuck 'em. Now that we're in Iraq, of course, he'd say we should go kick some more asses." She stops to consider her words. "How do I say this without sounding like an asshole? You know, a lot of country singers are just fuckin' *dumb*. Let's go ahead and say it. It's a problem!" she laughs. "A lot of rock & roll singers are fuckin' dumb, too. A lot of musicians don't have sense to come in from the rain, because they're just people, after all."

Nanci Griffith's Non-Emigrant Status

Nanci Griffith was supposed to be in Ireland by now. If a lot of her fellow Nashvillians had their way, she would be, nursing her grudge against George W. Bush "from a distance," to quote an old song of hers.

Instead, she's nursing a beer and a smoke at Brown's Diner, far from the heart of Dublin. Almost directly overhead is a TV quietly playing the Shania Twain–Billy Currington "Party for Two" video, as if to mock the Nashville loyalism of Griffith, whose brand of sensitive, pacifistic, accessible, but not terribly commercial Americana is far from the kind of product usually associated with the city. But she means it when she sings "I Love This Town." For that matter, Griffith loves Shania ("She's one of my favorite songwriters"), too. Even the drunk babbling incoherently into a cell phone at the next table can't drown out her ongoing enthusiasm for her hometown of the last fourteen years.

Nowadays, at her concerts, she lets leftist Pacifica Radio outlets set up tables in the lobby. But it was a different kind of radio that sparked her musical imagination. "I grew up in Austin, Texas, huddled next to my transistor radio every Friday and Saturday night to listen to the Grand Ole Opry," says Griffith. "It was hard to get WSM in Austin—it would go back and forth with some station in Juarez. So the first time I met Loretta Lynn, I said, 'I have to tell you that not only were you the inspiration for me becoming a songwriter, but I learned how to speak Spanish waiting for you to come on the Opry.' It's a magical experience for me, to get to be on the Opry, and they're so welcoming; they treat you like you should have always been there."

The city as a whole hasn't necessarily extended the same welcome wagon. In the fall of 2004, the *Tennessean*'s Peter Cooper did a roundup of country or quasi-country artists and their views on the election. Griffith was foolish and impetuous enough to opine that if her fellow Texas native got reelected, her faith in the country would be so shattered that she would have to move to Ireland. The remark sparked offers to hook her up with a good travel agent, naturally.

"Boy, was there a barrage of letter writing from people, and most of it was 'Good riddance!' 'Get out!' 'Love it or leave it!'" She *did* ask for it, but still . . . "I thought, is this 1966 or 2004?

"I make a lot of political jokes on stage, but I've never endorsed anyone on stage, unless it was a rally. I deal with it with humor. Every time I would talk about Bush/Cheney, I would say 'Nixon/Agnew' and then correct myself. So I received over a hundred Nixon/Agnew buttons in the mail from different fans. It's all been in good fun," she explains, still baffled by the sudden outcropping of bad will from her many critics.

"One day I ran into Brenda Lee. It was after all the hoopla in the newspaper and the letter writing, and Brenda came up and said 'You can't leave! We need you at the Opry! We're so few and far between, I won't let you leave!' Brenda talked me out of leaving the country, and the *Tennessean* wrote another article about that"—prompting a lot of

"Curse you, Red Baron!"–type missives now directed at spoilsport Lee (who, for the record, was not sorry).

As we speak, Griffith is just weeks away from releasing her twelfth album, *Hearts in Mind*. It seems safe to surmise that the title is an intentional allusion to the famous motto of soldiers in Vietnam ("Grab 'em by the balls, and their hearts and minds will follow"); the Bush administration more recently used a "hearts and minds" slogan vis-à-vis Iraq, conveniently leaving out the testicular part. Vietnam and, by inference, Iraq both figure in Griffith's album. The songs "Heart of Indochine" and "Old Hanoi" stem from her repeat visits to that part of the world. Having been properly sensitized to the feelings of survivors on both sides by her ex-husband, Eric Taylor, a veteran, Griffith started working with the Vietnam Veterans of America foundation in 1998.

"We had the moment of a lifetime in Seattle, doing an outdoor concert there at the zoo, with seven thousand people sitting out in the rain. After I finished playing 'Traveling Through This Part of You'"—a 2001 song about a younger woman trying to understand the inner turmoil of a Vietnam vet—"I see this one guy down in front struggling to get up with a cane, and when he finally got to his feet, he said, 'Nanci Griffith, that's my song.' And he gave his years of service—'67, '68. What followed was like a wave. It brings tears to my eyes even now. All these guys started standing up—and women, too, who had been nurses—and they all gave their years. It went on for about five minutes."

Though she probably loses more than a few vets by being against even "just" wars ("I am a pacifist. I think our government should be evolving. We should have a Department of Peace"), they make up a much larger contingent of her audience than they might for your average daisy-wielding radical peacenik, thanks to her cognizance that the ill will afforded returning soldiers in the Nixon years contributed to the eventual downfall of any real counterculture.

"I think we have to remember some lessons from the sixties. When Vietnam veterans came back, they were called by their peers 'baby killers.' We're not that many years removed from that being the attitude of the average American about a Vietnam veteran, or from thinking that all Vietnam vets are homeless and out on street corners."

Hearts in Minds ends (not counting bonus tracks) with "Big Blue Ball of War," which is basically this album's "From a Distance," with a more gynocentric slant.

A reformation might just save us all
A voice of harmony and open heart
Where the women teach the song
These men of evil deed can be proven wrong
If we join hand to hand with Abraham
So not a soul falls off

She genuinely believes the world's women could teach the menfolk to study war no more. Of course, *Lysistrata* was a wacky proto–musical comedy, not an actual peace plan, and the forced feminization of hawk culture probably isn't much more feasible now. But hey, a gal can dream. "'Big Blue Ball of War' came to me because I had reached a point of saturation. It was a matter of, okay, boys, since Abraham it's been all about you and your garbage and your dirty socks. It's time for you to load up your garbage, take it to the curb, and let the women do this for a while, because you obviously don't know how . . ."

"I don't have any children—that I know of." Rim shot. "But for me, it's all about America's children who are being sent to Iraq to die for a mistake. Remember what John Kerry said in 1971 when he addressed Congress: How would you like to be the last man to die for your country's mistake? After hearing that, I did research to find out who *was* the last man to die in Vietnam, and I wrote a song called 'The Last Name on the Wall.'"

You would think that Griffith would have learned from her earlier mistake, and might want to avoid making empty emigration threats. But she just can't help herself.

"I've been hearing rumors that Newt Gingrich is considering running for president in 2008. I'll just say straight out that if Newt Gingrich even gets nominated, I definitely am leaving the country. Brenda Lee will be leaving with me. We'll come back once a year and play the Opry."

Patterson Hood's Pennsylvania Avenue Drive-by

Patterson Hood, the driving force of Drive-by Truckers, is red. In the face. This occurs only when he breaks his recently self-imposed rule about keeping his blood pressure down by not watching TV news

anymore. Other than that, this disillusioned Alabaman is the quintessential azure guy swimming against a thoroughly crimson tide.

"I feel blue, that's for sure," says Hood. "I feel blue every time I
turn on the goddam TV and see that moron doing something else stupid that my children and grandchildren are gonna have to pay for the
rest of their lives." (As we speak, his wife is about a week away from
delivering their first child.) "I feel *real* blue."

The Truckers' music started out as a savage mixture of gothic satire
and tragedy. More recently, it's been heavier on the tragedy, sans
kitsch—full of family farms being sold and abject poverty and alcohol
abuse and every other kind of bad luck or abuse that could afflict the
rural South. Even in the din of a nightclub and without benefit of a
lyric sheet, you'd think fans would get the idea that this is music about
how screwed up things are, that no one comes out looking good in
Hood's worldview—least of all the prevailing powers. But apparently
it does still come as a surprise.

"We got booed cross-country in October. It's funny, because I've
never wanted to be that douchebag that stands on stage telling people
how to vote or feel or think. And, uncomfortably, I ended up doing a
little bit of that in this last tour, mainly just out of voicing my rage.
That's what I do for a living is talk about things I feel, and I felt too
strongly at this juncture not to. I never stopped the show or gave any
big political rants, but no one who reads my lyrics is probably for long
gonna doubt my feelings about some stuff. And in a lot of cases, I
would do the song 'Puttin' People on the Moon,' and somebody would
boo me, so I would say something sort of as a result of that, and a couple of times it got even a little more heated than that.

"One night I was in a particularly nasty mood, and there was a guy
directly in front of me going 'Fuck you!' the whole time. It was my
nineteenth day without a day off, and my back hurt, and the guy
pissed me off, so I said a little bit more than I normally say and probably wasn't too tactful. Some person wrote a letter to *No Depression*
about it, and I felt bad that I had kept somebody from having a good
time, because when people spend however much tickets cost nowadays, they want to come see a rock show.

"But another thing that drew us more into the fire this time is the fact
that because we're from the South, so many people assume, 'Well, you
must be Republicans.' But even an overwhelmingly Republican-voting

South means there's still a good 40 percent in any given state that feel strongly the other way. I wanted to speak up and have myself counted as among those. Also, we did that record that dealt with the folklore and mythology that surround Lynyrd Skynyrd"—the concept album *Southern Rock Opera*—"so a lot of people who don't know a lot about our band associate us with that. And Lynyrd Skynyrd, or the band that calls itself Lynyrd Skynyrd, was out there playing damn Bush and Republican convention stuff."

The low point in the history of Skynyrd is a recent number called "Red, White, and Blue," written by country's own Republican Warren Brothers. (Lyrical highlights: "My Daddy worked hard, and so have I / Paid our taxes and gave our lives to serve this great country / So what are they complaining about . . . if they don't like it they can just get the HELL out!")

"I hate that fuckin' song," says Hood. "In 2003, for some end-of-year poll, I was asked what my favorite and least favorite songs were, and that was my *Catwoman* song of the year. I got hate mail for that, too. But Lynyrd Skynyrd's following nowadays is probably closer to Toby Keith's than Bruce Springsteen's. That's how they market themselves. The record we made was about a band that hasn't existed since the plane crash in '77," in which three members died.

He points out that his mailbox "isn't flooded with death threats," yet the cards and letters keep coming. "I got a nasty letter today from someone who lives in Huntsville, saying that I was giving their town a bad name with 'Puttin' People on the Moon,' that the town's not as economically depressed as I've implied, and I should be ashamed of myself. It's like, whatever—it's a fuckin' song!"

> Double-digit unemployment, TVA be shutting soon
> While over there in Huntsville, they're puttin' people on the moon . . .
> Mary Alice got cancer just like everybody here
> Seems everyone I know is gettin' cancer every year
> And we can't afford no insurance, I been ten years unemployed
> So she didn't get no chemo so our lives was destroyed
> And nothin' ever changes, the cemetery gets more full
> And over there in Huntsville, even NASA's shut down too

The Truckers also got booed during a recent gig in Little Rock, when they revived a Clinton administration–era song called "The President's

Penis Is Missing." It's difficult to know which political persuasion was responsible for the catcalls; though the title is irreverent enough, the lyric was anti-impeachment, sardonically running through a long list of the confirmed peccadilloes and alleged cold sores of all the presidents of yore before making a conclusion about the climate of the late nineties: "This whole world is consumed by hunger and meanness / Meanwhile we're concerned about the president's penis."

Hood has written an unusually lighthearted new song called "Uncle Phil and Aunt Phyllis in the Month After the Election," which he plans to record for a solo album. "It's about a couple who have ended up on opposite ends of the political spectrum after years and years of marriage. The song itself is neither red state nor blue state. It makes fun of both of 'em; it's about the things one of them does to sabotage the other's attempts at canceling their vote." In Patterson Hood's lyrical world, a marital spat that ends merely in a political draw and not suicide, cancer clusters, famine, or the loss of the family homestead counts as a lark. Maybe impending fatherhood is good for him after all.

James McMurtry's Austin Pity Limits

James McMurtry had never written an overtly political song before, though there was plenty of the covert variety to go around. He aimed to make up for lost time with "We Can't Make It Here," issued as a free MP3 before the 2004 election. Aside from the obvious triggers—like Bush's popularity level in McMurtry's home state of Texas—why start now?

"I heard that Steve Earle was busting his ass trying to get a whole album out before the election, and I thought, well, if he can do that, at least I can get one song out," says McMurtry. "I was always afraid to get political, because I thought it was a good way to kill a song. But Earle was an inspiration, because he's always done a very good job of getting his point across through characters without making his songs into sermons." Initially, the title phrase refers to job migration:

> Wow I'm stocking shirts in the Wal-Mart store
> Just like the ones we made before
> 'Cept this one came from Singapore
> I guess we can't make it here anymore

And then, a more fatalistic "Masters of War"–type verse lends the title more existential overtones:

> They've never known want, they'll never know need
> Their shit don't stink and their kids won't bleed
> Their kids won't bleed in the damn little war
> And we can't make it here anymore

He's written some songs about his home turf that rival any of the literature turned out by his literary-icon dad, Larry McMurtry, for local detail that manages to be both sympathetic and sardonic. Among McMurtry's songs that examine the American divide, his masterpiece is "Out Here in the Middle," an early-nineties tune that he revived for his 2004 live album. "That song predates the concept of red and blue states by many years. People hear it wrong, especially those who listen to the Robert Earl Keen version, because they seem to think it's a rehash of 'Stuck Up Here with Dixie on My Mind,' if you remember the Hank Williams Jr. hit from the late eighties, which talked about being in New York and wanting to be in the South. We were starting to attract a lot of frat kids at our shows in Austin—which is good, because then we can get a crowd that will actually come out at midnight on a weeknight— and they scream and holler at that song. But I don't think they really get the fact that it's ironic. I say, 'Wish you were here,' but I'm really saying, 'I wish I was *there*, my love.'" Indeed, McMurtry pulls off some unexpected twists here, knocking urban climes in the first verse, which mocks car stereo thefts and snooty downtown restaurants, only to offer the exurban alternative in unexpectedly ironic, not idyllic, terms.

> We got tractor pulls and Red Man chew
> Corporate relo refugees that need love too
> We ain't seen Elvis in a year or two
> We got justification for wealth and greed
> Amber waves of grain and bathtub speed
> We even got Starbucks
> What else you need?
>
> Out here in the middle
> Where the center's on the right
> And the ghost of William Jennings Bryan preaches every night

To save the lonely souls
in the dashboard lights
Wish you were here my love

"We have a regular gig at the Continental Club every Wednesday at midnight when I'm home, and for a while it got really big with those frat guys even though they don't care for my politics. Somebody told me that Jenna Bush came in with a bunch of people. When I used to play 'Levelland,' I would do this whole big anti-Bush rap. (It's actually on my live record, as 'Maxus Theorem.') It's said that the guys who escorted Jenna to the club got pissed off and they all left en masse. I never saw 'em."

McMurtry has always felt like an alien, he says, having grown up and settled in urban Virginia and Austin, respectively, oases of blue amid the red. He doesn't hold much hope for reclaiming the nation's midsection. "The Democrats have been identified with Yankee elitism for as long as I can remember. And Bush talks with enough of a twang that nobody recognizes the fact that he is himself one of the Yankee elite. When I go hunting, I run into my cousins, who are died-in-the-wool Republican voters. I remember that when the 2000 recount was happening, they were convinced that Gore was trying to steal the election from *them*. I didn't get into it very far with my cousins, because we all had guns. But at least they don't mind me shooting out of their tree stand, regardless of my political leanings."

As for sensitivity to the needs of Texas and the South to hear the recognizable language of traditional morality and religion from the Democratic party? "*Fuck* that," says McMurtry. "I think it needs to expose religion for the power trip that it is. No, the Democrats need to be a genuine opposition party. They're not gonna out-Republican the Republicans, ever, in eons."

His only advice—not that the party has been asking, but just in case any of those Austin frat boys grows up to be a Democratic operative—is this: For God's sake, stop nominating senators. "I think the way elections are going, it's gonna be almost impossible to elect anyone out of the Senate. They labeled Kerry a waffler. Any senator can be labeled that, because of the way those bills are put together. If you stay in long enough, you're gonna have to vote against a popular bill at one point or another, because there's gonna be a rider attached that's not gonna be good for your constituents. But when he first ran, Bush didn't have anything you could pick on him about, because all a Texas governor gets to do is kill people. And nobody's gonna complain about *that*."

Rosanne Cash Plays the Spiritual Stock Exchange

Rosanne Cash has been a blue-stater for a while, so she doesn't want to speak for Nashville or the South. She did a good part of her growing up with her mother in Ventura, California, where, in 1972, though not old enough to vote, she campaigned for McGovern. For years now, she's lived in New York City, but during the period when she lived with her dad, Johnny, and got to experience Southern politics, she witnessed the joy in the Cash household in Henderson, Tennessee, on the night Jimmy Carter got elected.

There was no such joy in Mudville, or Manhattan, this latest election. "The classic thing I read is that they did a poll asking whether you thought Bush had divided the country, and half said yes and half said no," she laughs. "To me, that kind of summed it up. Yeah, the day after the election was depressing for me. It took me a few days to shake off my funk. But then I thought, stop whining about it. You know, you can still give money to progressive causes. Nobody stopped you from doing that. And there still is a system of checks and balances in our government. It's not as strong as it used to be, I don't think, but all is not lost.

"I grew up in Southern California, so I've had a blue-state mentality for my whole life. But there was divisiveness even in my own family. I would say that most of us are pretty hardy Democrats, but there are a few more conservative members, and we had to be very careful with each other, and respectful, and sometimes just not go there— even though I don't believe in the Bush agenda *at all*. Sometimes, in my worst moments, I believe what John Adams said, that all democracies will eventually destroy themselves. It takes mental muscle to maintain democracy. You have to allow for things that you can barely tolerate, because that's how things are in a democracy. The religious right getting themselves involved in politics makes me very nervous. That's a cancer on democracy that can lead only to destruction. I have this fear that the fundamentalists want the world to end, so they're trying to hurry things along."

Cash has been working on a new song called "Company" that she says is "kind of political in a very personal way. I think it's going to weed out the riffraff right off the bat," she laughs, sounding a tad nervous. "It starts out, 'I wish I was a Christian and knew what to believe, I could learn a lot of rules,' and then it goes through a series of things. I kind of give the same weight to wanting union with God or a sense of being religious as wanting money and wanting diamonds and wanting children and wanting to move—that constant sense of unease and dissatisfaction that so many people seem to feel. I gave the search for God equal weight because, to me, that's what religion has been reduced to in modern society. It's become just some other kind of addiction, like going the mall. The end of the song says, 'I wish I was a Christian, but I cannot believe / Because no one in the Bible craves my company.' And I thought, well, hell, *that's* gonna draw a line in the sand—but I don't care.

"I'm drawn more toward Buddhism than anything, because they don't want a market share. Every other religion does. And I can't trust that."

Todd Snider's East Side Story

Todd Snider used to get a lot of visitors coming backstage at his concerts, on the prowl. They weren't on the lookout for blow or groupies, but for telltale signs of holiness, as there was a pernicious rumor going around that Snider was a righteous rocker.

"My brother is in Christian rock"—sibling Mike Snider is the agent for top acts like Mercy Me and Audio Adrenaline—"so sometimes I am around those people, but they're all drunks, too. I do a few gospel songs that used to bring a lot of youth pastors backstage. Horrible people, unfortunately. Can't say the word 'Jesus' without these people trying to put you to work. They are always shocked and appalled at the dressing-room scene. I say, ever meet Hank [Williams] III? My dressing room looks like a goddam Fellowship of Christian Athletes meeting compared to his. Go bug him."

Snider found a way to finally rid himself of that element, by writing a singalong called "Conservative Christian Right Wing Republican Straight White American Males."

Diamonds and dogs, boys and girls, living together in two separate
worlds
Following leaders of mountains of shame, looking for someone to
blame.
I know who I like to blame:
Conservative Christian, right-wing Republican, straight, white,
American males,
Soul-savin', flag-wavin', Rush-lovin', land-pavin' personal friends
to the Quayles
Quite diligently workin' so hard to keep the free reins of this
democracy
From tree-huggin', peace-lovin', pot-smokin', barefootin'
folk-singin' hippies like me.

"So far I haven't been booed for the song. I thought I might be, and
I was very curious to see the reaction. The responses that I've been
getting to that song tell me that most of my crowd are tree-huggin'
bumper-sticker liberals like me. I've received a couple of 'I'm not listening to you anymore' letters, but I got the same kind of letters for
putting horns on an album."

He can confirm some stereotypes. "The *No Depression* crowd is
mostly liberal and the CMT crowd is mostly conservative." He has a
little experience with both, having recorded for MCA before going indie, and having had his songs covered by mainstream artists. "Rednecks and hippies don't mingle like they used to back in Willie's day. I
blame Garth Brooks. To me, seventies outlaw country was the last
batch of cowboy liberals. That movement grew to be as predictable as
today's, and I always thought that it was George Strait who came along
with a heart full of talent and gave them a much-needed kick in the ass
in the eighties. But before the outlaw types could get back on their
feet, Garth came along with a head full of marketing savvy, and was
willing to push so many easy buttons that anyone not willing to play
the Republican American family-values routine was forever relegated
to the four-hundred-seater circuit. Garth's willingness to be a shill first
undercut everyone in country who didn't want to be a shill at all. He
literally raised the new artist's promotional workday from an expected
ten hours to an expected eighteen. *Artistes* like Charlie Robison are
not gonna work eighteen-hour promo days. Very few liberal artists

will. There is a nice wave somewhere between mystery and arrogance that somebody like Willie never falls off of.

"The thing is, however, I really like Garth Brooks's music. Still listen to it; think he's great at it. One of the best. But he lowered the bar for how subtle or 'artistic' you could be, and liberal people flee from shit that feels more like product than art. I think he scattered the hippies. I like him; he gave me a bunch of money once. But, you know, I ran with the hippies."

Garth gave Snider money? "He called me up unannounced. It took him twenty minutes to get me to believe it was really him. Then he told me he was gonna record my song 'Alright Guy.' I thought, great, I'm rich! Then he told me about this Chris Gaines idea, which took another twenty minutes to believe. He cut it, and I played guitar and harmonica. The song got pulled from the record about a week before it was released, which Garth felt guilty about." Something about chickening out over having a positive pot reference in a song. (Gary Allan later recorded it and made it a country radio hit.) "So Garth then sent me ten grand. I thought he was a great guy; he treated me very well. We talked about Dylan. The first thing he did when we met was to read me a poem. The first thing Steve Earle did when we met was ask about my distribution, and then he answered his cell phone. The two events confounded my expectations of how artists worked, and I came away having more respect for both guys, for some reason."

The album which includes "Conservative . . ." is *East Nashville Skyline*; the title is a play on Dylan that honors that gentrifying eastern section of town's status as Music City USA's own Silverlake-in-progress.

"I like East Nashville and seldom cross the river. It's bean-counter country over on the other side, and the guys who work there all sleep out in Franklin at night. Ask a guy in East Nashville how things are going with the band, and he'll tell you about the new song or the new fiddle player. Ask a guy on the Row how things are going with his band, and he'll tell you about the pending deal or the new lawyer. East Nashville is where we made our record and where Loretta made hers. It's all working musicians over here—that and queers. We have a blast over here, and we even have a gang sign that we flash: 'Ring finger to the palm, right hand to the chest! Let 'em know what side of town you love the best! East side of Music City, where we don't fuck around! Just look at your map, we're on the right side of town!'" Snider issues a gang warning: "If Big Kenny comes up missing, well, you know what I'm saying."

He's taking a benign attitude toward the second half of the Dubya epoch. "My beef with my own party is that so many of us 'peace' people hate hate *hate* George Bush with such intense passion that we get nowhere. But as we know, he's going the distance, so Operation Nothing I Can Do About It Now is now in effect. If there's grass around, I can tolerate some of that conservative bullshit. And there is always grass around here."

Snider feels a little guilty about his conservative Caucasian-bashing anthem, and not just because of his brother. "The weird thing is, I'm a Christian, but I must've got a defective Bible or something. Mine didn't tell me to change anybody, or tell me to hunt and destroy all sin. Mine said forgiveness was the most important thing there was and pride was the worst. Mine said if someone takes your shirt, give them your coat. Mine said it was easier for a rich man to pass through the eye of a needle on a camel's back than it is for him to enter the gates of heaven. Passing through the eye of a needle on a camel's back is the American dream."

Adrienne Young as Joni Appleseed

Adrienne Young, a rising folk-bluegrass singer and picker, has a title for the sophomore album she's about to record, but it's not going over all that well in the left-leaning circles she tends to travel in. "My record's gonna be called *The Art of Virtue*," she explains, "but that really freaks people out. I actually had somebody tell me, 'You're gonna turn people off if you have virtue in the title.'" We're having dinner on Martin Luther King Jr. Day, which coincides with Robert E. Lee Day in a few southern states. This year, Kins Day also—quite serendipitiously, as far as she's concerned—happens to fall on Benjamin Franklin's birthday. Young may be Franklin's most dedicated young American acolyte; it was his proposed alternative political party, the United Party for Virtue, that inspired her proposed CD title.

"Franklin thought that the problem with society of his time—and it's the same today—is that all of the effort is put on the outside, on appearances, on what your bankbook says or what you've accomplished or how big your name is, as opposed to true virtue, which is of the soul."

Young is a bit of a hippie chick, but a dangerously educated one. This characteristic ties in with the most pointedly political song on her first album, which was called "Blinded by Stars"—as in, the stars on the flag, and the stars on the covers of the tabloids. Celebrity obsession and nationalism: twin American neuroses. The lyric was cowritten with Alice Randall, the African American novelist who penned the controversial *Gone with the Wind* spoof, *The Wind Done Gone*.

Young believes in planting seeds with each record she sells. Literally. In an organic variation on the "value-added" packaging that major labels have been experimenting with, this self-described "existential transcendentalist" has given purchasers of her indie CD a bonus in the form of a packet of wildflower seeds inside each jewel box. She's a spokesperson for the Food Routes Network, which encourages buying local produce and is affiliated with Farm Aid. "So many eating disorders develop these days because the food people are eating has no soul and no vibration. Our bodies crave soul nourishment that used to come from a nurtured plant with the wind blowing over it. We're not being dealt nourishing sustenance, so we're becoming gluttonous as a nation because we're trying to fill the hole."

This organic thing is both a rebellion and a (literally) back-to-roots fixation. "I'm a seventh-generation Floridian, and my parents didn't garden. Are you kidding? My grandparents did, and I longed to be with them. I would cry for days before I'd have to leave my grandma's at the end of the summer to go back home to the world of Domino's pizza and MTV and my mom putting the twenty-dollar bill on the table before she left for her real estate meeting, like, 'Order out!' There was no homespun anything . . . The sad part is that a hundred years ago, we were a rural country, 95 percent of America. Now only a fraction of a percent of family farms are left operating. If country music is really about simple people working the land to take care of their families without excessive grandeur, it's ironic how the agri-corporations have shut that down."

Young has gone through an evolution of her own during the past year. Touring with her band before the 2004 election, assuming her audience was on her wavelength, the youthful ideologue would throw out a question each night. "All I ever did was ask 'Who's voting for Bush?' Nobody would raise their hand, and we'd all laugh and clap." Except, presumably, the fans too chicken to risk humiliation. "I didn't even have to say anything anti-Bush for people to understand where I was coming from, obviously. But I remember we played a packed little club in West Virginia, the Purple Fiddle, and I asked that question, and there was this one table where everybody raised their hand. Everyone turned around to look at them, and I was like, 'We love you anyway, man!' And then I tried to make a funny. Later I got an e-mail from a guy at that table, and he said 'I will never again buy a record of yours or come to one of your shows. I come to hear music to escape the realities of life, not to be force-fed your political opinions.'"

Young is of two minds about that. "I e-mailed back very politely, 'Thank you so much for taking the time to share your opinion with me. But I don't understand how, as a writer, I could separate my views. Spiritual, political, social—there are no walls there for me. It all has to do with acting and living in a way that serves the greater good. So whatever T-shirt you want to put on it, whichever party truly has the greater collective benefit, is where I want my energy to go towards.'" And yet . . . it made her reconsider. "The funny thing is, Willie Nelson won't talk about politics on stage, but he's an incredibly political figure, which is fascinating. I have thought about adopting that approach, because I want to be able to touch people universally, and not everybody's ready. If I went to a concert and the first thing they said was, 'Man, I love George Bush!,' I'd be turned off. So if somebody comes to one of our shows—it could be my grandmother, who votes Republican—and I'm force-feeding her my opinion, I actually may close the door on myself, when they've opened it for me by saying 'I want to hear your music.' I don't need to tell you to vote for Kerry or Bush, just to go put your hands in the earth and watch something grow."

Bruce Robison wrote a comic song whose theme and title were "What Would Willie Do?" Adrienne Young is going to see how it goes, actually living by that guiding principle.

Raul Malo Keeps Tabs on the Right

Raul Malo, once and future Maverick, has his own tactic for dealing with being a blue guy in a red world.

"I have a lot of Republican friends. And I came up with a plan right after the election. I said to them, 'Obviously, it's a scientific fact that the Republicans have all the money. And obviously you guys wanted four more years of this. Well, guess what? For the next four years, drinks are on you.' So I make my Republican friends buy drinks, buy dinner, and for the next four years, I look forward to a pretty light bar tab. It's not much of a plan, but hey, it's better than the other ones I've heard. And I'm serious. I make them. Oh, yeah. *Oh*, yeah," he laughs. "It hurts a lot less."

The Mavericks' frontman can laugh about it now, but he got a little scared in 2004. "I did a solo acoustic tour and while I drove through the Midwest and along the East Coast right before the election, I'm listening to AM radio and it's nothing but hatred—and I mean *hatred*—for Democrats. And it goes uncontested, unanswered, unfiltered. It fades as you leave one small town, and you pick it up in the next. It's on all day, and there's not one left, liberal, non-conservative answer, not one rebuttal anywhere to be heard. It's Orwellian and it's creepy. A lot of people still don't have cable and don't get Fox News, but that AM stuff is nonstop, full of horrible things that should not be allowed to be said about anybody. But since the Fairness Act got overturned, there's no responsibility."

For a guy who has such a famously sweet, Orbisonesque singing voice, Malo gives good rant. If Steve Earle ever relinquishes his Air America slot, Malo could take it over, easy.

"Nobody comes out and says what really needs to be said. Which is, for one thing, 'You know what, people? Abortion is a non-issue. Government is not gonna get in on this. This is between a woman, her family, and her doctor.' As far as gay rights, I want to live in a country where people can get married to whoever the hell they want, because it's not gonna affect any one of us. We live such isolated lives anyway. Do we really know who our neighbors are? Do we really care if they're married or divorced? My neighbor could die tomorrow and be rotting in that house for months, and I would never know. That's just the world we live in. So what difference does it make who gets married to who, as long as they don't get married to you? As a matter of fact, let them get married and pay taxes like everybody else does.

"And as far as taxes are concerned, guess what, American fuckin' people: If you want to live in Disneyland, you gotta pay—it's that simple. If you want your streets cleaned, your police and your teachers paid, your sewage and park services, the money has to come from somewhere. But no politician touches the subject, because it won't get them elected, because the American public can't handle"—a prissy voice—"'ooh, the tax word.' Give me a freakin' break. Grow up. We have to pay taxes.

"I'm religious, but I don't force it on anybody and I don't think it should be part of government. To hear our president invoke the word of God is a frightening thing. Obviously he doesn't care what our allies think, because in other industrialized nations, no leader ever invokes the word of God, ever. If he did, he'd be ruled out, because people would not stand for it. Because they're tolerant societies and they feel that the leaders of their countries should not impose religion at all. Faith is a personal, private issue, but we turned it into a political agenda and a deciding factor in the vote of a nation. Incredible.

"I heard a conversation the other day that frightened me more than anything I've heard in a long time, and it was by two seemingly intelligent women working at the airport here in Nashville. They were talking about how God's gonna come down and take the believers up to heaven, which means that if you're on an airplane with a pilot that believes and he gets swooped up to heaven, the nonbelievers will come crashing down. What day and age is this? Do you people know that the earth is round and not flat, and that we have electricity . . . ? Don't get me wrong, man. Faith is a great thing, and I love it when people have faith and it gets 'em through their day. I wish I had more of it. But this was beyond belief. I started to think, wow, Canada is looking really good right now.

"I don't feel especially proud to be an American at the moment. And I just got back. I played for the troops in Bosnia and Germany and got to hang out with people who had just come back from Iraq and hear firsthand accounts about what's going on. It was frightening to see these young people who are being called back to duty—after serving, they've gotta go back. All for what? So we can save, what, ten cents on a gallon of gas, which we haven't, because gas has gone up anyway? And our troops are now depleted. And the states that have nuclear weapons, God forbid we're gonna attack *them*."

Why did he do a USO tour, feeling the way he does about the futility of America's efforts there? "These guys are much braver and tougher than I am and certainly a lot more patriotic than I am, and I admire that. When I was graduating from high school, the Cold War was over and there was no real enemy anymore, so I didn't go into the armed services. But if I were eighteen and this was happening, I might feel differently—I don't know. So the motivator was just to give them a little thank-you and go entertain them in some shit remote part of the world. Not that Germany is, but Bosnia's a shithole, now. So selfish reasons, karma points—call it whatever you want. Just to look them in the eye and see what that's all about."

He never let on about his anti-war feelings with the troops he met. "If all they have is their patriotism and that's what gets them through the day, I don't want to impose my politics and my agenda on them. All I'm gonna do is aggravate them, and I certainly don't want to do that. They've had enough shit imposed on them that may cost them their lives."

Slouching Toward Washington with Buddy Miller

The woman manning the counter at Nashville's Bongo Java rings up Buddy Miller's tally. The total comes out to exactly $7.77. "Wow!" she says. "A spiritual number."

"Yeah, I guess it is," says Miller, getting his order to go.

"Most of the time, if it's anything like that, it comes out to $6.66," she notes, seeming to regard this as a positive omen in the struggle between good and evil waged daily at this very brewhouse. (You can't discount such assumptions entirely out of hand, because Bongo Java *is* the coffeehouse that achieved world renown in 1996 for producing a cinnamon bun that, within its creases, seemed to bear the likeness of Mother Teresa.)

It would be untoward to say that Miller is on a mission from God. After all, the centerpiece of his most recent album is an indictment of that kind of presumption: a blazing cover of Bob Dylan's "With God on Our Side" that slowly, over nine minutes, roasts the politicos who would confuse even the best-intentioned nationalism with a divine mandate.

The context for Miller's version of this song lends it far more power than it would have in most any agitprop-prone alt-country-rocker's arsenal. Appearing early on in what is otherwise nearly a straightforward gospel album, *Universal United House of Prayer*, the song conveys a strong sense of indignation as a reflection of actual religious belief, rather than as pure agnostic venom.

In *No Depression* magazine's annual critics' poll, Miller's album was voted the second-best album of 2004, behind Loretta Lynn's *Van Lear Rose*. It was another validation of Miller, formerly best known as a guitar-hero sideman for Emmylou Harris and Steve Earle, as a major artist in his own right. For coeditor Grant Alden, his was "hands down the best record of the year. He absolutely caught the essence of things, down to the fact that the liberals simply do not respect the power of religion—to work for them, and against them." Alden gives Miller's album the nod over Steve Earle's more overtly and thoroughly political one. "Earle has become entrenched in his own polemics. I have deep respect for Steve, but there isn't very much lasting art to be created by addressing current events—some, but not much."

But *Universal United House of Prayer* is the kind of album that makes some people, well, *project*. Back in Miller's home studio a few blocks from Bongo Java, I let him sip his coffee while I recite for him excerpts from an essay that appeared in *No Depression*. In it, critic Geoffrey Himes (who also writes for the *Washington Post*) praises Miller's album as the perfect manifestation of blue-state progressivism circa 2004, and a richly realized expression of liberal theology and politics . . . as opposed to, say, an album of Christian devotion, which it mostly seems to be, the Dylan song and war anxiety notwithstanding.

Himes wrote: "Whatever else He may or may not be, God is not a meddling micromanager who determines the outcome of human decisions. And He certainly can't be used as justification for the genocidal slaughter of Indians . . . The God of Dylan, Miller, and John Kerry is a hands-off God, a God who treats human beings like adults who must bear the consequences of their decisions, a God who allows the laws of evolution, physics, meteorology, and sexual attraction to play themselves out without interference. By contrast, the God of Toby Keith, Darryl Worley, and George W. Bush is a hands-on God, a God who treats humans like children who can't handle nuance or dilemmas, a God who regularly contravenes the laws of nature to make sure the good guys win and the bad guys lose. These two different views explain the difference not just between the blue states and the red states, but also between alt-country and mainstream country."

Miller seems a bit taken aback at this reading of his album, but he isn't about to object. "Well, you can take the record actually anywhere you want to take it, I guess," he says quietly. "That's just what happens." Later, he elaborates a little. "I figure, when gospel songs come from somebody that believes it, that bugs people, sometimes. They have an easier time taking it from people that don't really believe it."

This album, he says, was "not about 'the war.' I didn't want it to be about the war and the election, or something that would be irrelevant after November. But there were a couple of songs that resonated with that." Another is the opening track, "Worry Too Much," an entirely secular statement of wartime angst written by the late Christian rock dynamo Mark Heard at the time of the first Gulf War, when Miller was engineering Heard's album. "You've gotta scratch your head and wonder about what's going on. And why is that Dylan song more relevant now than it was forty years ago? Gospel songs seemed to me like a way to connect dots, and I'd wanted to make a gospel record anyway." Miller's brother-in-law had died in a bizarre accident, and between that loss and the growing tension over Iraq, he decided to make a record in which angstfulness was next to godliness.

Getting Miller to talk about the election is like pulling teeth, if quieter and less bloody. He wants to play along—he really does—but it seems almost physically painful to him. Considerable wincing ensues.

"I'm not a Democrat or Republican. I just don't like any of it," he finally says in a barely audible voice. "I wasn't a big Bush-hater. Wasn't one of them. It seemed like the hatred toward Bush was so blindly strong in this last year. I didn't understand that. I didn't like the guy. I thought that it was one missed opportunity after another on his part, to bring the world and the country together. But the real hatred people had toward him, I don't know where it comes from, because there are a lot of good Republicans, good folks on both sides. I think people start out with good intentions, but the presidential campaign was just so ugly. Man, anybody who tries to be the president has got real problems, don't you think? If you want that job, there's gotta be something wrong with you.

"I told Emmylou I would do anything for her; any benefit she does, I would do for nothing—except anything political. Causes like Campaign for a Landmine Free World, I do, but when it was coming up to the election, if there's anything that she's doing, count me out, because I didn't want to have anything to do with any of it. You know, I'd pay money to play with her every night. I love it. I've had the best gig in the world, these last few years with her. Just none of *that stuff*."

The previous night, Miller and Harris, along with Gillian Welch, David Rawlings, and Patty Griffin, played the Grand Ole Opry together. He had wanted to play a Jerry Garcia song, "Deal," just to sneak the Grateful Dead into the Opry's international telecast. At the last minute, Miller settled on a substitute, "You Can't Judge a Book by Its Cover," by bluesman Willie Dixon, because he wanted to introduce it by saying, "This is a Willie song." He does have a bit of a subversive streak.

Of course, "You Can't Judge a Book by Its Cover" is a political statement, too. It's not hard to see why some critics, or Grammy committees, can't necessarily judge Miller by his cover. *Universal United House of Prayer* is a gospel album disguised as a political statement disguised as a gospel album. He's an acclaimed singer/songwriter disguised as an alt-country guitar hero-for-hire disguised as wife Julie Miller's duet partner. And he's a guy who, despite presumptions some might make about his politics from the company he keeps, sits in the muddled and vaguely disgusted middle. Both conservatives and liberals prefer to think of themselves as the silent majority, but it seems more likely that, the recent era of polarization aside, the real majority of the country might be made up of former and future swing voters who are silent because they're baffled by an overly simplistic divvying up into teams. Count Miller into that count-me-out crowd.

"I didn't like the way it seemed that Christians had to be aligned with a certain political party," Miller says. "If you believed this, then you had to believe that. You couldn't be any mix of something, you had to be one or the other. I can't align myself with the Democrats, who support that late-term abortion. I can't go along with that. That's the one thing I haven't been able to understand about the Democratic party, how they seem to believe it's okay to do that right up to the day before you have a baby. Why do they say that's okay?" He's not asking rhetorically, either. "*Do* you know? I mean, I'm just asking. Everything in there, you have to check it off. Gotta line up with all of that. And why the Republicans turn a blind eye to so many issues, it just kills me. If you're Republican, landmines—yeah, they're great. It's just things that don't make sense in each camp you've gotta go along with. I think there's some good people out there, but all they do is yell at each other. I don't understand, so I go play guitars and hope for the best."

His bafflement is both parties' loss.

"Except," Miller suddenly remembers, "I gotta admit, I did play for Patrick Leahy. I know I said 'anything but politicians,' but I leave him out of that column."

How did Leahy, a Democratic senator from Vermont, earn a pass?

"Well, you know, he's an ex-Deadhead."

Johnny Cash and Merle Haggard, widely revered as the two male giants of country music throughout the 1960s, 1970s, and beyond, shared a certain political iconoclasm. Country singer-cum-photojournalist Marty Stuart snapped this rare shot of the dynamic duo near the end of Cash's life. PHOTO BY MARTY STUART

8

Deep Purple

Haggard and Cash, the Omnipoliticians

When you're in the market to pick up a T-shirt with a flapping American flag on the front and LOVE IT OR LEAVE IT as the accompanying motto, or you develop the sudden need to find a "Fightin' Side" baseball cap with an embroidered eagle, a Bob Dylan show has historically not been your one-stop shopping source. But things have changed, as the man says. Merle Haggard is the opening attraction on Dylan's spring 2005 tour, and in the lobby of L.A.'s Pantages Theater, Hag's merchandise booth is almost as busy as Bob's. The fiftysomething fans who are snapping up these souvenirs probably realize that Haggard was always a bit more of a counterculturalist than a redneck at heart. And that handful of virulently patriotic, dove-baiting tunes Merle had hits with during the Vietnam era? In the minds of Dylan fans, most likely, these can be explained away—or embraced, judging from the T-shirt sales—as period kitsch. Anyway, there's definitely something historic going on when veterans of a previous generation's culture wars can hear "Masters of War" and "Fightin' Side of Me" performed on the same bill, and not by some perverse cover band.

In Haggard, Dylan picked as a support act one of the few other major figures in popular music whose sets are as freewheeling as his own. Last night, Haggard's show included "Fightin'" but no "Okie." Tonight, it's the other way around, as he responds to shouted requests. "Somebody once asked me why I wrote 'Okie from Muskogee,'" he teases the crowd. "I told him, because I was the only one that knew the words." Haggard may be a test-tube synthesis of Bob Wills and Woody Guthrie, but there's a little Henny Youngman in him, too. He suggests a "Muskogee" sing-along, and when much of the packed crowd at this old movie palace delightedly acquieses, the singer reacts with mock alarm: "This is Bob Dylan's audience! You're not supposed to be smoking—I mean singing—along with that!" He further ingratiates himself with fleeting commentary about the president, who he calls "G.W.": "I wish he would just get one smirk into a complete smile." Later in the rant, Haggard wonders, "Is *he* the jerk that invented work?" (a reference to that golden oldie, "Big Rock Candy Mountain"). After a bit more Bush-bashing, he figures, "I better shut up before the men in black come after me."

If only the webmasters who post Haggard's name as a card-carrying GOP member on their celebrity-Republican websites could see him now.

You can't really blame them for presuming he's one of their own. There's something about Haggard, and the late Johnny Cash, too: Everybody wants to claim them, and they're ambiguous enough that almost everybody can. If you're a member of the Grand Old Party, these twin titans almost certainly were or are conservatives in good standing. If you're a liberal, they must be, too. Hawks? Doves? Christians? Universalists? Hippie sympathizers? Love-or-it-or-piss-off patriots? All of the above were convinced that country's leading men were unassailably on their side, and, for all we know, there are secret enclaves of renegade John Birchers and neo-Stalinists proudly counting J.R. and Hag among their honorary rolls. These two belong to America—all of America. How else to explain their seemingly contradictory impulses over the years, the apparently irreconcilable positions that led to all those overlapping bragging rights from special interest groups? Cash and Haggard were mavericks who predate today's easy polarization, independents who boldly claimed their issues where they found them, without feeling boxed in by anyone else's ideological shorthand. Well, either that, or the maverick thinking we like to label as cowboy individualism was really just a sign of a couple of deeply confused, conflicted souls. But wouldn't there be something profoundly patriotic, signifying the beginning of wisdom, even in that?

At the Pantages, Haggard is playing around with some of his old lyrics. "Are the Good Times Really Over for Good?," from 1982, is a song that waxes nostalgic for a time "back before Nixon lied to us all on TV / Before microwave ovens, when a girl could still cook, and still would . . ." A few feminists have objected to that line over the years, and perhaps in reaction, or just out of silliness, Haggard now sings, "When a girl could still cook, and chop wood . . ." "Okie" also gets a slight update: "We let our hair grow long and shaggy, like the hippies out in San Francisco do," sings Haggard, with one level of irony—adding another when he doffs his hat to show just how far things have receded. The man does love a mixed message.

Indie Country

Haggard may be up for spoofing himself these days, but he isn't the first one to mess with the lyrics of "Okie." His pal Kris Kristofferson used to sing a half-affectionate, half-parodistic version in concert, as heard on *Live at the Philharmonic*, recorded in 1972, where he added additional lyrics such as, "We don't shoot that deadly marijuana / We get drunk like God wants us to do." Kristofferson ends the vintage live version "with apologies to our friend Merle Haggard, who is neither a racist or a redneck; he just happens to be known for the only bad song he ever wrote."

Kristofferson says now, "'Okie' wasn't a bad song. It was just a song that I didn't agree with. But he's always been one of my favorites. Just the other day, I was wishing Haggard would sing this song of mine, 'Anthem 84.' I'm pleased to see the stuff he's coming out with. Merle's stepping out and speaking these days," he says, referring to some recent Haggard anti-war statements, "and that's the Okie from Muskogee!"

Neither does Steve Earle, upon scratching heroes Haggard and Cash, find the blood of reactionaries. "These guys, none of 'em ever voted Republican in their lives," Earle insists. "They were probably what my uncle used to call 'yellow-dog Democrats.' But they were also hipsters, and they changed as they got older. I know Merle Haggard, and I knew Johnny Cash, and I promise you, if you look at Merle's last record [*Haggard Like Never Before*], you can see the change. By the time the Vietnam war was over with, he, like a lot of people, including my father, completely understood that we'd been had and that we needed to get out. His writing 'Okie from Muskogee' is the same thing as me writing 'John Walker's Blues.' He creates a character that isn't necessarily him. It's part of him, and to some extent it's who he was at the time, but it's not all of him. It is a fictitious character."

Cash was a little hard to figure, admits Kristofferson; sometimes Cash stood with him on issues and sometimes he landed squarely to his right. That's okay. "People don't need to fit into a neat box. John was a very concerned guy who always spoke the truth as he saw it, and he believed in fighting for the underdog. I know he supported some people whose views he probably thought were wrong—like maybe when he was defending me. He might've felt what I was saying was wrong, but he fought for my right to say it." Kristofferson mentions an early-nineties concert where, as Cash's opening act, he antagonized the crowd more than he realized with some diatribes against American foreign intervention; Cash not only refused to accept his apology, he brought Kristofferson out during the encore to sing "Why Me," so the audience wouldn't leave hating him.

The two artists found a point of agreement in wartime at the end: "One of the last things he said to me," Kristofferson recalls, "when we were bombing Afghanistan, was, 'I'm with you on this one. We're bombing a tribal people.'"

Cash's daughter, Rosanne, says, "The two of them, my dad and Kris, had their disagreements in the past. But oh, Dad was so opposed to this war. It broke his heart. It really did. I think that people appreciate people who follow their own truth, and what was so beautiful about my dad is that you knew he was an honest guy who was seeking out his own truth and living his own pain and his own life and his own joy. You have to respect that, no matter who you vote for. I always felt that Dad was an aberration, and also an iconoclast. No, I never thought he was the norm in country music or our family was the norm. Although back in the seventies, that contingency of Southern Democrats were strong and powerful, and there were a lot of us in there, Dad being one of them. Dad always remained a Democrat. But he never registered, you know. He never affiliated himself with a party, but he definitely was liberal in his social and political views."

But it's undeniable that he was ambiguous or conflicted enough for conservatives to believe he was one of their own. "Mm-hm. Yeah, he was complex, and he followed his own truth. You know what's so fascinating?" says Cash. "I did this press conference with David Byrne, Russell Simmons, and Lou Reed, right before we invaded Iraq—it was part of Moveon.org, this subgroup called Musicians United to Win Without War—and we said why we were against it. I got so much hate mail after that. Not just 'I disagree with you,' but really vicious name-calling. And this one guy wrote, 'Well, I'm just gonna stick with the *real* Americans like Merle Haggard and your dad.'" This cracks her up. "And I'm thinking, *they're* both as liberal as I am!"

Rodney Crowell, Johnny Cash's former son-in-law, by way of Rosanne, and a friend up till the end, agrees with her. "I think if you explore Merle Haggard, you'll find a liberal. And Johnny Cash was an eloquent conservative individual who was socially liberal. I know for a fact that George Bush drove Johnny Cash around the bend. He was no fan of that man. He said so to me, more than once!

"With stuff like 'Mama's Hungry,' Merle Haggard is a real post-Depression poet. He's a Steinbeck Okie. I think 'Fightin' Side of Me' or 'Okie from Muskogee' was Merle Haggard being a really great songwriter who tapped into something that was true about being an American during the Vietnam war. It was perhaps uninformed, be-cause in the late sixties, we weren't really learning about how duped we were in the Vietnam war. From the mid-seventies on, when Michael Herr started writing *Dispatches*, we started to put two and two together about how deceived we were."

Returning to Cash, Crowell says, "His patriotism was informed. He wore black as a political statement. He was critical of the American government for what it did to the American Indian, and his Christian-ity was compassionate and forgiving, not the ideology of the church. Billy Graham endorsed him, and therefore he had credibility during what was, for my tastes, a more enlightened Christian era. Through several traditional forms or archetypes—Christianity, patriotism—he filtered enlightenment, and in doing so therefore he resonated with conservative and liberal alike. Show me somebody who does that now, who has the audience's attention. Bono is the only one I can put my finger on immediately, in entertainment. Bruce Springsteen, maybe, although he doesn't introduce Christianity to it. *My* Christianity does not have any real archetypal form—my relationship with God is without religion, so I can't address an audience through that kind of Christian language.

"I don't see anybody in country music nowadays that is playing toward enlightenment, like Haggard and Cash were. Kristofferson did. Dylan electrified everybody with enlightenment; even if it wasn't what he intended, he couldn't help it. I really get moved by those kinds of artists, where what they do takes root and grows into something else. In the country music mainstream, it's just not there. That's why I hated to see the Dixie Chicks get their legs chopped out from under 'em, because those girls are articulate and smart and funny and sarcastic and metaphorical. It's almost like how, when the enlightenment was coming on with the Kennedy brothers and Martin Luther King, they just went out and killed it. 'Okay, that's out of the way, we can get on with our business.' This was not the same thing, but it's a metaphor for the smaller situation. The Dixie Chicks were the one dissenting voice, and it got chopped down."

Not everyone would be so quick or eager to put the Chicks and Haggard in the same ideological camp, though. One of Hag's biggest fans offers his opinion:

"We do 'Fightin' Side of Me' every night," says Toby Keith, a fellow Okie and recent duet partner. "Merle Haggard was the *original* angry American, and that was the original angry American song. I added a couple of verses of that song for our encore. It's in the same key, so I just slow it down and kick it right into 'Courtesy of the Red, White and Blue.' It's a nice segueway." Haggard loves Toby back; they duet on each other's most recent albums.

Conservatives who have made efforts to associate themselves with Cash after his death have sometimes run into resistance from the lawyers representing the singer's estate. An anonymous Bush supporter made a bizarre music video using one of Cash's last recordings, "The Man Comes Around," as audio for an illicit assemblage of material that was widely disseminated on the right-wing Free Republic website. The song recounts an apocalyptic vision of the second coming of Christ; the anonymous video director made the song a soundtrack for celebratory footage of the president and the war in Iraq, making "the man" of the title a vengeful wraith named Dubya instead of the Lord Jehovah. Same difference, right? Cash family attorneys didn't think so and eventually got around to quashing the video's online dissemination. There was also the matter of a political shindig that was held at Sotheby's for the 2004 Republican convention delegates. The auction house was hosting a Cash exhibit at the time, and Cash's photo was included on the invitation to the Republicans' confab. "That got out to the press, and people went ballistic," says Rosanne Cash, "and *I* went ballistic. Lamar Alexander is an old friend of Dad's and a friend of the family, and we respect him a lot, and he wanted to have this party there, and that was fine, but the lawyers made that group withdraw the invitations." Ease up, everybody: "Nobody used Dad to advance the Republican platform—although they would have liked to."

Bill C. Malone, the country music historian, doesn't think that conservatives are clueless for trying to claim Haggard and Cash as their own. As a liberal himself, he would like to think these two were warriors for the left, but he just doesn't see it.

"It's hard to find anything in either Haggard or Cash that's very brave or radical," says Malone. "You don't find any strong anti-war statements in Cash's stuff. It's always pretty oblique, and when he does take a strong stand on something, they're usually pretty safe issues, like convict rights, Indian rights, that sort of thing. It amazes me when people try to make Johnny Cash out as either a liberal or an outspoken radical. You've got the 'Ragged Old Flag' song, and at the most critical moments during either the Vietnam War or the wars in the Middle East you don't find any strong statements by him. The same with Willie Nelson; after he sang 'Whatever Happened to Peace on Earth' at one Kucinich campaign stop, I don't think he ever sang it again."

The songs that made a lot of folk enthusiasts fall in love with Haggard in the early sixties were numbers like "Hungry Eyes," which explored poverty as eloquently and unflinchingly as popular music ever has, and not as something that the American dream is about to override.

> I remember daddy praying for a better way of life
> But I don't recall a change of any size;
> Just a little loss of courage, as their age began to show
> And more sadness in my mama's hungry eyes

And then, of course, Haggard blew whatever Guthriesque image he might have been developing straight to hell for at least a few years with "Muskogee" and "Fightin' Side."

> I read about some squirrelly guy,
> Who claims, he just don't believe in fightin'.
> An' I wonder just how long,
> The rest of us can count on bein' free.
> They love our milk an' honey,
> But they preach about some other way of livin'.
> When they're runnin' down my country, hoss,
> They're walkin' on the fightin' side of me.

"People want to believe the best of Haggard," says Malone. "I was the same way. I was such a strong Merle Haggard fan in the 1960s, and became really disappointed." He was willing to forgive him for his first sop to conservatives, figuring it was an accident. "You can see him sort of stumbling into a position with 'Okie from Muskogee.' Haggard wrote it as a joke, and then he got a better reaction to it than he ever anticipated. But then he sat down and deliberately wrote 'Fightin' Side of Me' to exploit the audience that he found out existed. People will also mention 'Irma Jackson,' talking about his sensitive defense of interracial feelings"—Malone chuckles, not sure the song was that sensitive—"and some of his earlier songs that harken back to the 1930s when the Okies were being persecuted. But you find hardly anything that really fits today's world that can be described as politically activist. Even with 'That's the News'—there's not much to that song," says Malone, getting almost heretical. "Liberals, though, always liked him, and want to see things that are not there. They keep hoping that Haggard's gonna really come out one of these days and say something."

Crowell has an answer for Malone: "I guarantee you, man, at the core of Haggard is a common-man Democrat. But you know, that common-man Democrat is also the guy who will stand up and say, 'You long-haired hippies are full of shit.' *That's* also being part of being Democratic. The Democrats have lost their bite. I don't help," laughs Crowell, "because I don't have that kind of bite, either."

"That's the News" is the tune that put Haggard back in the news in mid-2003 and belatedly restored him to the good graces of some liberals who'd written him off three decades earlier. At the time, he was being distributed by a small alt-country label, so there was never any danger of the song getting much mainstream play, even if the lyrics had been what country radio had wanted to hear. But the press, eager to find any country-music figure brave enough to buck the conservative tide in the wake of the Dixie Chicks' stigmatization, converged on the single—even though the lyric was more an indictment of TV news' obsession with celebrity, and how quickly this obsession was reasserted in lieu of war coverage, than about the Iraqi conflict itself.

> Suddenly celebrity is something back in style
> Back to running tabloid for a while
> Pain's almost everywhere, the whole world's got the blues
> Suddenly the war is over: that's the news
> Suddenly the cost of war is something out of sight
> Lost a lotta heroes in the fight
> Politicians do all the talking: soldiers pay the dues
> Suddenly the war is over, that's the news

It's not quite Country Joe's "I-Feel-Like-I'm-Fixin'-to-Die Rag," but the song does implicitly indict the war machine almost as much as the media machine. Kristofferson thinks this is monumental; Malone thinks it's incidental.

Time to conclusively settle this debate, fix Haggard's place in the political firmament, and engage him in a round of pin the tail on the . . . well, what kind of animal would he be, exactly?

Transcendental Blues

Haggard's tour bus is parked outside a studio on a nondescript Burbank side street. He has just arrived to do one last day of recording for a new Capitol Records project that'll represent his first batch of original material for a major label in more than a decade. He's squeezing in the valuable studio time on a day off from the Dylan tour. Between sessions, producers Jimmy Bowen and Mike Post can't help but query their client about what kind of run-ins he has or hasn't had with Dylan, as rock's reclusive bard is famous for having little, if any, communication on the road with his handpicked opening acts, even when they're as legendary as he is.

"Has he been . . . friendly?" asks Post.

"Yeah, but strangely so," answers Haggard. "I met him once before, and back then he just sort of grunted. But he's Bob Dylan! You don't know what's going on inside him. He's like the Einstein of music. He

might be working out physics while he's talking to you." The two
have had minimal exchanges on this tour so far, "but I know he tells
people he's doing this to expose me to his audience," says Haggard,
still a bit curious about it all himself.

There seems to be a running motif to the pair's fleeting encounters.
"He comes up to me at one point and says"—Haggard breaks into a
classic Dylan imitation—"'So, uh, I've been reading your book [the
autobiography *Sing Me Back Home*], and, uh, you *stole* a lot of stuff.'"
Haggard, of course, spent some time in Folsom Prison in the late
fifties for his petty felonies. Later in the tour, some musicians were
looking at a guitar that formerly had belonged to fellow Bakersfield
country legend Buck Owens, which had recently been procured by a
member of Dylan's band. Dylan came over to admire it, as well. "I paid
for half of it, you know," Haggard bragged to Dylan—who quipped
back, "Maybe you *stole* your half."

At various times, Haggard recalled, Dylan would say to him,
"You're gonna have to teach me how to hop a freight someday," or "I
want you to teach me how you stole cars." "I said, 'Well, Bob, I haven't
stolen a car in a long time, you know.'" That's where they left it, but
Haggard sent Dylan a message from the stage a few nights ago. He'd
like to see the inside of the headliner's tour bus, because he's been
thinking of getting one like it, but he's had to call Dylan's handlers to
put that request in, and so far he hasn't gotten a reply. So a few nights
ago, Haggard upped the ante by telling the audience, "Bob Dylan invited me on his show, but he's afraid to have me on his fuckin' bus,
'cause he's afraid I'll *steal* something!" Haggard chuckles and says,
"We'll see if that gets a rise out of him."

Back to work, and an interesting afternoon of labor it is. Haggard
and the musicians were supposed to be wrapping up overdubs today,
but Haggard stepped off the bus with a new song he just wrote this
morning, and he wants to record it immediately. "If there's one thing
better than sex, it's to write a good song. The climax never ends, you
know what I mean?" he says. While Hag and his guitarist and fiddler
work out the parts, Bowen laughs and mutters, "That's the thing about
working with Haggard. If you try to figure out what's gonna happen
next, you're wasting your time." Within minutes, they're recording
the elegiac ballad "Some of Us Fly," which is almost in the vein of
something like Dylan's "Every Grain of Sand."

Some spiral down in a circle
Some climb too steeply and stall
Some take the bet, some ponder it yet
Some pass, some raise, and some call
Some play it smart
I had a ball
Some of us fly . . . all of us fall

After three takes, they've got it. Now it's on to the regularly scheduled vocal overdubs. Haggard has one decidedly political new song they're wrapping up, called "Let's Rebuild America First." He insists he had to be talked into including it on the new album. "I said, 'Why don't we just leave that stuff off, and for once do an album that's totally about music and doesn't have any political undertones or overtones?' But Bowen says he thinks that the American Merle Haggard fan wants to hear about my opinions as much as they want to hear the music, so we should have it in there." Bowen adds, "He felt people were tired of it all"—meaning politics. "I felt that way, too. But by the time the album comes out, it'll be a year after the election, and people will just be gearing up for the next one!"

The song starts off provocatively enough: "Why don't we liberate these United States / We're the ones who need it the worst . . ." There are references to "highways and bridges falling apart," and Haggard tries to make it clear that he knows whereof he speaks: "Well, you think I'm blowin' smoke / Boys, it ain't no joke / I make twenty trips a year coast to coast." He proceeds to lay into the overextended U.S. military and what he feels are the dangerous constrictions of the Patriot Act:

Hey, who's on the hill
Who's watching the valley
And who's in charge of it all
God bless our army and God bless liberty
And dad-gum the rest of it all

Heyyy, men in position are backing away
Freedom is stuck in reverse
Let's get out of Iraq and get back on the track
Let's rebuild America first

"Time to come home!" he barks as the verse leads into an instrumental break that's all fiddle and banjo and martial snare, as if alerting the band to head for the coda *and* personally recalling the troops from the Middle East all at once.

With that tune a wrap, and a cover of "Everybody's Talkin'" scheduled to be recorded next, studio talk inevitably turns to the era when Nilsson first had a hit with that song, and to President Nixon object of some of Haggard's greatest ire. Nixon was known to be such a fan of "Okie from Muskogee" that he asked Johnny Cash to perform it during a visit to the White House; Cash turned him down, though that may have had less to do with disavowing its politics than feeling insulted by a royal request to impersonate a rival.

"If they took a poll of the top three assholes of all time, who would they be?" wonders Haggard. "It'd have to be Hitler and Nixon, and then G.W. would be in there right under 'em."

"I've met a bunch of them," offers Bowen.

"Mike Curb would be in the top five," says Haggard. Curb presumably has multiple strikes against him, having been the Republican lieutenant governor of California, Haggard's home state, at a time when schools and services went into decline, *and* the owner of a Nashville label who has withheld a cache of unreleased Haggard recordings since the singer bolted the company. "I'd just like one chance to get my songs back," Haggard declares, shaking his head sadly.

He grabs the lyric sheet off the console, taking an a cappella run at nailing Fred Neil's vintage lyric. "Everybody's talkin' at me / But I can't hear a word they're sayin' . . ."

Why We Fight

Conservatives, liberals, Democrats, Republicans—they all want to think Merle Haggard is one of them, I tell him, when we get down to talking.

"Well, I *am* one of all of them," he declares. "I represent all of them with their hearts and their souls, and I'll leave their politics and religion to them. I have *my* politics and *my* religion. Not to put the Dixie Chicks down any more than they already have been, but I'm not gonna do what they did. I'm not gonna jump up and put my well-known foot in my mouth about anything having to do with the chief executive or what's going on."

Which, of course, is precisely what he spends much of the next hour doing. He doesn't even take a breath after the preceding disclaimer before starting in.

"You know, I'm going to say as an American that I think they've been disingenuous with the public about the reasons why we're in Iraq. And I think the United States of America is mature enough to understand the real reasons. With the knowledge the commander in chief was given, he felt the invasion was necessary, but I don't think he told us *why*. If Americans are gonna have to suffer sanctions to our freedom, then we ought to know the entire picture. They ought to say 'Hey, we need that oil,' or whatever the real reason was. And if they've got the Ark of the Covenant over there or something and we need to have it, then I think the American public—Republican and Democrat alike—would appreciate honesty, straightforward honesty. He'd be the biggest president since Abe Lincoln if he'd only step up and say, 'Okay, we're gonna cut all the well known crap, and here's the real deal. I don't have any control at all,' or, 'This is what happened, and I'm a lame duck, and I'm out of here, but I'd like to leave here an honest president' . . . But it's like the old joke, the one where the guys are talking about Bush and Hussein and one of them says, 'He's a mass killer, he has weapons of mass destruction—but remember, he *is* our commander in chief.'"

Steve Earle was right when he said Haggard never voted for a Republican in his life. But that statement needs a footnote.

"I wouldn't have voted for John Kerry. There wasn't really anybody opposing Bush that could step into the shoes of what it takes to be president of the United States. So had I voted, I *would* have voted for G.W. I have never voted. They took away my right to vote when I was an ex-con, and I got used to it, and I just never did register after that."

Did Haggard get much flak over "That's the News"? "I didn't see anybody oppose it. It is a *fact* that the news media reported that we were basically over with the war, when he came down on the ship and said 'The major conflict is over. We've invaded and we've captured Iraq.' I probably do get a lot of flak because I'm not for this Patriot Act. But listen, it's been a long time since 9/11. We didn't react to World War II this long! It's sure time that we went back to being normal. God forbid we put people out of work in security, but it's like 1939 in Berlin in some places in America right now! And the further east you go, the worse it gets. I don't want to be on the front lines of a war right now. I'm sixty-seven years old. I don't want 'em patting me down," he laughs. "I'm too old to feel it."

In "Are the Good Times Really Over for Good?," Haggard had that pointed lyric about Nixon lying to the country. Seems fair to surmise that presidential disingenuousness is a pet peeve.

"Well, Nixon had a choice of being a snitch or a liar. And if you've got to choose between the two, he should have been a snitch. He should have told the people, 'Well, they went over here and they went in this building,' and shook his head two or three times, and turned 'em in! I'm sorry, I hate snitches, too." (Once an ex-con, always an ex-con, when it comes to certain ways of looking at things.) "But if you've got to turn state's evidence, boy, that was the time to do it, instead of lying to the people and saying he didn't know anything about it. That's forever what we'll remember Richard Nixon for. And he was an extremely intelligent man. I played for him and 300 dignitaries, and he introduced everybody in my entourage to them and everybody in their entourage to us, and remembered all their names and their children's names, and was telling me about his life and asking me about mine while he had about eight other conversations going on. He was just a brilliant guy. And all-American. But he cheated." A pause. "I guess that's part of being an American. We all cheat a little bit. Maybe we're a little too critical on the presidents, I don't know. That's why at the end of everything I say about George Bush, I add: But he is the commander in chief, and we must respect that. If we don't, we're foolish."

We regret to inform Steve Earle, Rosanne Cash, and other liberal defenders that, when asked to name his favorite president, Haggard replies: "Kennedy was on his way to doing good, but he got too big for his britches. I think Ronald Reagan really did the job best." It may not be coincidental that, as governor, Reagan gave Haggard a full pardon. But he cites a master thespian quality that he thinks is intrinsic, not antithetical, to the job. "Reagan had the talent of carrying himself right that was necessary for the rest of the world to see what an American is. Our current president has done a terrible job of that; he should have taken some acting lessons. After 9/11, he pissed off 120 countries with his arrogance. And while our freedom has been infringed upon, and we're looking up each other's dresses, he walks around with his head up in the air."

Nowadays, there's a presumption that anyone singing patriotic material is a Republican, whereas in a previous era there was no reason not to imagine that the guy singing "Okie" or "Fightin'" was a Democrat.

"There are things I go for on both sides of the fence. I can't be called one or the other. Both of 'em disappoint me. America is being sold out right beneath our feet. Our way of life is going away. Each attempt is named something. Now it's the Patriot Act. How many years should this thing go on, until we go back to being real Americans? I feel sorry for my kids and grandchildren. The brand of freedom they're settling for is different from the kind we had."

Haggard's musical freedom included the liberty to zig just when everyone expected him to zag—especially in the late sixties and seventies when he would alternate material that some saw as impossibly right-wing with stuff that struck others as progressive. "My mother summed all that up with one word. She said somebody asked her, 'Can you describe your son in a paragraph?' And she said, 'I can describe him in one word. Unpredictable.' And I come by it honestly. But I also plan it. I intend to be taking a different route this morning to wherever I'm going than I did yesterday morning, and I'm not gonna leave at the same time. And I'm not gonna worry about the show I'm doing this weekend till I get on stage. I just have always been that way. I think it's the best way to protect yourself against a robbery," he laughs. "And you might even trick the devil once in a while, if nobody knows what you're gonna do."

After more than thirty-five years, Haggard is surely tired of being asked to defend "Muskogee," but he rises to the task with fresh aplomb.

"Not every song is about the guy who's singing it. That song was really about somebody like my dad, who got up at five in the morning to go to work and came home and ate supper and went to bed and did the same thing the next day and had nothing else to look forward to. And was happy with a Sunday afternoon together with the family and church. This whole country was full of people like that. The little hippie thing that was occurring in the big cities did not reflect the true majority of America. They called 'em the silent majority. They were just sitting there with their mouths open, watching all this crap come down. My dad had been dead for several years, but I thought, if he was alive, he'd like this song. It was kind of for my dad, because *he* was the Okie from Muskogee. He came from Oklahoma to California, and I was born out here, sort of an afterthought in our family."

He's not surprised that Dylan's audience has embraced this song. "I think everybody has finally accepted the positive message in that song, which is: Whatever you are, be proud to be it. 'Muskogee' doesn't put anybody down. It doesn't say 'They don't.' It says '*We* don't.' And we *don't* smoke any marijuana down there in Muskogee, you know!"

Time to let him get back to it. "Well, I hope I didn't say something to piss everybody off. You know, I'm sixty-seven, and I'm supposed to be dead when I'm seventy—so hell, so be it, you know. But look, I love this country as much as anybody you ever talked to in your life. I've enjoyed my life in it. And somebody needs to be aware that things are changing and we are eroding as a nation."

Anything else, Senator? Just one last plug for his old "Pancho and Lefty" duet partner, Willie Nelson. "Willie does a lot of things. For example, he pushes this thing, biodiesel, some sort of a vegetable fuel that's grown by farmers. He has an army of transportation, and he burns a combination of diesel and vegetable oil—French-fry oil from these quick food places around the country—in his automobiles and buses and trucks. Sensible things like that oil of his are totally possibilities now, not just probabilities or pie in the sky. There's all kinds of things to do for fuel that would put inner America back to work. God, why does something that's so simple have to be so involved?" Well, that's the oldest question in country music.

See you out on the road, Pancho. Or is it Lefty?

Epilogue

Four More Beers

Polarization and Its Discontents

There's a star-spangled banner waving somewhere, as Elton Britt, Dave Dudley, and so many other country singers have reminded us over the years, reviving that old World War II favorite. Tonight, Old Glory is waving over the annual Country Radio Seminar, of all places. In a ballroom inside Nashville's convention center, Big & Rich have brought a flag out on stage as part of their midnight showcase. A crowd of two thousand radio programmers and DJs is being asked to display some musical patriotism, which might not require all that much cajoling even if they all weren't about on their fifth open bar of the night.

"Well, y'all," Big Kenny tells the audience, "something that's always been important to us since the beginning of mankind is that we respect a little bit of where we come from. And one place that I think a lot of us come from in here—any of you who don't, well, you're welcome to sing along anyway—is from the good old U.S. of A. Out on tour all year long, we've been singing a little song every night, one everybody's probably heard, called 'The Star-Spangled Banner' . . . Let's just give it up one time! All of y'all sing together!"

"By the way," adds his partner, John Rich, "we're looking for your add on this single right now."

At the time, it's a joke. But John Philip Sousa, call your royalty accountants. A few months after this, in time for a Fourth of July network appearance with the Boston Pops, Big & Rich, Gretchen Wilson, and Cowboy Troy will record and make available as a free download "Our America," which makes a Stars-on-45 medley out of the preamble to the Constitution, Martin Luther King Jr.'s "dream" speech, the Pledge of Allegiance, the Declaration of Independence, and, of course, the national anthem.

By the summer of 2005, even something this safely patriotic has become an anomaly in country music. What Joe Galante thought would happen at least a year earlier has finally come true: the fans seemed burned out on political, topical, and even patriotic material, at least for the time being. Toby Keith's new album has come out, and aside from a reference to his USO trips to Iraq and Afghanistan in the autobiographical single "Honky Tonk U," there's nary a soldierly moment on it. Singles that do refer to current events have gone bust.

This even includes Terri Clark's "I Think the World Needs a Drink," a song that does a fairly clever job of being spirited in the service of ennui:

> Politicians flingin' dirt
> Got dissension in the church
> Another lawsuit in the works
> Man, you talk about a mess
> Too much tension between Miss Liberty and the Eiffel Tower
> It's about time we all made up at some big happy hour
> I think the world needs a drink . . .

Clark's single stalled at No. 26 on the chart. Apparently, people are even tired of songs about how tired we are of politics.

But surely it's just a lull. Merle Haggard's producers were able to convince him that, by the time a year had passed after the 2004 election, folks would be gearing up for infighting again and ready to hear something like his "Let's Rebuild America First." Meanwhile, we see little skirmishes breaking out, like the one in Texas, where some Republican politicos made a partisan show out of refusing to name a new tollway after Willie Nelson because of, you know, his partisanship. Simultaneously, the musician-cum-novelist who has long described himself as "the Texas Jewboy," Kinky Friedman, is indulging in the ultimate quixotic quest, running for governor of the Lone Star State, going on Bill O'Reilly's show and playing down his presumed liberal Democrat leanings.

Can Friedman really pass himself off as a centrist in Texas? Might he even be one? It'd be intriguing to see a true strain of political independence emerge from some unexpected pocket. It's easy to idealize someone as politically unpredictable as a Merle Haggard and wish that mercurial streak could translate into the real world of elections and deal-making. But that could just be nostalgia, not just for the Bakersfield sound but for a pre–Fox News, pre–Air America era. You could argue that the polarization that many of us find so alarming is actually a sign of national maturity, if maturity means that an electorate that previously didn't know any better than to wade through the wishy-washy middle is at last sufficiently well-informed enough to choose a side and stick with it. Perhaps political independent-mindedness now should be considered an outdated flaw at a time when the way to push things through the political process is clearly to decide which of the dominant philosophies you most naturally align with, jump on board, and not be bothered by less significant party planks that might seem inconsistent or hypocritical.

For anyone who believes that country music isn't nearly openly conservative enough, there's a new duo made up of a couple of Music Row songwriters, Frank Highland and Aaron Sain, who call themselves the Right Brothers. They decided there was a market for music that cuts out all the pussyfooting and *only* deals with divisive issues.

The Right Brothers know they don't have much hope of getting on country radio in the near future. There'll be listeners even in the most Republican areas who won't want to hear songs like "The Waffle House" (their ode to John Kerry's flip-flopping), "The Illegals" (they're against 'em), "Hey Hollywood" (they're angry at it), "It's My Money" (they're for keeping it), "You Can't Racial Profile," and "Trickle Down." But they hope to pursue a whole new model of promotion. They just got back from the 32nd annual Conservative Political Action Committee Conference, where they headlined the Reagan Banquet. Their "I Want to Live" video, in which ultrasound accompanies an adoption scenario—narrated by a fetus—was downloaded 400,000 times from various anti-abortion websites during its first week and a half online. They're taking their act not to country radio but to right-wing talk radio. The Right Brothers may be just one Sean Hannity booking away from a breakthrough, and even their liberal acquaintances in Nashville are in awe of how they identified an obvious niche and proceeded to fill it.

In tunes like "Tolerate This," the Rights do a fairly slick job of manifesting the manifesto of the right:

> I heard you found a new religion that's got nothing to do with God
> Your politically correct liberated little sect self-appointed tolerance
>   squad
> You say that you've been enlightened and the problem lies with people
>   like me
>> You say that you're tolerant and open-minded
>> Well, here's your chance to prove it to me
>> Tolerate this
>> I believe in marriage between a woman and a man . . .
>> I believe in driving the biggest car I can . . .
>> A good old-fashioned spanking is necessary, not cruel
>> You're preaching tolerance to me while you're standing there
>>   shaking your fist
>> Well, tolerate this

Try to imagine Tim Robbins's Bob Roberts character trading in his acoustic guitar for a mixture of honky-tonk and Southern rock and you've just about got it. If the Right Brothers don't make converts, that's okay—it's about galvanizing the faithful. "We're really kind of preaching to the choir with our stuff," admits Frank Highland. "We're not trying to book shows where we get a mixed audience that arrives and all of a sudden finds out we're singing bait and switch. People know upfront, before they come to see us play, what we're about." But it's not as if they're batting for the losing side. "This country is coming down to two competing philosophies, and which one are we gonna take. It's almost like you're on one side or the other. I don't know that that's good." Wait a second—what *is* he saying? Highland corrects himself. "Um, maybe it *is* good, that at some point it all comes to a head. One philosophy has got to win. I don't want us to be a country in gridlock." Right now, the conservative philosophy is winning out. In the arena of ideas, they're the ones getting elected, not just presidentially, but all across the country.

The Right Brothers also have a song called "I Want My Country Back." If there's a little déjà vu in that, you may be remembering the title of the Music Row Democrats' theme song, "Takin' My Country Back." Sounds like a dogfight, all right.

Hanging up the phone after chatting with the Rights, I decide on a whim to e-mail an acquaintance from the left, Bobby Braddock, just to check on what he's been writing since Bush began his second term. It turns out he just penned a new song, a radically bipartisan one titled "Thou Shall Not Kill." The lyric describes a fictional conversation overheard between a Republican and Democrat who cop similar and yet utterly opposite attitudes toward the sanctity of life. Finally, God himself sorts it all out . . . sort of.

"Just pitched it today to a major artist," Braddock informs me. "It's on hold—no guarantee, of course. What's amazing, though, is that friends and associates from the hard left to evangelical right have all reacted very positively to it. For one thing, it's in the third person, and therefore doesn't preach; it lets you draw your own conclusions. Even the God part is in the form of a dream."

The Republican's part of this symbolic argument is recounted in the first chorus:

> Thou shall not kill little babies living in their mommas' womb
> Thou shall not kill little ladies who can't use a fork or spoon
> Thou shall not kill those who want to die to just escape the gloom
> Thou shall not kill

The Democrat character claims he knows his Bible equally well and, a couple of verses later, gets in his own "pro-life" licks:

> Thou shall not kill helpless children in some crazy war somewhere
> Thou shall not kill by injection, gas chamber or the chair
> Thou shall not kill with poisoned water or polluted air
> Thou shall not kill

And then, the not entirely conclusive deus ex machina capper to the song:

> I got home at midnight and I climbed into my bed
> The words that I had heard that night kept running through my head
> Then I dreamed the clouds rolled back and lightning filled the sky
> And there stood God Almighty looking me right in the eye
>
> Thou shall not kill
> What did you mean, Lord, and who did you mean it for

Thou shall not kill
He said you read it right, I said it right before
Thou shall not kill
If that were not enough I would have told you more
Thou shall not kill

I tell Braddock that I wonder whether this will be a song that strikes the folks in Nashville as an obvious smash, something that most country music fans might see as validating at least some of their own positions. Or, conversely, whether a lyric that deigns to be truly fair and balanced and attempts to give a proper hearing to each opposing side is something that'll be too inherently hot for any young hat act to touch with a ten-foot Tin Pan Alley South tent pole.

"Me too," he writes back.

Acknowledgments

In the course of researching and writing this book, mostly over the course of a few intensive months at the end of 2004 and beginning of 2005, I did, on a few occasions, spend some time with folks outside the country music bubble. I would bring up the book a bit begrudgingly, if at all, assuming it might be of limited interest over in the rock sphere, only to be surprised by the real curiosity that even northeasterners—and people as far to the north and east as London—seemed to have about the intersection of politics and country. Take Chris Martin, frontman for the British band Coldplay. He appreciates country enough to have written a song, "Kingdom Come," expressly for Johnny Cash, though Cash never got around to recording it and Coldplay's version ended up as a hidden track on their *X&Y* album. (Cash didn't record the song "either because it was shit or because he died, depending on whether you like Coldplay or not," the singer joked.) Martin was full of questions. "The whole pride-in-America thing really confuses me," he admitted. "And I think particularly in country music, it feels really isolationist. But we love country, too, and we're from England. Sometimes it's upsetting to feel like a lot of country musicians won't acknowledge that there's anywhere else other than Texas, basically. Do you know what I mean? Why is that?" He really wanted to know. "Where do you think that comes from?" Finally, Martin—who's done some well-reported Bush-bashing—pressed me for some partisan buying tips: "*Are* there any country stars who aren't Republicans?" he wondered, making a mental list as I dutifully ticked some off. If the next Coldplay album turns out to have a Tim McGraw influence, it's my fault.

Of course, you really have to spend some time with a foreigner to become aware just how alien a concept deep and abiding patriotism is beyond the Atlantic. Regardless of how much the rest of the world hates, resents, admires, or is jealous of the United States, above all else they have few real reference points for relating to our outsized, wounded sense of self-esteem. But while nationalism and regionalism have their ugly sides, the pride most Americans feel is an incredible luxury, and a wonderful indulgence based not just in team spirit but, for most or all of the artists profiled in this book, heartfelt perspectives about how a nation can really embody the principles of life and liberty. Merle Haggard's "I Take a Lot of Pride in What I Am" is a song most Americans could sing along with—even the ones who might kill each other if locked in the same room—and here's hoping the chorus of voices singing in different keys in this book adds up to a tune that makes some harmonic sense to an inquisitive gus like Martin.

There's an old gag in Nashville that's supposed to serve as a sort of Rosetta stone for the niceties you run into there: the phrase "Well, bless your heart!" should usually be translated as "Fuck you!" Even with that decoding process in mind, I'm fool enough to believe all the goodwill directed my way on my frequent visits was genuine. A few of the interviews were done under the auspices of *Entertainment Weekly*, but the vast majority were done out of the goodness of the heart, or need to vent, of artists who saw fit to sit with me even without a record to promote. And they had every reason to be wary. When Ronnie Dunn asked me, in an exaggerated drawl, "So, are you one of those left-coast liberals?," it was intended as an ice-breaking joke, but, on some level, it was just as much a legitimate question—one I would've asked, anyway. The goal, I assured anyone who asked, was to present a variety of fairly unfiltered voices without too much undue editorial superimposition. I'm hoping we achieved that, and if there ended up being a few more liberal voices than conservative ones in the book, that was more a function of the underdog side generally tending to be more crankily quotable than the party in power. My chief hedge against deck-stacking bias or setting up straw men was choosing almost exclusively to interview figures that I either personally like or feel have made valuable contributions to country music—and in most cases, both. Your mileage and sympathy may vary, of course.

Deep thanks are due the following folks who deigned to ignore the advice on the walls of the bars where Gretchen Wilson grew up and talk politics: Grant Alden, Cindi Berger, Kathy Allmand Best, Big & Rich, Bobby Braddock, Jimmy Carter, Rosanne Cash, Mark Chesnutt, Rodney Crowell, R.J. Curtis, Charlie Daniels, the Dixie Chicks, Tim DuBois, Ronnie Dunn, Steve Earle, Sara Evans, Steve Fishell, Chet Flippo, Fletcher Foster, Joe Galante, Tracy Gershon, Holly Gleason, John Grady, Nanci Griffith, Merle Haggard, Sean Hannity, Patterson Hood, Martha Hume, Marcus Hummon, Alan Jackson, Toby Keith, Kris Kristofferson, Luke Lewis, Mike Long, Loretta Lynn, Raul Malo, Bill C. Malone, Tim McGraw, James McMurtry, Buddy Miller, Allison Moorer, Craig Morgan, Nelly, Willie Nelson, Joe Nichols, Kristyn Osborne, Brian Philips, Simon Renshaw, the Right Brothers, Bruce Robison, Linda Ronstadt, Nancy Russell, Dave "Mudcat" Saunders, Tamara Saviano, Ricky Skaggs, Todd Snider, James Stroud, Bob Titley, Travis Tritt, David Wild, Gretchen Wilson, Lee Ann Womack, Paul Worley, Chely Wright, and Adrienne Young.

I also need to express profound gratitude to these executives and publicists, who were instrumental in helping set up interviews or otherwise offering emergency assistance: Pamela Adamson, Kathi Atwood, Lisa Gladfelter Bell, Allen Brown, Todd Briginski, Craig Campbell, Donica Christensen, Kay Clary, Paula Erickson, Jim Flammia, Danny Goldberg, Cynthia Grimson, Jim Havee, Regina Joskow, Allisse Kingsley, Susan Levy, Jason Owen, Tresa Redburn, Logan Rogers, Elaine Schock, Regina Stuve, Traci Thomas, Amber Williams, and Jules Wortman. Dawn Oberg, librarian at the Country Music Hall of Fame and Museum, was an enormous help in pulling the right research.

At *EW,* I'm grateful to editors and colleagues including but not limited to Rick Tetzeli, Mary Kaye Schilling, Rob Brunner, Dulcy Israel, Jason Adams, Kristina Feliciano, David Browne, Sarah Saffian, Thom Geier, and Ben Svetkey, along with alumni John McAlley and Jim Seymour. Thanks to Robert Hilburn and Richard Cromelin at the *Los Angeles Times* for assigning me so many Haggard and Jones shows back in the day. Also, thanks to Alanna Nash, Michael Wright, Steven Smith, Larry and Melissa Krikorian, Todd Coleman, and Alan Elliott. My gratitude to Cynthia and Hadley for not making too big a fuss over losing me to Nashville, physically and spiritually. Gracias, also, to

Mom and Dad for setting more in motion than they could have imagined by playing "Cattle Call" over and over during my Idaho childhood.

For support, patience, and ongoing guidance, a particularly profound hat-tip to my agent, Sarah Lazin, and everyone at The New Press, especially Lizzie Seidlin-Bernstein, Sarah Fan, and Colin Robinson, the last of whom wondered aloud how Willie and Steve Earle were getting along in the current political climate, broaching the idea that should have been staring a Dixie Chicks groupie in the face all along.

And to the reader, for your interest: Bless your heart. No, really.

Selected Discography

Following is a list of some—but hardly all—of the country and alt-country songs over the years that have dealt with topical subject matter, grouped by decade. For songs that made *Billboard* magazine's country chart (which began in 1944), peak positions and year of release are listed. LPs have not been included, except in a few instances where the bulk of the material on the album were "message" songs of a political, topical, or patriotic nature.

1920s

Bentley Boys, "Down on Penny's Farm"
Fiddlin' John Carson, "Tom Watson Special," "Honest Farmer," "Dixie Division"
Dutch Coleman, "Gonna Raise Some Bacon at Home"
Vernon Dalhart, "The John T. Scopes Trial," "Eleven Cent Cotton, Forty Cent Meat," "Farm Relief Song"
Frank Hutchison, "Miner's Blues"
Uncle Dave Macon, "Farm Relief," "From Earth to Heaven," "Buddy Won't You Roll Down the Line," "The Bible's True," "Eleven Cent Cotton and Forty Cent Meat"
Bob Miller, "Eleven Cent Cotton, Forty Cent Meat," "The Farmer's Letter to the President," "Farm Relief Blues," "The Dry Votin', Wet Drinkin', Better-Than-Thou Hypocritical Blues"
Charlie Poole, "White House Blues," "The Battleship of Maine"
Blind Alfred Reed, "There'll Be No Distinction There," "Why Do You Bob Your Hair Girls," "How Can a Poor Man Stand Such Times and Live?," "Money Cravin' Folks," "Why Don't You Bob Your Hair Girls No. 2"
Lowe Stokes & His North Georgians, "Wish I Had Stayed in the Wagon Yard"

1930s

Roy Acuff, "Old Age Pension Check"

Carolina Tar Heels, "Got the Farm Land Blues"

Fiddlin' John Carson, "Taxes on the Farmer Feeds Them All," "Little Mary Phagan"

Carter Family, "No Depression in Heaven," "There'll Be No Distinction There"

Bill Cox, "NRA Blues," "The Democratic Donkey's in His Stall Again," "Franklin D. Roosevelt's Back Again"

Dixon Brothers, "Sales Tax on the Women"

Oscar Ford, "Farmer's Dream"

Woody Guthrie, "Talking Dust Bowl Blues," "This Land Is Your Land"

Fisher Hendley, "Weave Room Blues"

Lee Brothers Trio, "Cotton Mill Blues"

Light Crust Doughboys, "On to Victory Mr. Roosevelt," "Blue Bonnet Governor"

Uncle Dave Macon, "All In and Down and Out Blues," "Governor Al Smith," "Wreck of the Tennessee Gravy Train," "Run Nigger Run"

Bob Miller, "The Rich Man and the Poor Man," "Five Cent Cotton," "Bank Failures," "1930 Drought," "I Can't Go to the Poorhouse," "The Poor Forgotten Man," "Page Mr. Volstead"

Jimmie Rodgers, "No Hard Times Blues"

Slim Smith, "Breadline Blues"

Lowe Stokes & His North Georgians, "Prohibition Is a Failure"

Hank Warner, "The Death of Huey P. Long"

1940s

Eddy Arnold, "Mother's Prayer"

Gene Autry, "Don't Bite the Hand That's Feeding You"

Elton Britt, "There's a Star-Spangled Banner Waving Somewhere"

Buchanan Brothers, "Atomic Power" (#6, 1946)

Denver Darling, "Cowards over Pearl Harbor," "The Devil and Mr. Hitler," "When Mussolini Laid His Pistol Down"

Red Foley, "Smoke on the Water" (#1, 1944)

Boyd Heath, "Smoke on the Water" (#7, 1945)

Karl and Harty, "When the Atom Bomb Fell"

Tex Ritter, "Deck of Cards" (#10, 1948)

Carson Robison, "1942 Turkey in the Straw," "Hitler's Last Letter to Hirohito" (#5, 1945), "We're Gonna Have to Slap the Dirty Little Jap (and Uncle Sam's the Guy Who Can Do It)," "Mussolini's Letter to Hitler," "Get Your Gun and Come Along (We're Fixing to Kill a Skunk)," "Hitler's Reply to Mussolini," "Remember Pearl Harbor," "I Don't Work for a Living"

Riley Shepard, "Atomic Power"

Ernest Tubb, "Soldier's Last Letter" (#1, 1944)

T. Texas Tyler, "Deck of Cards" (#2, 1948)

Hank Williams (as Luke the Drifter), "No No Joe"

1950s

Roy Acuff, "Advice to Joe," "Douglas McArthur"

Rex Allen, "Cold Cold War"

Gene Autry, "Old Soldiers Never Die" (#9, 1951), "The Bible on the Table and the Flag Upon the Wall"

Jasper Blake, "Red Deck of Cards"

Elton Britt, "The Red We Want Is the Red We've Got in the Old Red White and Blue," "Rotation Blues"

Harry Choates, "Korea Here We Come"

Cowboy Copas, "Smoke on the Water"

Little Jimmy Dickens, "They Locked God Outside the Iron Curtain"

Jim Eanes, "Missing in Action"

Ferlin Husky and Jean Shepard, "A Dear John Letter" (#1, 1953), "Forgive Me John" (#4, 1953)

Grandpa Jones, "I'm No Communist"

Happy Fats LeBlanc, "Dear Mr. President"

Shorty Long, "No Wars in Heaven"

Louvin Brothers, "Great Atomic Power," "The Weapon of Prayer," "Broadminded," "Don't Let Them Take the Bible Out of Our Schoolrooms"

Lulu Belle and Scotty, "I'm No Communist"

Wink Martindale, "Deck of Cards" (#11, 1959)

Jimmie Osborne, "God Please Protect America" (#9, 1950), "Thank God for Victory in Korea," "Ballad of Robert A. Taft"

Sonny Osborne, "A Brother in Korea"

Terry Preston, "Let's Keep the Communists Out"

Cactus Pryor, "Point of Order"

Tex Ritter, "The Red Deck of Cards"

Curly Seckler, "Purple Heart"

Sons of the Pioneers, "Old Man Atom"

Merle Travis, "No Vacancy" (#3, 1946), "Reenlistment Blues"

Jimmy Wakely, "The Red Deck of Cards"

1960s

Red Allen, "Purple Heart," "Down Where the River Bends"

Hoyt Axton, "Soldier's Last Letter"

Bobby Bare, "Detroit City" (#6, 1963), "Times Are Gettin' Hard" (#30, 1965), "What Color Is a Man," "Law Is for Protection of the People," "If There's Not a Hell (There Ought to Be)," *Bird Named Yesterday* (LP), "God Bless America Again" (#16, 1969), "Somebody Bought My Old Hometown"

Glen Campbell, "Galveston" (#1, 1969), "Universal Soldier"

Sara and Maybelle Carter, "I Told Them What You're Fighting For"

Johnny Cash, "The Ballad of Ira Hayes," (#3, 1964), *Bitter Tears; Ballads of the American Indian* (LP), "The One on the Right Is on the Left" (#2, 1966), *From Sea to Shining Sea* (LP), "Roll Call"

Tommy Cash, "Six White Horses" (#4, 1969)

Johnny Darrell, "Ruby Don't Take Your Love to Town" (#9, 1967)

Mac Davis, "Bad Scene," "I Protest"

Jimmy Dean, "Dear Ivan" (#9, 1962), "P.T. 109" (#3, 1962), "There's Still Time, Brother"

Senator Everett McKinley Dirksen, "Gallant Men" (#58, 1967)

Dave Dudley, "What We're Fighting For" (#4, 1965), "Talkin' Vietnam Blues" (#12, 1966), "Soldier's Last Letter"

Harry Griffith, "The Battle in Vietnam"

Merle Haggard, "Hungry Eyes" (#1, 1969), "Workin' Man Blues" (#1, 1969), "Okie from Muskogee" (#1, 1969)

Tom T. Hall, "Strawberry Farms" (#40, 1969)

Ray Hildebrand, "Hello Vietnam"

Jan Howard, "My Son" (#15, 1969)

Autry Inman, "The Ballad of Two Brothers" (#14, 1968), "Ain't I Right," "Must We Fight Two Wars," "Who Am I?," "Vietnam Blues"

Stonewall Jackson, "The Minute Men Are Turning in Their Graves" (#24, 1966)

Wanda Jackson, "Little Boy Soldier" (#46, 1968)

Ivan Kavanovich, "Dear Jimmy"

Louvin Brothers, *Weapon of Prayer* (LP), "There's a Grave in the Wave of the Ocean," "At Mail Call Today," "I Died for the Red, White and Blue," "From Mother's Arms to Korea," "Searching for a Soldier's Grave"

Loretta Lynn, "Dear Uncle Sam" (#4, 1966)

Jimmy Martin, "God Guide Our Leader's Hand," "Guitar Picking President"

Charlie Moore & Bill Napier, "Is This a Useless War?"

Willie Nelson, "Jimmy's Road"

Jim Nesbitt, "Please Mr. Kennedy" (#11, 1961), "Looking for More in '64" (#7, 1964), "Still Alive in '65," "Heck of a Fix in '66," "Clean the Slate in '68," "Social Security"

Minnie Pearl, "What Is an American"

Jerry Reed, "Fighting for the USA"

Don Reno & Benny Martin, "Soldier's Prayer in Viet Nam" (#46, 1966)

Kenny Rogers, "Ruby Don't Take Your Love to Town" (#39, 1969)

Marty Robbins, "Private Wilson White" (#21, 1966), "My Native Land," "Ain't I Right"

Sgt. Barry Sadler, "The Ballad of the Green Berets" (#2, 1966)

Johnny Sea, "Day for Decision" (#14, 1966)

Hank Snow, "Letter from Vietnam (to Mother)"

Red Sovine, "Pledge of Allegiance"

Ernest Tubb, "It's for God and Country and You Mom (That's Why I'm Fighting in Vietnam)" (#48, 1966), "It's America (Love It or Leave It)"

Porter Wagoner, "I Dreamed I Saw America on Her Knees"

Wilburn Brothers, "Little Johnny from Down the Street" (#37, 1970), "Vision at the Peace Table," "The War Keeps Dragging On"

Doc Williams, "Freedom Monkey"

Lawton Williams, "Everything's OK on the LBJ" (#40, 1964)

Hal Willis, "The Battle of Vietnam"

Johnny Wright, "Hello Vietnam" (#1, 1965), "Keep the Flag Flyin'" (#31, 1965), "American Power" (#66, 1967)

1970s

Rusty Adams, "Hippy from Mississippi"

Bill Anderson, "Where Have All Our Heroes Gone" (#6, 1970)

Bobby Bare, "Red-Neck Hippie Romance" (#85, 1977), *Hard Time Hungrys* (LP), "Back in Huntsville Again" (#23, 1975), "The Farmer Feeds Us All," "Daddy's Been Around the House Too Long," "Two for a Dollar," "Warm and Free," "Able Bodied Man," "The Unemployment Line," "Mama Bake a Pie (Daddy Kill a Chicken)," "Good Christian Soldier," "Finger on the Button"

Travis Bell, "Welfare Cadillac"

Glen Campbell, "God Must Have Blessed America" (#39, 1977)

Johnny Cash, "What Is Truth?" (#3, 1970), "Man in Black" (#3, 1971), "Singing in Vietnam Talking Blues" (#18, 1971), "Ragged Old Flag" (#31, 1974), "Sold Out of Flagpoles" (#29, 1976), *America* (LP)

Tommy Cash, "The Tears on Lincoln's Face" (#36, 1970), "Unpatriotic Itchin' Needs a Patriotic Scratch"

David Allen Coe, "Longhaired Redneck" (#17, 1975), "How High's the Watergate Martha," "Fuck Anita Bryant"

Ben Colder, "What Is Youth?"

T. Tommy Cutrer, "The School Bus"

Charlie Daniels, "Uneasy Rider" (#67, 1973)

Guy Drake, "Welfare Cadillac" (#6, 1970), "The Marching Hippies," "Politickin' Pete"

Lester Flatt, "I Can't Tell the Boys from the Girls"

Kinky Friedman, "Sold American" (#69, 1973), *Sold American* (LP), "We Reserve the Right to Refuse Service to You," "High on Jesus," "Top Ten Commandments"

Merle Haggard, "The Fightin' Side of Me," (#1, 1970), "The Farmer's Daughter," "Jesus Take a Hold," "Soldier's Last Letter" (#3, 1971), "I Wonder if They Ever Think of Me" (#1, 1972), "If We Make It Through December" (#1, 1973), "A Working Man Can't Get Nowhere Today" (#16, 1977), "Irma Jackson," "They're Tearing the Labor Camps Down"

Tom T. Hall, "100 Children" (#14, 1970), "I Want to See the Parade," "Girls in Saigon City," "America the Ugly," "Hang Them All (Get the Guilty)," "The Monkey That Became President" (#11, 1972), "Mama Bake a Pie (Daddy Kill a Chicken)," "Watergate Blues" (#16, 1973)

Arlene Harden, "Congratulations (You Sure Made a Man Out of Him)" (#49, 1971)

Harlan Howard, *To the Silent Majority with Love* (LP), "Uncle Sam (I'm a Patriot)," "Three Cheers for the Good Guys," "Better Get Your Pride Back Boy," "Mister Professor," "A Little More Time," "We Didn't Build This World"

Kris Kristofferson, "Why Me" (#1, 1973), "Okie from Muskogee" (live), "The Law Is for the Protection of the People"

Loretta Lynn, "Rated X" (#1, 1972), "The Pill" (#5, 1975)

Loretta Lynn and Conway Twitty, "God Bless America Again"

Byron Macgregor, "Americans" (#59, 1974)

Jim Nesbitt, "Pollution," "Spiro," "Havin' Fun in '71"

Johnny Paycheck, "Me and the IRS," "All-American Man" (#23, 1975)

Webb Pierce, "The Good Lord Giveth and Uncle Sam Taketh Away"

John Prine, "Sam Stone," "Your Flag Decal Won't Get You into Heaven Anymore"

Tex Ritter, "The Americans (A Canadian's Opinion)" (#35, 1974)

Doug Sahm, "You Just Can't Hide a Redneck (Under That Hippy Hair)"
Billy Joe Shaver, "Christian Soldiers"
Jimmy Snyder, "The Chicago Story" (#30, 1970)
James Talley, "Are They Gonna Make Us Outlaws Again?" (#61, 1976)
Tanya Tucker, "I Believe the South Is Gonna Rise Again" (#18, 1975)
Leroy Van Dyke, "Mister Professor" (#71, 1970)
Jerry Jeff Walker, "Up Against the Wall Redneck Mother"
Freddy Weller, "Betty Ann and Shirley Cole"
Faron Young, "Are You Hungry—Eat Your Import"

1980s

Moe Bandy, "Americana" (#8, 1988)
Bellamy Brothers, "Kids of the Baby Boom" (#1, 1987)
Johnny Cash, "Song of the Patriot" (#54, 1980)
Charlie Daniels Band, "Long Haired Country Boy" (#27, 1980), "In America" (#13, 1980), "Simple Man" (#12, 1989), "American Farmer" (#54, 1985), "Still in Saigon"
Lee Greenwood, "God Bless the USA" (#7, 1984)
Merle Haggard, "Are the Good Times Really Over (I Wish a Buck Was Still Silver)" (#2, 1982), "Amber Waves of Grain"
Tom T. Hall, "Everything from Jesus to Jack Daniels" (#42, 1983)
The Highwaymen, "Deportee (Plane Wreck at Los Gatos)," "Welfare Line"
Waylon Jennings, "America" (#6, 1984), "Will the Wolf Survive" (#5, 1986)
Kris Kristofferson, "They Killed Him" (#67, 1987), *Repossessed* (LP)
Kathy Mattea, "From a Distance"
Willie Nelson, "Living in the Promiseland" (#1, 1986)
John Prine, "Paradise"
T.G. Sheppard, "War Is Hell (On the Homefront Too)" (#1, 1982)
Statler Brothers, "More Than a Name on the Wall" (#6, 1989)
Don Williams, "Good Ole Boys Like Me" (#2, 1980)
Hank Williams Jr., "Dixie on My Mind" (#1, 1981), "A Country Boy Can Survive" (#2, 1982), "American Dream" (#5, 1982), "If the South Woulda Won" (#8, 1988), "Mr. Lincoln," "The Coalition to Ban Coalitions," "I've Got Rights"

1990s

Bill Anderson, "Deck of Cards" (#60, 1990)
Austin Lounge Lizards, "Gingrich the Newt," "The Ballad of Ronald Reagan"
Chad Brock (with George Jones and Hank Williams Jr.), "A Country Boy Can Survive (Y2K Version)" (#30, 1999)
Garth Brooks, "The Thunder Rolls" (#1, 1991), "We Shall Be Free" (#12, 1992)
Charlie Daniels Band, "(What This World Needs Is) A Few More Rednecks" (#56, 1990), "America, I Believe in You" (#73, 1993), "Let Freedom Ring"
Iris DeMent, "Wasteland of the Free," "There's a Wall in Washington"
Dixie Chicks, "Goodbye Earl" (#13, 1999)
Drive-by Truckers, "The President's Penis Is Missing"
Steve Earle, "Copperhead Road," "Christmas in Washington"

Nanci Griffith, "From a Distance"

Merle Haggard, "Me and Crippled Soldiers"

The Highwaymen, "American Remains," "Anthem '84"

Alan Jackson, "Little Man" (#3, 1999)

Waylon Jennings, "The Eagle" (#22, 1991)

George Jones, "50,000 Names Carved in the Wall"

Kris Kristofferson, *Third World Warrior* (LP), "The Eagle and the Bear," "Third World Warrior," "Aguila Del Norte," "The Hero," "Don't Let the Bastards (Get You Down)," "Love of Money," "Third World War," "Jesse Jackson" (with Willie Nelson), "Mal Sacate (For Maria)," "Sandanista"

Tracy Lawrence, "Time Marches On" (#1, 1996)

Jerry Martin, "Letter to Saddam Hussein" (#71, 1991)

Martina McBride, "Independence Day" (#12, 1994)

Montgomery Gentry, "Daddy Won't Sell the Farm" (#17, 1999), "Tattoos and Scars"

Gary Morris, "Somebody Lives There," "Time Will Tell"

Eddy Raven, "Someone's Tearin' the Flag"

Sawyer Brown, "Cafe on the Corner" (#5, 1992)

Billy Joe Shaver, "Good Ol' USA"

Aaron Tippin, "You've Got to Stand for Something" (#6, 1990), "What This Country Needs" (#47, 1999)

Randy Travis, "Point of Light" (#3, 1991)

Travis Tritt, "Son of the New South," "Sign of the Times," "Lord Have Mercy on the Working Man" (#5, 1992), "Blue Collar Man"

Waco Brothers, "Bad Times (Are Comin' Round Again)," "Plenty Tuff Union Made"

Hank Williams Jr., "Don't Give Us a Reason" (#27, 1990)

2000s

Trace Adkins, "Welcome to Hell," "Arlington"

Big & Rich, "Love Train," "Rollin' (The Ballad of Big & Rich)"

Clint Black, "Iraq & Roll" (#42, 2003)

Brooks & Dunn, "Only in America" (#1, 2001), "Holy War"

Johnny Cash, "Drive On"

Tommy Cash, "Thoughts on the Flag"

Donovan Chapman, "There Is No War" (#58, 2003)

Terri Clark, "The World Needs a Drink" (#26, 2005)

Charlie Daniels, "This Ain't No Rag, It's a Flag" (#33, 2001)

Dixie Chicks, "Long Time Gone" (#1, 2002), "Travelin' Soldier" (#1, 2003), "Truth #2"

Rodney Crowell, "Give It to Me," "The Obscenity Prayer," "Ignorance Is the Enemy"

Dusty Drake, "One Last Time" (#26, 2003)

Drive-by Truckers, "Birmingham," "The Southern Thing," "The Three Great Alabama Icons," "Wallace," "Puttin' People on the Moon," "Sands of Iwo Jima"

Dave Dudley, "Don't Mess with U.S. Truckers"

Steve Earle, "Amerika 6.0 (The Best That We Can Do)," "John Walker's Blues," "Conspiracy Theory," "Jerusalem," "The Revolution Starts Now," "Rich Man's War," "Home to Houston," "Condi Condi," "F the CC," *The Revolution Starts Now* (CD)

Robbie Fulks, "Countrier Than Thou"

Mary Gauthier, "Mercy Now"

Billy Gilman, "One Voice" (#20, 2000)

Lee Greenwood, "God Bless the USA" (new version) (#16, 2001)

Nanci Griffith, "Traveling Through This Part of You," "The Last Name on the Wall" "Heart of Indochine," "Big Blue Wall of War," "Old Hanoi"

Merle Haggard, "That's the News," "Yellow Ribbons," "Let's Rebuild America First"

Emmylou Harris, "Time in Babylon"

Faith Hill, "We've Got Nothing but Love to Prove"

Alan Jackson, "Where Were You (When the World Stopped Turning)" (#1, 2001)

Cledus T. Judd, "Don't Mess with America," "Martie, Emily and Natalie" (#56, 2003)

Toby Keith, "Courtesy of the Red, White and Blue (The Angry American)" (#1, 2002), "Beer for My Horses" (with Willie Nelson) (#1, 2003), "American Soldier" (#1, 2004), "The Taliban Song," "Honky Tonk U" (#8, 2005)

Shelby Lynne, "You're the Man"

Lynyrd Skynyrd, "Red, White and Blue"

Neal McCoy with General Tommy Franks, "Last of a Dying Breed"

Tim McGraw, "Red Rag Top" (#5, 2002)

James McMurtry, "Out Here in the Middle," "Max's Theorem," "We Can't Make It Here Anymore"

Buddy Miller, "With God on Our Side"

John Michael Montgomery, "Letters from Home" (#2, 2004)

Montgomery Gentry, "You Do Your Thing" (#22, 2004)

Allison Moorer, "All Aboard"

Craig Morgan, "Paradise," "Where Has My Hometown Gone," "God, Family and Country" (#49, 2001), "Blame Me"

Willie Nelson, "Whatever Happened to Peace on Earth" (Internet only)

Joe Nichols, "If Nobody Believed in You" (#10, 2004)

Dolly Parton, "Welcome Home"

John Prine, "Some Humans Ain't Human"

Rascal Flatts, "Mayberry" (#1, 2004)

Right Brothers, *Right Brothers, Right Brothers II* (CDs)

Ray Scott, "Makin' My Way"

SheDaisy, "Please Come Home Soon" (#14, 2004)

Todd Snider, "Conservative Christian, Right Wing, Republican, Straight, White, American Males"

Son Volt, "Endless War," "Jet Pilot," "6 String Belief," "Joe Citizen Blues"

Ray Stevens, "Osama Yo' Mama (You in a Heap o' Trouble Boy)" (#48, 2001)

Luke Stricklin, "American by God's Amazing Grace"

Marty Stuart (with Merle Haggard), "Farmer's Blues"

TMCB Band, "Takin' My Country Back" (Internet only)

Keni Thomas, *Flags of Our Fathers—A Soldier's Story* (CD)

Aaron Tippin, "Where the Stars and Stripes and the Eagle Fly" (#2, 2002)

Randy Travis, "America Will Always Stand" (#59, 2001)

Travis Tritt, "Livin' on Borrowed Time," "Country Ain't Country" (#26, 2003), "What Say You" (#21, 2004), "When in Rome"

Warren Brothers, "Hey Mr. President" (#28, 2003)

Hank Williams Jr., "America Will Survive" (#45, 2001)

Gretchen Wilson, "Politically Incorrect"

Gretchen Wilson, Big & Rich, and Cowboy Troy, "Our America"

Darryl Worley, "Have You Forgotten?" (#1, 2003), "Awful, Beautiful Life" (#1, 2004), "Wake Up America"

Chely Wright, "Bumper of My SUV" (#35, 2004)

Adrienne Young, "Blinded by Stars," "Hills and Hollers," "Walls of Jericho"

Space doesn't permit listing all the LPs and CDs where these songs might be found, but a few collections in particular will be invaluable for anyone collecting this type of material:

Various artists: *Hard Times in the Country: Down and Out in the Rural South—Songs & Tunes from 1927 to 1938* (County Records, 2002). This single-disc celebration of economic disadvantage includes numbers by Uncle Dave Macon, Blind Alfred Reed, and lesser-known proto-hillbilly acts. With liner notes by Bill C. Malone.

Various artists: *Country Shots: God Bless America* (Rhino, 1994). Hard-to-find tracks, mostly from the Vietnam era, by Ernest Tubb, Autry Inman, Bill Anderson, Stonewall Jackson, and Dave Dudley. Out of print, but worth finding for the wealth of material on one disc, much of it otherwise unavailable on CD.

Various artists: *There's a Star-Spangled Banner Waving Somewhere: Music to Invade By* (Bear Family, import only, 2003). In the Bear Family tradition of eclectic compilations, this has eleven different versions of the World War II–era smash, including variations rewritten for Korea and Vietnam. (Conservatives beware: the liner notes of this British import have a field day with supposed American imperialism, as the cynical subtitle suggests.)

Various artists: *America's Country* (Columbia, 2002) and *Patriotic Country* (BMG, 2004). These two sets collect some of the more treacly go-America material of recent vintage from Lee Greenwood's "God Bless the USA" forward.

Johnny Cash: *Patriot* (Columbia, 1990). Single-disc collection of Cash's war- and patriotism-themed tunes, now out of print but often available on eBay. *The Essential Johnny Cash* (Legacy, 2002). All the key Columbia-era hits on two discs.

Merle Haggard: *Down Every Road, 1962–1994* (Capitol, 1996). A must-have four-disc boxed set that includes material from all the labels he's recorded for (except, of course, Curb).

Tom T. Hall: *Storyteller, Poet, Philosopher* (Polygram, 1995). Nearly all of Hall's most pointedly topical early 1970s songs are reprised in this two-disc boxed set.

Blind Alfred Reed: *Complete Recorded Works in Chronological Order, 1927–1929* (Document, 1998). A single-disc roundup of everything Reed cut in his blink-of-an-eye career.

Hank Williams Jr.: *America (The Way I See It)* (Curb, 1998). Single-disc compilation of some of Bocephus's most patriotic—and some would say most reactionary—celebrations and provocations.

Notes on Sources

Quotes appearing in this book derive from the author's own interviews, except when otherwise noted. Following is a list of outside sources that were consulted, along with recommendations for further reading.

Preface: The Red Carpet

The *Entertainment Weekly* "nude" cover that further aggravated many protesters accompanied my cover story, "Stars and Strife" (May 2, 2003). The Diane Sawyer television interview with the Chicks that also upset some of the demonstrators was broadcast on ABC the same day that *EW* hit newsstands (*Primetime Live*, April 26, 2003). Jerry Falwell's "French hens" comment, as appropriated by one of the protesters, appeared in an Associated Press story, "Falwell Sings Anti-Dixie Chicks Tune" (April 30, 2003). Further coverage of the alternative concert in Spartanburg headlined by the Marshall Tucker Band can be found in "Packed Crowds Roar Approval at Chicks, Anti-Chicks Shows" by Paul Alongi in the *Greenville News* (May 2, 2003). My own brief coverage of the opening dates of the Chicks' 2003 tour ran on EW.com as "The Maines Event" (May 2, 2003) and in the pages of *EW* under the heading "Tour de Force" (May 16, 2003).

Introduction: Row Rage

Bill C. Malone has written several essential books about the history of country music, but the one that proved most invaluable as background for the writing of this book—particularly the introduction and chapter 5—is *Don't Get Above Your Raisin': Country Music and the Southern Working Class* (University of Illinois Press, 2002). As more contemporary concerns go, an Associated Press piece, "Country Music Sales Up 12 Percent in 2004" (January 7, 2005), was one of many articles to trumpet the good year the genre had right after SoundScan released its annual figures, which showed that country acts sold 77.9 million units in 2004 versus 69.3 million the previous year. Meanwhile, plummeting ratings for "music's biggest night," the Grammy Awards, were covered in *Daily Variety*'s "Grammys See Less Tune-in" (February 14, 2005). A *Tennessean* article, "Country Radio Gathering on Stable Ground" by Jeanne Anne Naujeck (March 2, 2005), surveyed the healthy state of the format on the eve of another edition of the Country Radio Seminar. The Chet Flippo "Nashville Skyline" column arguing that conservatives and liberals are both well-represented in the genre ran on CMT.com under the headline "Germs and Jesus and Country Music: Presidential Politics & Red-Blue States Debate Linger" (November 25, 2004). Critic David Browne's EW.com column about the lack of rockers protesting the impending Iraq war was titled "The Sounds of Silence" (March 4, 2003). The Bush administration's policy of being particularly helpful to battleground states—while withholding the same favors from unshakably blue states—was detailed in a *USA Today* story, "Bush Policies Follow Politics of States Needed in 2004," by Susan Page (June 16, 2002).

Chapter 1: Plucked

The Dixie Chicks/Toby Keith feud got officially under way with Natalie Maines's critical comments about "Courtesy of the Red, White, and Blue" in a Los Angeles *Daily News* story, "Natalie Maines Bashes Toby Keith's Patriotic Anthem," by Fred Shuster (August 8, 2002). Her London stage patter was fatefully first reported in a review by Betty Clarke in *The Guardian*, under the simple heading "The Dixie Chicks" (March 12, 2003). The Cox radio chain's cancellation of a syndicated radio show that included Chicks music was covered in *Radio & Records* (March 20, 2003). Travis Tritt's broadsides against his embattled labelmates spread through multiple news stories (including "Travis Tritt Slams Dixie Chick, Antiwar Celebs," NBC10.com, March 18, 2003). Comedian Larry the Cable Guy's disgust for Maines was registered in two essays posted at his website: "Dixie Sow" (www.larrythecableguy.com/commentary/2003/march/0317a.htm, March 17, 2003) and "Libs & Bitchin'" (www.larrythecableguy.com/commentary/2004/february/0205a.htm, February 5, 2004); the latter is also available on his site as an audio link. The controversial edition of Chet Flippo's regular "Nashville Skyline" column at CMT.com was titled "Shut Up and Sing?" (March 20, 2003). Bill C. Malone's rebuttal, "Guest Viewpoint on Chicks Controversy," was posted to the site in Flippo's usual column space one week later. The civic enthusiasm for the Chicks in liberal Madison, Wisconsin, was reported in numerous articles, including Launch.com's "Chicks Embraced by Wisconsin City Council" (April 9, 2003). The banning of all Lloyd Maines–produced records by a Texas radio chain was reported by *Paste* magazine's website in "Kevin Deal: Trouble in Texas" (June 9, 2003). In an edition of his weekly *New York Times* column titled "Bowling for Kennebunkport," Frank Rich quoted Michael Moore and cited *EW* as a source for his outdated information on the Chicks' supposedly still healthy record sales (April 6, 2003). Michael Moore's open letter facetiously inviting the world to boycott both him and the Chicks was posted on his website (April 7, 2003). After being laid into for supporting the Chicks, Vince Gill was compelled to restate his support for the president in Brad Schmidt's *Tennessean* column "Brad About You" (April 10, 2003).

The Chicks' ill-timed and ill-prepared interview with New Zealand's TV One was transcribed and then reprinted on some country radio and political websites. I haven't been able to locate a copy of the tape to confirm the accuracy of the transcript, but among the comments Maines is said to have made about the then-nascent controversy, belying the band's lack of awareness of the trouble that awaited them back home, are these: "Uh . . . I said . . . what did I say? I said . . . um . . . we're embarrassed . . . just so you know, we're embarrassed . . ." Maguire corrected her: "Ashamed." "Oh, we're ashamed that the president is from Texas . . . Is that what I said? . . . And it was a joke and it wasn't planned. And it was really funny at the time. It got lots of cheers and that's what it was meant for . . . You see the trouble that you can get into if you speak religion or politics. It gets people very upset. But, um, UN approval would have been nice."

It was in a *Vogue* magazine spread celebrating "Heroines 2003" that Maines finally admitted she was sorry she ever issued a public apology of any sort (January 2004). In a Salon.com essay titled "Chicks Against the Machine," Charles Taylor compared the Chicks to rock's riot grrrls, and sharply denounced Diane Sawyer's interrogation techniques (April 28, 2003). The congressional hearings on deregulation were reported in *Billboard*'s "Radio Under Fire: Chicks Ban Comes Back to Haunt Chain" (July 19, 2003). Mike Lawrence, a Texas DJ, made his plea for the return of the Chicks to the airwaves in a *Country Weekly* guest column, "Sounding Board: Bring Back the Dixie Chicks!" (February 2005). Yet another Cledus T. Judd tirade against the Chicks, this one explaining her FUTK T-shirt, was reported in an *Indiana Statesman* concert review with the headline "Rascal Flatts Thrills Hulman Center Crowd" (January 26, 2004).

Chapter 2: Courtesy of the Red, White, and Formerly Blue

Toby Keith's point of view about the war was alternately questioning and complacent when he spoke with the *Los Angeles Times* shortly after the invasion of Iraq: "This war here, the math hasn't worked out for me on it. But I'm smart enough to know there's people smarter than me. Condoleezza Rice, Colin Powell, George Bush—this is their job, and I have to trust in them" (July 2003). He explained his politics a bit more in a *Boston Globe* profile, "Singing Out: Chest-Banging Keith's Jingoistic, Country Rants Belie a Secret: He's a Democrat," by Steve Morse (August 20, 2004). Among his statements: "I'm probably the most right Democrat in the world . . ." His support for Oklahoma's Democratic governor was mentioned in an AP article, "Toby Keith Doesn't Stray Far from His Roots" (November 15, 2004). Keith's and the governor's mutual support for a gaming law, Senate Bill 553, was trumpeted in a press release on the Oklahoma state website (www.governor.state.ok.us/display_article.php?article_id=237& article_type=1).

Two *Los Angeles Times* stories provided useful information on the Democrats' sometimes contradictory attitudes toward winning back key red states: "GOP Has Lock on South, and Democrats Can't Find Key," by Peter Wallsten and Nick Anderson (November 6, 2004), and "Democrats Map Out a Different Strategy," by Ronald Brownstein (December 15, 2004). Articles profiling Democratic strategist Dave "Mudcat" Saunders included the *Christian Science Monitor*'s "Maybe a Democrat Can Win in the South," by Patrik Jonsson (November 8, 2004), and the *New York Times*'s "Huntin' for Nascar-Lovin', Moon-Pie-Eatin', Bluegrass-Listenin', Shotgun-Totin'

Democrats," by Matt Bai (September 15, 2002). The *Roanoke Times* covered Saunders's successful attempt to find Virginia governor Mark Warner a bluegrass theme song in "Mark Warner Stumps to a New Campaign Tune," by Todd Jackson (April 5, 2001). During the Gore/Bush contest, the AP ran lists of who was stumping for whom in "Country Stars Not Supporting Gore" (August 23, 2000), which included the news that pop singer Jewel had been chosen over country stars to provide entertainment at a Nashville Gore/Lieberman rally. The presence of country stars like Sawyer Brown at Tipper Gore's forty-eighth birthday party at the Ryman four years prior to that was recounted in *USA Today*'s "Nashville Throws Tipper a Party" (August 20, 1996). Author James C. Cobb argued that the "outlaw" movement represented a safer, apolitical 1970s version of a counterculture party in his book *Redefining Southern Culture: Mind and Identity in the Modern South* (University of Georgia Press, 1999). Willie Nelson's song "Whatever Happened to Peace on Earth?," which was performed once at a Kucinich rally and officially available briefly and only on the Internet, was covered in a Reuters article, "New Willie Nelson Song Condemns War in Iraq" (January 1, 2004). Jimmy Carter's open letter to a former friend and Georgia Democrat, "Letter to Zell Miller: 'You Have Betrayed Our Trust,'" appeared in the *Atlanta Journal-Constitution* (September 8, 2004).

The *Two Americas: Our Current Political Deadlock and How to Break It*, by Stanley B. Greenberg (Thomas Dunne Books, 2004), is a fascinating nonpartisan breakdown of the various factions that make up contemporary America, examining which strata and substrata are open to political change and which are already locked down. Several of the statistics in this chapter are borrowed from Greenberg's book. Also useful in researching this chapter, albeit altogether more partisan than *The Two Americas*, was *What's the Matter with Kansas: How Conservatives Won the Heart of America*, by Thomas Frank (Metropolitan Books, 2004). Someone who presumably thinks Kansas is just fine as it is, meanwhile, is Charlie Daniels, whose *Ain't No Rag* (Regnery Press, 2004) is a collection of editorials that have appeared on his website.

Chapter 3: Opryland, D.C.

A *USA Today* story that ran the day of the 2005 Black Tie and Boots ball confirmed that Neil McCoy is "one of the favorite performers of Karl Rove, Bush's chief political adviser" (January 19, 2005). In 1990, then-President George H.W. Bush's love letter to country music first ran in *Country Music* magazine and was reprinted in the *Washington Post* under the headline "George and the Oval Office Do-Si-Do: Heck, a President Ain't Nothin' but Just Folks" (October 7, 1990). Bush the father, as the newly elected president, spoke further about his love of country in a 1988 *New York Times* column, "Bush Loves His Country Music, But Can't Dance" (November 10, 1988), written by future family nemesis Maureen Dowd: "'George Bush says he likes country music and it's written in the Houston paper, "Who's he trying to kid, this Ivy League elitist?"' the vice president says, talking about himself in the third person, as he likes to do, and sounding annoyed . . . 'You know what you can do?' Bush suggests eagerly . . . 'Have Barbara Bush take you to our bedroom and you turn on the automatic button, the left hand button, on the machine right there, and it's going to be 98.7 [a Washington country station] and it never moves from there.'"

Chapter 4: Of Boots and Bumper Stickers

The rave by Salon.com writer Eric Boehlert for Alan Jackson's "Where Were You" appeared in "Stuck in a Moment" (February 28, 2002). The *Tennessean* article that broke the news about the questionable activities of Chely Wright's fan club was "Campaign of Deception Used to Push Patriotic Song Up Charts," by Jeanne Anne Naujeck (December 19, 2004). The same reporter produced a follow-up story, "Fan Club Pros Say Wright's Went Too Far," two days later. A third story by Naujeck, headlined "Money Behind No. 1 Hits Raises Crucial Eyebrows" (January 30, 2005), tangentially mentioned Wright. This one was about pay-to-play tactics that helped get a Reba McEntire single to the top of the charts, and the Wright comparison was actually a favorable one. ("'Bumper' is one of the only songs on the country charts right now without labels stuffing money into radio. It's the cleanest airplay in the nation," said Brian Jennings, program director for KZKX in Lincoln, Nebraska, noting that Wright had no promotion arm behind her, save her fans.)

Chapter 5: Town & Country, Jungle & Trench

Several books merit special mention as crucial for this chapter coming together, particularly in alerting me to historic recordings I might not have otherwise have heard. One is Bill C. Malone's *Don't Get Above Your Raisin': Country Music and the Southern Working Class* (University of Illinois Press, 2002). Another is *Country Music Goes to War* (University Press of Kentucky, 2005), a collection of essays edited by Charles K. Wolfe and James K. Akenson. One area that isn't really covered in that book—oddly enough, as the editors admit—is the Vietnam era. That gap is made up for, and then some, by *Battle Notes: Music of the Vietnam War* (Savage Press, revised edition 2003), in which author Lee Andresen covers all popular genres but inevitably spends a good deal of time examining country. A 1971 essay by Jens Lund, "Fundamentalism, Racism, and Political Reaction in Country Music," collected in the book *The Sounds of Social Change*, edited by R. Serge Denisoff and Richard A. Peterson (Rand McNally, 1972), also provided useful background material. Finally on the book front, any serious country fan will want two expensive but invaluable collections of stats, *Top Country Singles 1944 to 2001* and *Top Country Albums 1964–1997*, both put together by Joel Whitburn under the auspices of *Billboard* magazine, and the source of most of the chart information here.

Loretta Lynn's remark about not knowing how to pronounce Dukakis's name comes from a report on president-to-be George H.W. Bush's campaign stumping, "Bush Parades Small-Town Values," in the *Minneapolis Star-Tribune* (October 2, 1988). The *Newsday* article "Artists' Lives, GOP 'Values' Clash," by Myron S. Waldman, brought up the Tanya Tucker/Dan Quayle dichotomy (August 14, 1992). Linda Ronstadt's 1969 appearance on *The Johnny Cash Show* appears on a bootleg DVD; unfortunately, though ripe for anthologizing, Cash's historic series hasn't been issued for legal video consumption yet.

In an issue of *Time* that hit print September 12, 2004, Tim McGraw told the newsweekly's reporter, Josh Tyrangiel, "I want to run for the Senate from Tennessee. Not now, but when I'm 50, when music dies down a little bit. I know lots of artists and actors have those delusions of grandeur, but ever since I was a kid, it's been of interest to me. It'd be great to be in a position to do something good for people. Wouldn't

Faith make a great Senator's wife?...I love politics. I love Bill Clinton. I think we should make him king. I'm talking the red robe, the turkey leg—everything."

Jimmie Davis's life story has been entertainingly recounted in many places throughout the years, but the account that may strike the best balance between respect and a healthy skepticism is Jason Berry's "The Sunshine Man: A Tale of Stardom, Political Heat, and Legendary Music," in *Reckon* magazine (Fall 1995).

Chapter 6: The Donkey Under the Elephant in the Room

The "Open Letter to Hollywood" from Charlie Daniels that eventually led to the trouble between Tamara Saviano and GAC is available on Daniels's website and is also reprinted in his book, *Ain't No Rag* (Regnery, 2004). Saviano's firing was reported in Nashville's daily and alternative weekly papers: the *Tennessean*'s "Producer Fired after E-mail Blasting of Charlie Daniels' Iraq Stand," by Brad Schmidt (March 11, 2003), and—seeming to side with GAC over Saviano in the matter—the *Nashville Scene*'s "Crying Wolf: A Producer Disagrees with Charlie Daniels, Won't Let It Drop, Then Gets Canned," by Matt Pulle (March 13–19, 2003). *Newsweek*'s website wrote up the fledgling Music Row Democrats in "Getting Out the Music Lovers," by Jamie Reno (March 16, 2004). The *Tennessean* wrote up Janet Reno's (non-musical) appearance before the organization in "Reno Tells 'Music Row Democrats' She Shares Their Concerns" (June 5, 2004). The *London Observer* came across the ocean and covered the Music Row Democrats' Kerry-oke nights in "Country Swingers" (October 17, 2004).

Chapter 7: Steve Earle's Mouth Is Gonna Rise Again

The editorial in *No Depression* magazine urging votes for Kerry and against Bush appeared in the September–October 2004 issue. Letters condemning and supporting the stance appeared in several issues of the bimonthly publication after that. Nanci Griffith's plans to move or not move overseas were detailed in two stories in the *Tennessean* by Peter Cooper, "Should Singers Strike a Political Note?" (August 15, 2004) and "Even with Bush Win, Griffith to Stay in U.S." (November 7, 2004). Conservative alt-country fan Mike Long's favorable critique of the Drive-by Truckers' *Southern Rock Opera* album appeared on the *National Review*'s website, NRO.com (November 3–4, 2001). Patterson Hood told me he assumed he'd lost Long's support after it became evident how liberal he really was, but Long endorsed the group's follow-up effort, *Decoration Day*, at NRO.com, too (August 20, 2003) and continues to be a big supporter, polar-opposite politics aside. Geoffrey Himes's endorsement of Buddy Miller's album as a blue-state document was one of several essays accompanying the year-end critics' poll in *No Depression* (January–February 2005).

Two books proved to be particularly enjoyable reads as I researched the artists in this chapter and are highly recommended for fans of alt-country and/or vintage Southern rock. Jan Reid's recently updated version of *The Improbable Rise of Redneck Rock* (University of Texas Press, revised edition 2004), which focuses mostly on the Texas wing of alt country, includes new sections on figures like Bruce Robison. Mark Kemp's *Dixie Lullaby: A Story of Music, Race, and New Beginnings in a New South* (Free Press, 2004), a highly personal look at Southern rock as a lifeline for young people growing up in the region in a prejudicial age, includes a long appreciation of the Drive-by Truckers as righteous descendents of the author's past heroes.

Chapter 8: Deep Purple

Most books of musicians' lyrics end up demonstrating how ridiculous even the most respected songs can sound when shorn of their accompaniment. But two such lyrical compendiums, *Merle Haggard—Poet of the Common Man: The Lyrics* (Hal Leonard Corporation, 2002) and *Johnny Cash: The Songs* (Thunder's Mouth Press, 2004), are exceptions to the rule, making a solid case for these songwriters' truly poetic sensibilities. Both are edited by Nashville writer Don Cusic and feature short introductory biographies by him as well. More information on Willie Nelson's biodiesel fuel, as championed by his friend Haggard, can be found at http://www.wnbiodiesel.com.

Epilogue: Four More Beers

Kinky Friedman's proposed run for the Texas governorship was covered in a Chet Flippo CMT.com column, "Nashville Skyline: Kinky for Governor in '06?" (February 3, 2005) and a Fox News TV interview with Bill O'Reilly (March 14, 2005). In an *Austin American-Statesman* story titled "Willie: Thanks but No Thanks," Willie Nelson ultimately said he'd just as soon not have his name on a Texas tollway anyway: "Toll roads are not that popular. I'd put my name on an electric chair, too, but I don't think that'd be too great a thing. As far as the Republican opposition, I don't blame them. It all sounded political" (May 5, 2005).

Index